Measurement and Evaluation in Physical Activity Applications

Measurement and Evaluation in Physical Activity Applications offers the most accessible, student-friendly introduction to the principles and practice of measurement in physical activity available. Fully revised and updated, the second edition provides students with a clear guide to the obstacles to good measurement, and how to apply the principles of good measurement to a range of physical activity disciplines.

Spanning applications in exercise science, sports performance, physical education, sports coaching, athletic training, and physical activity and health, the book also includes chapters on the key principles underlying good measurement practice— validity, reliability, and objectivity—as well as an introduction to using statistics and qualitative measurement.

Structured to reflect single-semester classes, and involving students at every stage through its rich pedagogy and accessibility, this is a crucial resource for introducing students to the principles of best practice in measurement and evaluation. It is the ideal learning aid for any students studying measurement, evaluation, or assessment in kinesiology, exercise science, sports coaching, physical education, athletic training, and health and fitness.

Phillip A. Bishop is Emeritus Professor of Exercise Science at the University of Alabama, USA where he taught for over 30 years. He has taught, researched, and lectured in about 31 states and about 30 foreign countries. He has conducted research for NASA, the US Airforce, the US Army, and the US Military Academy.

Measurement and Evaluation in Physical Activity Applications

Exercise Science, Physical Education,
Coaching, Athletic Training, and Health

Second Edition

Phillip A. Bishop

Routledge
Taylor & Francis Group

NEW YORK AND LONDON

Second edition published 2019
by Routledge
711 Third Avenue, New York, NY 10017

and by Routledge
2 Park Square, Milton Park, Abingdon, Oxon, OX14 4RN

Routledge is an imprint of the Taylor & Francis Group, an informa business

First edition published by Holcombe Hathaway 2008

Library of Congress Cataloging-in-Publication Data
A catalog record has been requested for this book

ISBN: 978-0-8153-9224-8 (hbk)
ISBN: 978-0-8153-9225-5 (pbk)
ISBN: 978-1-351-19971-1 (ebk)

Typeset in Sabon
by Swales & Willis Ltd, Exeter, Devon, UK

Visit the eResources: www.routledge.com/9780815392255

This book is dedicated to my family, my colleagues in many places, my former undergraduate and graduate students, all of whom have taught me a great deal. It is dedicated to Jehovah, who provides all things.

Contents

PART 2

Numbers and Statistics in Measurement 33

Figures

Tables

Preface

More than 33 years ago, I walked into a college classroom to teach my first class: Measurement and Evaluation (M & E) as a new assistant professor. In those days, teacher education students were the primary target audience, and the courses and texts were aimed mostly at these future teachers. That demographic has changed, and I have found my classes increasingly filled with exercise science students who were not seeking teacher certification. I also noticed that many, if not most, of my students were not mathematically inclined. Thus, they often found M & E to be a daunting course. As a result of my teaching experiences, my goal has been to write a simple M & E book that fits the needs of all the diverse students who take this course.

Measurement and Evaluation in Physical Activity Applications is written for your students, some of whom may have an aversion to mathematics. It focuses on what students will need to succeed, now and after graduation, in physical activity and health and medically related fields. I have focused on the underlying principles of measurement and evaluation, believing that if students understand the principles, they will be able to apply the concepts in a variety of settings. This text also recognizes that most who teach this class are not measurement and evaluation specialists.

The book is divided into three parts. Part 1 introduces students to the measurement process. Chapter 1 explains the relevance of measurement and evaluation to their personal and professional lives, and Chapter 2 discusses error and introduces the concept of validity, with Chapter 3 introducing reliability and objectivity. Feedback from colleagues indicated that students learn measurement and evaluation best if a book integrates important measurement and evaluation concepts together with examples and statistics. Thus, Chapters 4 through 16 use this approach to further develop and explain the concepts of validity, objectivity, and reliability and how statistics can be applied in evaluating measurements. Students are presented with the hypothetical situation of determining the validity of a 12-minute run test as a predictor of maximal oxygen uptake. As they work through this example, they learn about tests of means, correlations, and predictions, and ultimately, they learn to perform a Bland-Altman analysis to evaluate the validity of this test.

Part 2 focuses on statistics, helping students understand numbers and introducing more advanced statistical calculations. Because many students are intimidated by mathematics, these more detailed chapters on statistics are positioned somewhat later, allowing students to develop confidence and enthusiasm before they encounter the more challenging work. Because of the rising interest in undergraduate research, a chapter on measurement and evaluation in research is also included as this is a situation nearly everyone encounters. From this treatment, students should be able to understand how the desire or need to know something about human performance flows from a question, to data collection (measurement), to statistical treatment, and eventually to evaluation and conclusions.

Part 3 presents measurement and evaluation applications with chapters on measuring physical fitness; measuring exercise, physical activity, and health; measuring psychomotor performance and sports skills; measuring in competitive sports and coaching; alternative approaches to measurement and subjective measurement; measuring and evaluating knowledge and assigning grades.

As reflected in the topics covered, this book considers the various interests of students enrolled in a typical university physical activity measurement and evaluation class. Discussions and examples show the relevance and application of measurement and evaluation in various physical activity and health-related professions, including athletic training, fitness/wellness management, exercise and sport psychology, exercise science, coaching, physical education, and physical therapy.

This book seeks to engage students and make them active participants in their education. Practical exercises that reinforce key points are included throughout the chapters as well as at the end of chapters. These exercises will help students recognize the relevance of measurement and evaluation skills to their professional lives. Many of the exercises are easily done and have been classroom tested. Where appropriate, chapters also include case studies that illustrate real-world examples of measurement and evaluation in sport and physical activity settings. Each chapter ends with a series of application questions to encourage further reflection on the chapter topics. Repetition is used throughout the text to illustrate applications and aid student learning.

The fundamental philosophy guiding this text is that measurement and evaluation are useful to all of us in many facets of our lives. I have made every effort to provide a reader-friendly and yet comprehensive text that students will find to be relevant and interesting. The book is designed to provide a firm foundation of knowledge for success in physical activity and health-related settings.

The rapid changes of the last several years make it clear that preparing for a *specific* future is difficult. Thus, I hope that teachers who use this text will be prepared to help students go beyond basic facts to higher orders of thinking: application, analysis, synthesis, and evaluation. If students acquire a thorough grounding in these important skills and in the fundamentals of measurement, they will be equipped to adapt what they have learned to their own individual situations.

Acknowledgments

I have learned a great deal in writing this text. First, that writing a technical textbook is a long and challenging, but rewarding, process.

I have also gained a greater appreciation for the many people who have helped me and supported me throughout my career and during the writing of this book. I especially appreciate the love and support of my wife Brenda and my five children, Kelly, Daniel, David, Andrew, and Anna Grace, my daughters-in-law, sons-in-law, and my grandchildren.

I also appreciate the great work of the fine staff of Routledge.

Above all I thank God, who gives meaning to life, purpose to work, and genuine hope for the future, and who will be the Ultimate Evaluator.

Part 1

Understanding the Measurement Process

1   Measurement and Evaluation for Your Personal and Professional Life

Abstract

Measurement (quantification or qualification), and evaluation (assigning value) are essential in being wise consumers and good professionals. We use measurement and evaluation most days, so the better our skills, the better our outcomes. Measures can be objective or subjective and can be norm-referenced or criterion-referenced. Measures can also be continuous or discrete. We make personal measurements and evaluations in finance, and as professionals we measure and evaluate to help humanity. Study hard, you will use this knowledge of measurement and evaluation in your personal and professional life.

Keywords: measurement, evaluation, objective, subjective, norm-referenced, criterion-referenced, continuous, discrete, quantitative, qualitative

The Value of Measurement and Evaluation

Measurement and evaluation skills are essential to both your personal life and your professional life. Why? Because, regardless of your profession, you will always be a consumer. And for most of the purchases you make, whether a sports drink, a new automobile, or a house, you will need to measure and evaluate. Lack of skill in measurement and evaluation will cost you money sooner or later, I guarantee it! Likewise, as a professional you will measure and evaluate athletes, students, patients, and clients, and the better you measure and evaluate, the better you will be.

Measurement and evaluation are most useful areas of study. "Everybody says that about their specialty area!" you might reply. Skepticism is a good quality in measurement, so you are already on your way to being good at measurement and evaluation.

For example, if you receive a generous gift of cash from your aunt and decide to make a down payment on a new automobile, measurement will be crucial to a good decision. Here are some questions you may ask:

- How much will it cost?
- What trade-in can I get for my old clunker?
- What does the warranty cover, and how long does it last?
- What's the gasoline mileage?
- How high are the payments?
- How much will I pay in interest over the loan's duration?
- How much will insurance cost?
- How fast will it go?
- Does it come in red?

All of these questions, even the last one, are measurements, and you will need these measurements to make an informed *evaluation* of which is the best automobile, which dealer has the best deal.

Measurement is the process of assigning a value (a number or quality) to the characteristic being measured. We gather measurement data by observation and by the use of measurement tools. We then decide which pieces of data ("How much will it cost?" for example) are most important. **Evaluation** is the process in which we combine all available data to make an informed decision. In most situations, we end up ranking choices based on our evaluations. Ultimately, we decide on our number one choice. If for some reason our first choice is not available, then we may have to settle for the one evaluated as second most desirable, and so forth.

When choosing a car to buy, you may ignore most of the measurements and evaluate the car based only on the last two questions: "How fast will it go?" and "Does it come in red?" If you fail to use good measurement and evaluation techniques, however, sooner or later you will likely become the victim of "buyer's remorse," facing the reality of having made an expensive, but bad, purchasing mistake.

Figure 1.1 Phil Bishop, your text author

Classifications in Measurement and Evaluation

If you go back and closely examine the possible questions to ask, and measurements to make, when determining which automobile to buy, you may notice that the measurements can be classified in two different types. For example, gas mileage can be measured objectively. This is an **objective measure**, because such a measure is independent of who is doing the measuring. Likewise, the warranty information for a car, which states the mileage and time period for coverage on the car, is objective. It doesn't change depending on who is reading the warranty. In contrast, if you ask your friends about which car color is best, you will probably get a variety of opinions. Measurements involving preference are **subjective measures**, because they depend on who is doing the measuring. These measurements are opinions, which will vary among observers. Similarly, the question, "Is this the best auto?" is subjective, because different people have different criteria for what constitutes the "best" vehicle.

Measurements can also be classified as norm-referenced or criterion-referenced. **Criterion-referenced measurements** are those measurements that compare a person's knowledge, ability, or performance against a standard or criterion that is considered essential for mastery. Criterion-referenced measurements determine whether one has a specified ability level. A person is evaluated to see if he or she meets certain criteria. These measures are usually evaluated as pass/not-pass.

Consider this example. If you take a cardiopulmonary resuscitation (CPR) class, you will probably have to pass both a performance test and a knowledge test to earn a CPR certification. You will have to demonstrate such things as knowledge of how to evaluate the safety of an accident scene and your ability to perform CPR effectively. Depending on the certification, you may have to demonstrate your ability to do CPR correctly on both an infant and an adult. You will have to demonstrate knowledge of certain cognitive aspects of CPR, such as the order in which certain things are done and the ratio and rate of compressions and ventilations for both infants and adults. You will have to pass all aspects of the testing in order to meet the criteria for certification. You will not be compared to other CPR test takers—you will simply have to demonstrate that you know enough and can do enough to be effective in rescuing a person in need of CPR. Since you either can demonstrate this or not, independent of others' abilities, this test is criterion-referenced.

In contrast, the test you took for admittance to college was norm-referenced. **Norm-referenced measurements** are those that measure an individual's performance in comparison to that of others. Although there may have been some minimum score (a criterion) for being admitted to your college or university, your score was "referenced" to those of all other test takers—that is, it was stated in terms of where your score fell compared to those of other test takers. You were likely given an interpretation of your score that was based on either all other scores or all scores in your grade level. It may have been the percentage of scores that were the same as your score or below it. (For example, "63%" would mean that 63 percent of test takers scored the same as or below your score.) When you take a fitness test, generally speaking, your score will be meaningless to you until it has been compared to the scores of other people of your gender and similar age. For example, if you did 50 push-ups in two minutes, is that good or bad? You don't really know, until your score is expressed relative to others. Test situations like these, where one score is evaluated with respect to others, are norm-referenced measurements.

It is important to recognize that being "average," or even in the top 25 percent or 10 percent, doesn't necessarily mean that the score is ideal or even desirable. For example, a person's body fatness might be "average" according to norm-based standards, but the person still might be overly fat. Because the United States' population is becoming increasingly sedentary and over-fat, the use of norm-based measures for fatness must be interpreted thoughtfully.

The CPR test and your height illustrate the difference between criterion-based and norm-based measurements and also illustrate the differences between discrete and continuous scores. A score on a CPR test is a **discrete measurement**, because there are only two possible scores: passed or failed. But your height can have many, many different values; this is an example of continuous scoring. In a true **continuous measurement**, it is possible to have an infinite number of scores, because the measurements can be anywhere on a scale, only limited by the precision of the ruler. For example, the star ratings for movies are *not* a continuous scale, because there can be only zero, one, two, three, four, or five stars (sometimes there is a half star, but that doesn't make the scale continuous). In contrast, your body weight is a good example of a continuous measurement, because your weight can be measured down to the fraction of an ounce—you can get as precise as your scales permit.

Measurement and Evaluation Applications in Life

If you become a teacher, a coach, a fitness professional, an athletic trainer, or a physical therapist, you will use measurement and evaluation often in your work.

As a teacher, you can measure your students early in the school year to evaluate what they know and at what level to begin instruction. As a fitness expert, you will make measurements in order to evaluate which exercises would be safe and useful for your clients. As an athletic trainer, you will make measurements to evaluate injuries and determine the best course of action—to have the athlete sit out a few plays, to call for medical transport, or to treat the athlete on the spot. As a physical therapist, you will measure patients' abilities, evaluate and select therapies, and monitor and demonstrate patients' progress. As a coach, you will measure athletes' fitness, strength, speed, and other abilities, as well as collect measurements to show the team's and the opponent's overall strengths and weaknesses. Measurements are essential to making accurate evaluations and good decisions in many fields.

In fact, we are constantly measuring and evaluating all day long, without even thinking about it.

- Will my car fit into that space?
- What are the odds I'll get a ticket if I park there?
- Can I pay all my bills this month?
- Can I afford to cut this class?
- Do I have enough money for an orange mocha cappuccino?
- Are my grades good enough to get into graduate school?
- How much will I have to study to keep my B in that class?

All of these are measurement and evaluation problems that we solve, hopefully correctly, every day.

1.1   Practical Exercise

There are 128 fluid ounces in a gallon. Find some common items (for example, canned soft drinks) and express their price on a per-gallon basis.

1.2   Practical Exercise

Give examples of how we could express measurements in ways that are helpful in making good evaluations. For example, how could we express the total costs of owning and operating things like automobiles, motorcycles, boats, cellular phones, and homes to help us evaluate them?

Applications in Research

To keep up to date as professionals, we must stay informed of current research. Like other professionals, researchers often face a primary challenge of obtaining good-quality measurements. Research into fitness, therapy, and coaching is generally limited by the variables that can be measured. In the past, research on education was largely limited to **quantitative measurement**—data which could be quantified so that it could be analyzed statistically to test hypotheses. More recently, however, research on education has expanded to include **qualitative assessments**—efforts to understand the processes that underlie various behaviors, through detailed, verbal descriptions of characteristics, cases, and settings, using observations and interviews to collect data.

Exercise was not scientifically studied systematically until the mid-1930s. This means we still have much to learn, and some of what we believe now is probably wrong. In fact, some commonly used measurements have never been closely evaluated for accuracy.

This isn't meant to be discouraging. Rather, the point is that there are still a great many unexplored areas and still much to be learned. We need research to develop better measurement and evaluation techniques to advance of our specialty areas.

1.3 Practical Exercise

What measurement problems exist in your specialty area? Think of three measurement challenges in your area, or ask professionals for at least three measurement issues.

Concluding Thoughts

This text will introduce you to the fundamentals of measurement and evaluation. It covers the essential points of knowledge that will serve you in your profession and in your life, including some very useful statistical skills. It should provide a foundation to help you learn what you will need in the future. Ideally, you will continue to observe and learn, and you will constantly become a better professional and a wiser consumer. Reading carefully will help you begin the learning process before you come to class. Asking good questions will help you progress. Most important, however, looking for ways you can apply what you learn to your own life will make this knowledge your own.

Application Questions

1   List three everyday examples of measurement and evaluation in your own life.
2   Give an example of how you or someone you know was intentionally or unintentionally cheated because of a measurement error.
3   What is the difference between a norm-referenced and a criterion-referenced test?

    a   Give an example of a norm-referenced test.
    b   Give an example of a criterion-referenced test.

4   What is the difference between a continuous and a discrete measure?

    a   Give an example of a continuous measure.
    b   Give an example of a discrete measure.

Additional Practical Exercises

1.4   Practical Exercise

Find a news article dealing with measurement and answer the following questions:

1   What was the measurement?
2   Was the measurement difficult to make?
3   Was it accurate?
4   What were the potential sources of error?
5   What were the key issues involved?
6   Did an evaluation arise from the measurement?
7   Does the evaluation, if any, appear reasonable and accurate? Why?
8   What might be the negative or positive ramifications of poor measurement in this situation?
9   What might be the positive ramifications of accurate measurement?

1.5   Practical Exercise

Interview

Choose ONE of the following areas:

- *Education:* School teachers or administrators
- *Adult Fitness:* Managers and employees of YMCAs, private fitness clubs, university gyms
- *Recreation Center:* Directors or employees of a campus recreation center
- *Allied Health:* Physical, occupational, or respiratory therapists, therapy assistants, physicians, phlebotomists, lab technicians

Identify an expert in the selected area and interview him or her (in person or by email or telephone). Ask permission to conduct a brief interview (should take no longer than 15 minutes). Record the person's answers to the following questions:

Name of person interviewed _____ Occupation _____

Phone or email _____ Date _____

What measurements does the person make in the course of his or her work?

_____

How are these measurements used?

_____

(continued)

(continued)

What additional measures would the person make if additional equipment, time, or resources were available?

_____

Is the person confident regarding the accuracy of the measurements and evaluations? Why?

_____

What skills and experience are needed to do the measurements this person uses?

_____

Who is affected (and how) if a measurement is poorly made?

_____

Ask an additional question of your own about this person's use of measurement and/or evaluation.

_____

Turn in your research findings.

2 The Challenge of Good Measurement
Validity

Abstract

Making accurate measurements and evaluations is harder than most of us realize. Much sport depends on accurate measures, yet all but the simplest measures have error. Good measurement is a result of minimizing error. Error is so important in measurement that we name measurement errors as validity, reliability, and objectivity. Validity means a measurement measures what it is supposed to measure, with acceptable error. And acceptable error is determined by the context in which the measurement is made.

Keywords: validity, acceptable error, true score

Measurement Error

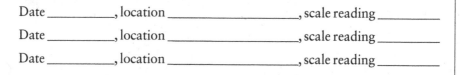

2.1   Practical Exercise

Before you read this chapter, weigh yourself on three different scales while wearing the same clothing, shoes, jewelry, etc., and record the results to the nearest one-quarter pound (or 0.1 kilogram) below:

Date _____, location _____, scale reading _____

Date _____, location _____, scale reading _____

Date _____, location _____, scale reading _____

Most likely, you recorded a different weight from each of the scales. How can you explain the different readings of your body weight on the different scales? What does this tell you about this common measurement?

Many of us make a big mistake regarding measurement. We assume, erroneously, that most measurements are accurate. We buy gasoline, or steak, or sugar, or gourmet fudge, trusting that we are getting the amount for which we paid. But, sometimes, we don't! Sometimes we get more than we paid for, sometimes less.

Only a few measurement situations involve zero error, and these are usually simple tasks. Counting tasks, the simplest measuring tasks, may have zero error. However, even in counting tasks, error can occur. If I ask you to count the tables or the desks in your classroom, error might result because it is not necessarily clear which things should be classified as tables or desks.

A counting task becomes more complex when the items to be counted are not well described. For example, the National Collegiate Athletic Association (NCAA) has an injury-reporting program. This program is useful, but it would be hard to judge the degree of error. When does an injury count as an injury? When it causes an athlete to miss practice? When he or she is able to do nothing at all? Should it count as an injury when an athlete has reduced performance but is on the court or field anyway? The definition of injury affects the injury count.

Error occurs even in "precise" measurements. For example, consider the task of measuring a coastline. If we measure an irregular coastline with a mile-long ruler, we will miss many of the curves and outcroppings and so we will come up with a shorter length. A 1,000-foot-long ruler will measure more of the indentations and, hence, give a measurement that is longer than the length using the mile-long ruler. Likewise, a yardstick will measure a longer coastline compared to the 1,000-foot-long ruler, because the yardstick measures in smaller, more precise increments, so it includes more indentations and irregularities. Thus, the coastline seems to get longer because the more precise yardstick incorporates smaller variations in the coastline. If we accurately remeasure the coastline with a foot-long ruler, we'll measure even smaller irregularities, and we will find the coast is longer yet. If we measure down to individual rocks, it is longer still. Finally, if we measure microscopically—that is, if we are able to measure the small irregularities in each grain of sand—our billions of tiny measurements will add up to a longer measurement. With each increase in the precision of our measurement, the coastline measurement increases. This is continuous measurement.

Trivia Question

World's Longest Measured Coastline

Here's a curiosity: Which country of the world has the longest measured coastline and why? (The answer is at the end of the chapter.)

Examples of Measurement Error in Sport

In many sports, the measurements involve what appears to be simple counting; however, even counting isn't always accurate. How many batters are out? How many goals, points, or runs have been scored? These sound like easy questions, and we may think it is safe to assume all sports scores are error-free. But consider other measurements vital in determining the score. In basketball, was a player fouled in the act of shooting (two free throws) or not (one free throw)? In softball or baseball, was the pitch a ball or a strike? Was the hit ball foul or fair? Was the base runner safe or out? All of these measurements are subject to error, and all are vital to "counting" the score.

In some sports, measurement is even more difficult (and subjective). For example, in gymnastics and diving, a panel of judges is required to make very precise measurements very quickly. This situation can result in serious disputes over measurement. In the 2002 Winter Olympics in Salt Lake City, Utah, for instance, a major scandal developed over the scoring (measurement) of the pairs ice skating.[1] Likewise, in a boxing match where the outcome is decided by points (based on successful punches to different parts of the body), major discrepancies can occur among judges.

Minimizing Error

2.2 Practical Exercise

Read the following paragraph and count the number of times the letter "f" appears in either upper or lower case. Record your count.

From feudal days, training farm hands for first-class farms has always been a lot of fun. They first need facts for facilitating farm livestock in fruitfulness, a friendly art. After this, the foremost priority of farm owners is to facilitate the function of fruitful finance. Since the forefathers of the farmers aforetimes, they functioned to foster farm hands in the first-class function of their farms. The farm owners, feeling fatherly, feel they should further the family tradition of training farm fellows to facilitate forward function on the fine farms to avoid foreclosure or failure, especially in the form of finances. Facts that facilitate forecasting facilitate profit. Fruitful fundamental farm function by aficionados, with or without frustration, is fully a function of avoiding futility.

(continued)

(continued)

Now repeat the process. Did you get a different number the second time? For most people, the count changes. Since the number of *f*s in the paragraph is unchanged, at least one of your counts must have contained error. Count again. Maybe this time you noticed some *f*s that you missed before, and your number went up slightly.

In fact, certain strategies allow us to reduce errors, including those in tasks like Practical Exercise 2.2. If we're very good, we may eventually reduce the error to zero (but remember that zero error typically occurs only for the simplest of measurements, such as counting).

One strategy for the *f*-counting task is to start counting from the last word and work backward. If we go backward, we cease to read and we see more *f*s. This is because as we read, we tend to skip "unnecessary" words such as "of." Another strategy is to hold a piece of paper over the text and read down each column of letters. We can circle every *f*, total each line, and add the numbers for a grand total.

The point is that although the simplest measurement is subject to error, we can use techniques to reduce error. Numerous strategies can help us reduce error to a tolerable level. For example, measuring twice reduces error. Better measurement techniques result in better measurements and smaller error. This text is devoted to helping you learn procedures, strategies, and techniques to minimize error, so that when you measure something you will do a good job of it.

Understanding Error

Because one of the fundamental issues in measurement is that every measurement contains some inherent error, we can think of any measurement as a two-part equation:

measurement = true value ± error

This equation can be expressed mathematically as:

$$X = T \pm E$$

where X is the measurement, T is the true value, and E represents the error.

This equation says that every time we measure something, the number that we get (X) is really composed of two separate parts. The part we really want is the true value (T). T, or true value, is a construct we wish to measure. Because we often can't measure T, we substitute some kind of measurement and use the observed score, X, as our best estimate. We will discover how good a job we have done of substituting X for T when we get an estimate of error and decide just how much error we can tolerate and still use X in the decision-making process.

As suggested above, we seldom know what T really is. We never know because some error (E), though it may be small, is always present, thus adding to, or subtracting from, the true value. E can be either positive or negative. On a close call on the football field, for example, the exact placement of the ball will determine whether or not a first down was gained. There is error in this measurement; it may be too long or too short. Once we get a good estimate of *E*, we can then determine if the error is acceptably small.

We know every measurement has error. Sometimes we know the *direction* of the error—that is, whether it adds to or subtracts from the true value. Most people tend to say they are taller than they actually are. Many male athletes tend to describe themselves as heavier than they actually are. Although sometimes we can *guess* the direction of particular errors, in most measurement situations we do not *know* the direction of the errors.

The challenge of good measurement is to minimize error. In fact, the most accurate measurements in the world simply keep the error very, very small. You may be thinking to yourself that the best measurement can eliminate *all* error, but that simply isn't possible for most useful measurements. You may also be asking "how do I know when an error is small enough?" For example, for reasons you will understand later, an error of 5 mg/100 mL on a measurement that is normally between 150 and 300 mg/100 mL for total cholesterol is a very small error, whereas an error of 5 mg/100 mL on a measurement that is normally between 12 and 18 mg/100 mL, e.g., for hemoglobin, is large. We'll discuss how to evaluate the size of the error in the next section.

How Much Error Can We Stand?

The next question to consider is: How much error is tolerable? The answer is, "it depends." For a backyard volleyball match, the exact court size isn't crucial. If the timing isn't exact for a local foot race, there will be no dire consequences. In contrast, if the pilot of a small aircraft mismeasures her cargo weight or how much fuel is on board, the plane may crash. If a medical lab tech mismeasures a crucial blood characteristic, a patient may suffer or die. Errors on many medical tests can cause unnecessary further testing, unnecessary procedures (e.g., surgery), or even failure to recognize a fatal disease.

Naming Measurement Errors: Validity

Good measurement is a result of minimizing error. Because error minimization is so critical, we have developed ways to classify measurement errors, as issues of **validity**, **reliability**, or **objectivity**. These are important qualities of measurements, and when you evaluate any measurement, you should consider all three. Fully understanding validity, reliability, and objectivity is the key to good measurement, and good measurement is vital to accurate evaluation.

Validity

Validity is the degree to which a measurement measures what it is supposed to measure, with acceptable error. We must also keep in mind that the ultimate goal is not simply to take a valid measurement but to arrive at a valid evaluation. Hence, to be completely valid, a measurement must not only be acceptably accurate, but also must be interpreted and applied accurately.

As an example of invalid testing, interpretation, and application of data in measuring fitness with field tests, body fatness may have such a large impact on other measurements that it greatly reduces their validity. Consider a student who lives on a farm, is overly fat, but has very great muscular endurance: he can throw 50-pound sacks of feed for hours. In school we attempt to measure his endurance with a pull-up test. We might accurately measure his ability to do pull-ups, but since he has to lift a lot of fat, he may receive a low score that inadequately (invalidly) represents his true muscular endurance. The same type of error can occur with step tests or other tests designed to estimate aerobic fitness. Many fitness field test items unintentionally include fatness in their measurement, and though fatness is a valid characteristic to measure, it often contaminates measures of other physical abilities.

A valid measurement, then, has *acceptable* error. It can be thought of as a refinement of the equation for a score:

valid measurement = true score $\pm$ *acceptable* error

or,

valid $X = T \pm$ acceptable E

How do we know what is "acceptable?" How much error will you accept? How good is good enough? The answer depends on what is being measured. For example, weight measurement is critical in competitive wrestling or boxing. As a result, we need a scale that is accurate within a quarter of a pound. The scales in your bathroom probably only need to be accurate within a pound or two, and maybe not even that good. The scales that weigh big trucks on the highway are valid only within about 60 pounds.

Examples of Validity

An umpire in a softball or baseball game must show some degree of validity in evaluating balls and strikes. No one expects that an umpire will be perfect, yet it would be extremely frustrating if the pitches called strikes were far outside the strike zone and the pitches called balls were well inside the strike zone. If the umpire's judgment of the strike zone doesn't accurately (validly) measure the strike zone, then neither the pitcher nor the batter can predict which pitch will be called a "strike" and which will not. The same would be true for fouls in basketball. If the measures of what constitutes a foul—that is, the validity of foul calls—were extremely bad, then it would be very difficult for players to play the game well.

Having a valid measurement only creates the *possibility* of a valid evaluation. If we accurately measure muscular endurance but misinterpret the measure as one of muscular strength, then we will not make a valid evaluation of strength. Appropriate circumstances such as maximal effort, fully rested participants and others must be considered before we can accurately assess someone's strength. Even then, the measure might reflect some other issue, such as sickness, lack of sleep, minor muscle soreness, or some other source of error that will create an invalid measurement.

You can probably think of many instances when your knowledge and abilities were tested and you did not feel the results were accurate. Whether it was a test of your knowledge or fitness, you may have felt the test was not valid. For example, if a test as a whole did not measure what it was supposed to measure, then the test was invalid.

Maximizing Validity

We try to make every measurement as valid as possible, but, often, we cannot be certain that a measurement is valid or invalid—only that there is strong evidence for its validity. We can't say that a given measurement is perfectly valid, but only that it is close enough for our application.

Nearly always, we have to make a trade-off between the accuracy of a measurement and its cost, the time it requires, or how much effort is required. Scales that can measure body weight to within a quarter-pound cost more than scales that are accurate only to one pound. In general, measurements that are more valid are more expensive, take longer, and require more equipment or more personnel than less valid measures.

In many physical education and athletics situations, the shortage of time, money, and personnel means that, to be practical, we have to settle for less valid measurements than we would prefer if the circumstances were better. For example, the better-trained, more experienced, and more highly certified referees are, generally the more they charge to officiate a competition, because they have a stronger claim to validity.

Sometimes, a lot of error may be tolerable at one point in time but not at another. For someone who is enjoying recreational sports, validity is important in official measurements, but it is not as important as it is for the Olympics. What is acceptable depends on the context in which the measurement is taken.

Regardless of the degree of accuracy required to meet the definition of validity, validity is obviously the most important characteristic of any measurement. If a measurement does not measure what it is supposed to measure (too much error), it is misleading. Validity is also often the hardest characteristic to establish. In fact, for most measurements, validity can never be *absolutely* established because it is impossible to determine absolutely the true measurement. That is, the exact size of the error always remains unknown.

In some situations, a measurement is declared to be valid because a great deal of effort has gone into minimizing error. In these cases, we believe that the remaining error is small enough to be unimportant. Of course, error still exists, as is reflected in the equation for valid measurement. It's just been decided that the error is small enough to disregard. Remember, however, that the equation tells us only that the *measurement* is valid, with some degree of acceptable error. To achieve a valid *evaluation*, we must interpret and apply the measurement correctly—and there is no equation for that!

Concluding Thoughts

A measurement's most important quality is its validity. Validity is seldom absolute for complex measurements; in most cases, it is a question of whether the measurement has an acceptable or unacceptable degree of validity. Whether the validity is acceptable depends on the situation. Validity may be evaluated through several types of evidence. The simplest (and least convincing) of these is content validity, which is verified by having acknowledged experts evaluate the measurement as valid. Construct validity is verified by examining the measurement's ability to assess key constructs. One way to do this is to compare individuals' known proficiency to test results (highly skilled individuals should score very well and unskilled individuals should score very poorly). When a criterion measurement is available, criterion validity makes possible a rigorous statistical evaluation of new measurement techniques and thus provides a strong argument for validity. Ecological validity refers to how well the context of a research measurement matches the actual application. External validity refers to how applicable research measurement is to a population or situations. These last two types of validity are important because they remind us that a measurement must not only be validly made, but also be validly interpreted and applied.

Application Questions

1   For the exercise on weighing yourself, a data collection sheet was provided. What are the advantages of data collection sheets?
2   Why is validity the most important quality of any measurement?

Answer to Trivia Question

Canada, because it has so many islands.

Note

1 https://en.wikipedia.org/wiki/2002_Winter_Olympics_figure_skating_scandal. Retrieved May 28, 2018.

3 Additional Challenges of Good Measurement
Reliability and Objectivity

Abstract

In addition to validity, there are two other key characteristics of measurement. Reliability means a repeated measure yields similar results with every repetition. Objectivity (inter-rater reliability) means a measure yields similar results when performed by different measurers. A measure may be reliable or objective and yet not be valid. Factors like learning, fatigue, and environmental changes may reduce reliability, and poor directions, bias, or lack of training may reduce objectivity. Good reliability and objectivity are *evidence* for valid measurement, but are not *sufficient* to ensure validity.

Keywords: reliability, objectivity, acceptable error, inter-rater reliability

Reliability

When the validity of a measurement cannot be fully established, we must try to accumulate enough evidence to trust that the measurement is indeed valid. One step to accumulating this evidence is to determine *reliability*. **Reliability** means consistency or repeatability. A valid measure will be reliable. With a reliable measurement, we can repeat the measurement over and over and get similar results each time. This is *consistent* error. Reliability can be expressed in terms of an equation, just as for validity:

reliable score = true score ± a consistent error

or,

reliable $X = T \pm$ consistent E

where X is the measurement, T is the true score, and E is the error.

The reliability of a measurement is largely determined by three factors:

- The validity of the score.
- The repetitions of the measurement (the more a measure is repeated, the better the reliability).
- The stability of the measured characteristic.

To understand the last factor, consider that some characteristics are more sensitive to internal and external influences than others. For example, fine motor skills like tracking and steadiness are more sensitive to fatigue, dehydration, and other influences than are gross skills like lifting a non-maximal weight. Hence, reliability tends to be lower for these sorts of measurements, unless the outside influences are carefully controlled.

If the error is acceptably small (valid), then the observed scores will be very consistent over different trials. The measurements need only be *about* the same for the measure to qualify as reliable, because for most measurements we are never going to get exactly the same scores. We don't expect perfect reliability on any measurement, but if this is a valid test of free-throw ability, then we would expect that, in general, performers will achieve about the same score whenever they are tested, unless their ability changed. This is a *reliable* test: it produces scores that do not vary much between trials. Reliable scores are *stable* scores.

Examples of Reliability

For all valid measures, good reliability is requisite. If, for example, we are measuring an athlete's recovery from an injury, we want to have a reliable measurement. That is, if the measurement shows that the athlete is rehabbing well, then we want the measurement to show that consistently. If the measurement doesn't show good reliability, that means we are not accurately (validly) measuring the rehab status. If the measures aren't reliable, we won't be able to say whether the therapy was effective.

If we are measuring the strength of an athlete, we also want a reliable measurement. If we measure bench press strength, we want a measurement that will give the same score each time, if the subject's bench press strength hasn't changed. If the measurement doesn't give consistent results, and chest and triceps strength aren't changing, then we are getting so much error that the measurement couldn't be very valid. That is, if the error is large enough to cause inconsistency, it is too large to result in a valid measurement.

Relationship of Reliability to Validity

If the reliability of a measurement is very good, we sometimes accept that as a rough indicator of the measurement's validity. It is not a *guarantee* of validity, because a measurement may evidence very high reliability without being valid. This can happen when an error is large but also very consistent (because reliability measures only the consistency, not the size of error). That is, it is possible to have a large, constant error and, therefore, have good reliability yet poor validity. Remember, validity requires acceptably small error, so a large consistent error means that the measurement is not valid, even though it yields good reliability.

Consider a situation in which a weighing scale for people is broken in such a way that it consistently adds 30 pounds to everyone's weight. This scale gives very consistent, very reliable results, which are invalid because the error is too large.

Factors that Affect Reliability

Some factors hurt reliability. In physical performance, a common factor that causes reliability errors is fatigue. If a teacher had her students run three miles and timed them, then had them repeat the run immediately, the results would show very poor reliability, for obvious reasons. The very fit students might only lose seconds, but the unfit might lose several minutes.

Of course, the opposite happens when students are improving in skill. Suppose we took a group of students who had never hit a golf ball before and tested their ability to chip by having them hit 30 balls at a target, then had them do it again. We would expect to get poor reliability simply because students would be learning and improving, even while we were trying to measure them. So, on the one hand, we must be cautious of effects which might change the true score (such as skill improvement), and we also have to be wary of changes in the test group (such as fatigue) which might increase error. If either the error or the true score changes, then the reliability of the measurement will be reduced.

Another common factor that can hurt reliability is environmental change. If we give a mile-run test in cool conditions and then give another test in very hot and humid conditions, the measurements will not be reliable, because an external factor changed performance.

Objectivity

Objectivity is sometimes called inter-rater reliability, because it is the reliability between different measurers or judges. Humans making the measurement are often biased or careless. Objectivity, as a quality of measurement, indicates the consistency among the measurers or raters.

Be careful not to confuse objectivity with objectives. Objectives are goals—things you are trying to accomplish. You would have *objectives* for a class you are teaching.

You would want to evaluate students *objectively* in order to give them *objective, as opposed to subjective,* scores.

A measurement has good objectivity when it does not matter who is making the measurement—the results will be the same, or close to it, regardless of the measurer. Expressed in terms of error, we can think of objectivity as follows:

$$\text{score with good objectivity} = \text{true score} \pm \text{acceptable error attributable to the measurer}$$

or,

$$X \text{ with good objectivity} = T \pm \text{acceptable } E \text{ due to measurer}$$

where X represents the score, T is the true score, and E is the error.

Objectivity is largely determined by three factors:

- The validity of the score.
- The availability of good, clear directions for administering the measurement.
- The ability and willingness of the measurer to read, understand, and follow the directions precisely.

Formal training for measurers (e.g., judges, referees, and umpires) is a means for helping to maximize objectivity.

A truly objective score is free of bias. That is, it doesn't matter who makes the measurement; the score is not affected by the measurer (although it may be affected by other sources of error). Measurement error due to lack of objectivity is more obvious in some situations than in others. If all the judges in a gymnastics competition are boosters or parents of one team, we would expect bias (low objectivity), regardless of their attempts to be impartial.

In sport, fitness, physical therapy, athletic training, and research, good objectivity is a goal. The investigator's biases should not influence the measurement of data or their evaluation. To maximize the objectivity of research, researchers often "blind" their subjects, meaning that they do not allow the subjects to know when they are receiving the experimental treatment or the placebo or control treatment. (The placebo or control is a "fake" treatment, against whose results the experimental treatment's results are compared.) This is called a "single-blind" experiment. In a "double-blind" experiment, neither the researchers nor the subjects know when they are receiving the experimental treatment and when the placebo.

For example, if we were testing a drug's impact on performance, we could test the subjects twice: once with the actual drug and once with a placebo. If the subjects didn't know which treatment they were getting, but the investigators did, it would be a single-blind experiment. If someone else besides the investigators administered the drug and concealed from both the subjects and the investigators when the subjects had taken the drug or the placebo, then it would be a double-blind experiment. Because neither the subjects nor the investigators would know which treatment was administered, neither group would be able to bias the results, thus helping ensure measurement objectivity.

Maximizing Objectivity

In situations where the probability of bias is high, the following steps help maximize objectivity:

1   Select measurers who are *not* associated in any way with the outcome of the measurement. For example, coaches are not objective when their own teams compete.
2   Devise clear, complete directions for scoring (for example, define terms clearly).
3   Train the measurers thoroughly so that all understand exactly what should be done and so that they have adequate experience doing it.
4   Monitor scoring and scorers for evidence of bias.

It is possible for a score to be objective but not valid, if the measurer is contributing very little error but there are other sources of error which result in an unacceptable total error. Objectivity only minimizes the error arising from the measurer. If the measure is not valid, then it doesn't matter whether or not it is objective, because the score already has too much error.

Neither high objectivity nor high reliability ensures that a measure is valid. However, if a measurement is unreliable or not sufficiently objective, you can be sure that it is not valid. Evidence of both reliability and objectivity is *necessary* evidence for valid measurement, but is not *sufficient* to ensure validity.

3.1   Practical Exercise

Think of examples of subjectivity (the opposite of objectivity) in sport and everyday life. For example, art competitions rely on subjective judgments of the art work in the competition.

Concluding Thoughts

Error is the enemy of good measurement. Errors can be either positive or negative, and typically we do not know the direction of the error. Fortunately, we can take steps to minimize error. Measuring multiple times may reduce the error. Better measurement techniques will result in better measurements and smaller errors.

Validity in a measurement is the primary goal. A measurement's validity is the degree to which it measures what it is supposed to measure, with acceptable error. Validity also requires accurate interpretation and application. What level of error is acceptable depends on what is being measured and the context of the measurement. Validity is supported, but not proven, by good reliability and objectivity. A measurement with good reliability has a consistent (large or small) error. If a measurement is valid, it will be reliable, but good reliability does not guarantee good validity. Objectivity describes the amount of error that is due to the measurer. If the error caused by the measurer is large, then the measurement cannot have an acceptably small error and, therefore, cannot be valid, at least for that measurer. Good measurement techniques will yield valid, reliable, and objective measurements.

Application Questions

1   Explain why a measurement cannot be valid if it is not reliable. Give an original illustration of this concept.

2   Explain why a measurement might be reliable and still not be valid. Give an original illustration of this concept.

3   If a measurement is not valid, why doesn't it matter whether or not it is reliable?

4   If a measurement is not objective, what does that say about its validity?

5   Give some examples from your own experience of biased judging, refereeing, or umpiring. How did it make you feel to be a victim—or beneficiary—of biased evaluation?

6   Give some examples from your own experience of biased grading. How did it make you feel to be a victim—or beneficiary—of biased evaluation?

7   Every measurement is composed of two parts: a true score plus or minus some error. Please explain in detail, using *original* examples (one example each), how *error* relates to each of the following concepts (circle the term in your answer):

   • Validity
   • Reliability (and how reliability relates to validity)
   • Objectivity (and how objectivity relates to validity)

8   *Validity, reliability, and objectivity are crucial for good measurement and evaluation.* Use the analogy of a darts contest (or another sport) to explain to a fellow student what this statement means. Discuss each term in the sentence. Be complete and clear in your explanation.

9   Explain all the ways a good measurement system could be used to improve *one* of the following tasks:

   a   Coaching strength and conditioning or basketball
   b   Managing a health clinic or recreation center
   c   Teaching PE on any level
   d   Directing adult fitness or recreation

Additional Practical Exercise

3.2   Practical Exercise

One of the keys to good objectivity is learning to follow directions exactly as written. Complete the exercise below.

Ability to Follow Directions

Your Name _____

Read everything before doing anything. The object of this test is to point out that directions are meant to be followed. Students often find an assignment difficult NOT because they cannot do the work, but because they have not followed directions. You may even decide to skip reading this preliminary paragraph, because you do not think it is important. This would not be wise. You may take longer to do this test than other students, but if you are one of the first to finish, turn your paper over and wait patiently for the others to finish.

1 Write your last name in the space provided where it says "YOUR NAME."
2 Draw a circle around your name.
3 Draw five small squares in the upper left-hand corner of this page.
4 Put an "X" in each square.
5 Draw a circle around each square.
6 Underline "ABILITY TO FOLLOW DIRECTIONS."
7 Draw a circle around each word in the directions of number six.
8 Place an "X" in the lower left-hand corner of this sheet.
9 Draw a triangle around the "X" you have just drawn.
10 On the reverse side of this page, in the top right-hand corner, write 8950 and 9803.
11 Call out your first name before writing any more on this page.
12 If you think you have followed all of the directions up to this point, call out, "I have."
13 Write your name in the middle of the bottom of this page.
14 Now that you have read everything before doing anything, as you were instructed in the opening paragraph, do only instructions number 1 and 14.

4 Understanding Validity

Abstract

Validity is the key quality of good measurement. It is established as construct, criterion, or content validity. Validity requires not only acceptably good measurement, but also correct interpretation and application of the measure (ecological and external validity). Validity is always context-specific and may be hard to establish for some measurements.

Keywords: construct validity, criterion validity, or content validity, ecological validity, external validity

Introduction

When a measurement has validity, we are measuring what we intend to measure and we are correctly interpreting and applying these measurements. Validity is the most important characteristic of any measurement. Therefore, establishing validity is of utmost importance.

Validity is not always established conclusively; instead, we collect evidence that suggests an acceptable degree of validity. In fact, the concept of validity itself is a continuous rather than a criterion measurement. That is, validity is never a yes-or-no issue; it is a question of degree. A measurement may appear to be highly valid or invalid, but it will seldom be 100 percent valid. If a measurement is very difficult, then we may tolerate a lower degree of validity. For example, measures of intelligence, anxiety, and emotion are very difficult, so we tolerate measurements with low, but acceptable, validity. Measures of aerobic capacity or sprint speed are easier to obtain, so we demand higher validity. In addition, the more crucial the measurement, the higher the validity must be. For example, if we are diagnosing cancer, we need a highly valid, discrete (yes or no) measure.

This chapter is the most important chapter of this book. If you do not grasp validity, you will not be good at measurement and evaluation.

Types of Validity

Construct Validity

The most fundamental approach to evaluating validity is construct validity. A construct is a characteristic that forms the foundation for the value being measured. For example, to measure wellness, we must identify and measure all of the underlying constructs that "construct" wellness. A person could be free from any physical disease and yet, if the person has a mental illness, he or she would not be well. To measure wellness validly, we have to measure the mental and physical, along with all the other, constructs that comprise wellness.

Construct validity refers to the correspondence between the constructs for a value and the actual measurement that is being used to measure that value. Because constructs are the fundamental principles that comprise (construct) the value we are trying to measure, we can think of a valid test as being one that evaluates the key measurement constructs. Some measurement experts argue that *all* validity is essentially construct validity. That is, the major errors in validity can be traced to either erroneous overrepresentation of constructs—that is, including things in the measurement that are not true constructs of the characteristic being measured—or failure to include important constructs.

It is helpful to think in terms of construct validity when making complex measurements. As an example, if we want to measure a person's ability to play soccer, we would consider the constructs needed to be a good player. What abilities does a competent soccer player need?

- Passing skills
- Dribbling skill
- Shooting skills
- Ball-trapping skills
- Tackling skills
- Defensive skills

- Running endurance
- Agility
- Leg strength
- Kicking power
- Speed

For elite soccer play, additional constructs are vital. Some of these may be difficult to measure:

- Attitude (How does the player interact with other players? How does she play when far behind on the scoreboard?).
- Sense of field position.
- Sense of who is "open".
- Teamwork.
- Ability to develop tactics and strategy.
- Ability to adjust to the other team's or other players' different tactics and strategy.
- Willingness to be coached.

If we want a truly valid test of soccer skill, we need one that tests most of the qualities listed above, so that it will have construct validity. We also want the test to weight the different constructs appropriately, because all constructs are not equally important.

One approach for establishing construct validity is to examine the scores of a large group of test takers with a variety of known ability levels. If we give the soccer skills test to some pro players, to some NCAA All-American players, to some high school players, to some elementary players, and to some nonplayers, we should be able to predict the results for each group. If players with much less practice, training, and experience score better than players whom we know to be proficient, then we have validity problems. If we have a valid test, then the players' scores should reflect their training and experience (key constructs) in soccer.

4.1   Practical Exercise

Do you consider yourself "fit"? What constructs constitute physical fitness?

In summary, constructs are the underlying factors that are fundamental to a capability. A measurement that fails to measure key underlying constructs is not valid. In order to develop valid physical performance tests, professionals must understand sport and exercise and movement's underlying constructs.

Criterion Validity

US taxpayers fund a little-known federal agency called the National Institute of Standards and Technology (NIST). This agency is responsible for the accuracy of standards and measurements. In the Office of Weights and Measures, the NIST maintains standards such as a meter stick that is extremely close to 1 meter long (but not exactly, because of ever-present error). The NIST can certify length measurements to a resolution of 1 nanometer (about 1/75,000 the thickness of a human hair) by comparing length measurement devices to their own carefully maintained master measurements.

These very precise standards illustrate criterion validity. A *criterion* is simply a "master gauge" measure. That is, it is a measurement sufficiently valid that we use it as a point of comparison. To establish **criterion validity** for a meter stick, we simply compare it to the one at the NIST. If they are the same length (or "close enough" for our usage), then we can say our meter stick has "criterion validity." If we have a very trustworthy criterion measurement (that is, if we can compare very accurately), then we will have very high confidence in the criterion validity of our own measurement device. Criterion validity is one of the most convincing ways to establish the validity of a measurement, but it requires that a criterion measurement be available for comparison.

Calibration is an application of criterion validity to evaluate a measurement device. For example, most states employ someone to visit grocery stores with a set of NIST-certified scale weights to check the store's scales and make sure we are actually getting a pound of steak when the scale indicates a pound. Similarly, a state employee visits our local gasoline stations to make sure we are getting a gallon of gas when we pay for one. Calibration simply applies the concept of criterion validity to a particular measurement device.

Sometimes, a complex measure of physical performance may attain the status of a criterion, meaning that the method of measurement is accepted as the most valid way to measure a particular characteristic. Open-circuit spirometry (maximal oxygen uptake, or $\dot{V}O_2$max, testing) when it is performed carefully with accurate (calibrated) measurements is accepted as the criterion measure for aerobic fitness. Mercury sphygmomanometers are considered the criterion for measuring blood pressure, when high-quality equipment is used carefully by a trained technician, because blood pressure in millimeters of mercury is the unit of measure.

Any measure's status as a criterion depends on it being performed carefully. That is, a criterion measure done carelessly can have unacceptably high error (it is invalid). Status as a criterion measure is not permanent. Newer technology sometimes replaces current criterion measures.

Unfortunately, many of the useful measurements in sport and exercise do not have a criterion measure available. For example, we may be able to establish criterion validity for a beam-balance weight scale if we have a trustworthy set of weights with which to calibrate the scale, but if we want to evaluate a measure of sportsmanship, we have no criterion measure with which to compare.

When criteria are not available as a means of establishing validity, alternative means must be used. For example, if we want to measure a student's ability to succeed in college, there are no criterion measures for ability and no universal agreement on what constitutes "success." We will have to use other forms of validity, such as content validity. These alternatives are considered next.

Content Validity

The simplest evidence of validity is termed *content validity,* also sometimes called *face validity* or *logical validity*. Criterion validity requires that we have access to a known valid measure (a criterion standard), which may not be available. In contrast, content validity requires only logic and comparison. A measure has **content validity** when careful inspection shows that it logically appears to measure what it claims to measure. If we are trying to measure long-jumping ability, and we devise a reasonable definition of this activity and a reasonable means of quantifying the distance leaped horizontally, we may be able to establish content validity for our long-jump measurement.

A definition is required and not everyone may be willing to accept our claim of content validity. The definition helps us to decide what, and how, to measure, particularly when it includes descriptive information. For example, take a moment to write your own definition of a long-jump. Your definition probably mentions the horizontal distance traveled. If you were very precise, your definition may also include issues like "take-off point" and specify the aspect of the landing that marks the terminus of the jump. The more precise the definition, the better it is for content validity purposes.

In practice, long-jumping in competition is done in a well-maintained sand pit. The take-off board and the jumper's mark in the pit help to maximize the validity of the measurement. If it is a high-level competition, measurements are carefully made with a certified tape measure. Clear rules must be followed, both in jumping and in the measurement of the distance jumped. The measure is valid only when the rules are followed completely.

Ecological Validity and External Validity

Both ecological validity and external validity are types of validity that are important, particularly in research experiments. Recall that validity means a valid interpretation as well as a valid measurement. Ecological validity refers to the methods, materials, and setting of a research experiment. To have **ecological validity**, the laboratory situation in which a measurement is being taken must be similar to the real-life situation that is being studied. **External validity** deals with the ability of a study's results to be applied to situations and groups.

A research study may not have ecological validity because the research conditions may not be similar in any way to the real-life situation being studied. For example, laboratory studies of how young athletes learn to use teamwork are designed to study how the subjects might act if they were players on the same sports team. Such a study might simply provide written descriptions of hypothetical situations, and the measurements might be made in a classroom setting. Because such an experiment does not approximate the actual circumstances and emotions of a real sports competition, it lacks ecological validity.

External validity means that appropriate measurements are applied to appropriate groups. A novice soccer test would be different from one for pros. External validity would be good, if the results from such teamwork studies can apply to a broad range of players, from inexperienced to highly skilled. Researchers strive for both good ecological validity and good external validity.

Application Questions

1 Why is validity always a question of degree?
2 Give examples of constructs for a swimming life-saving skills test.
3 Explain why someone might suggest that all validity is really construct validity.
4 Many sport governing bodies will allow a national, Olympic, or world record only when certain measurement procedures are followed (for example, the wind speed must be validly measured and recorded for certain sprint events). From a measurement perspective, why would this be so?

Part 2

Numbers and Statistics in Measurement

5. Evaluating Validity
Introduction to Statistics

Abstract

To establish the criterion validity of a measurement, we will use statistics. The most basic statistics are the descriptive statistics of mean, median, and mode. In describing a group of scores, we may find it to be a normal (standard) distribution. The standard distribution is very useful, because for this shape distribution, the percentage of data encompassed by each standard deviation is predictable. This allows us to make predictions and recognize data that is unusual. We will use inferential statistics to evaluate criterion validity, but we will start with basic statistics.

Keywords: descriptive statistics, central tendency measures, mean, median, mode, standard/normal distributions, standard deviations, samples, populations

Now that you know of ways to establish validity (construct, criterion, content, ecological, and external validity), you may be wondering how to evaluate the validity a measurement possesses. Before we do that, we will have to understand a few basic statistics.

Measures of Central Tendency

There are many situations wherein we want to "describe" a set of data. For example, if you are coaching a group of runners, you might want to get a general idea of how fast the group is. The *mean*, *median*, and *mode* are all considered to be **descriptive statistics** since their main function is to describe a set of data, which may also be called a distribution. Because the mean, median, and mode describe the "center" of a distribution, they are also referred to as **measures of central tendency.**

Mean

The most common way to describe a set of data is to calculate the average, also called the **mean.** In statistical terms, the mean is expressed as follows:

$$\text{Mean (average)} = \frac{\Sigma x}{n}$$

where Σx = the sum of all the numbers

and n = the number of scores

Thus, the mean of 1, 2, 3, 4, and $5 = (1 + 2 + 3 + 4 + 5)/5 = (15/5) = 3$.

The mean is easy to calculate and easy to understand, but it can be deceiving. If one or two of the numbers are very different from the others, the numbers that are very large or small will contribute much more to the mean than the others. For example, if you have a group of basketball players and most of them score only a few points in a game, but one can shoot like Michael Jordan, the very good shot will inordinately raise the overall average and give you a false impression of how good your shooters are as a group.

The mean of 1, 2, 3, 4, and $5 = (15/5) = 3$, but

the mean of 1, 2, 3, 4, and $50 = (60/5) = 12$.

As you see, the mean's disadvantage is that it is influenced greatly by any numbers in the data that are very different from the mean. When you have "different" numbers mixed with a group of similar numbers, it is usually better to use the median to describe the group, which we'll discuss next.

5.1 Practical Exercise

Calculate the mean of the following standing broad jump scores.

3 feet 6 inches

3 feet 9 inches

3 feet 9 inches

4 feet 0 inches

4 feet 6 inches

Median

The **median**, unlike the mean, is not influenced by atypical numbers. It is simply the middle number in a group of numbers, half of which are above the median and half below. Consider the following examples:

1, 2, 3, 4, 5

mean = 3, median = 3

1, 2, 3, 4, 50

mean = 12, median = 3

If there is an even number of numbers in the set, the median is the average of the two middle numbers. For example, for 1, 2, 3, 4, 5, and 6, the median is the average of the two middle numbers, 3 and 4. The average of 3 and 4 is 3.5, so 3.5 is the median of the set of 1, 2, 3, 4, 5, and 6.

Even in these simple examples, you can see that there are advantages and disadvantages to the median. The median is unaffected by unusually large or small scores, so in some situations it may be more representative of the group than the mean, which *is* affected by these scores, especially when there isn't much data. On the other hand, because it *is* so stable, the median doesn't give the clearest picture of the data. That is, the median isn't responsive to the size of the individual numbers in the data set; it is simply the middle-valued number in an ordered list of numbers, regardless of what is going on around it.

How do we decide which number to choose, the median or the mean? Sometimes we decide to use whichever number best fits the argument we are trying to make. For example, suppose you become involved in a discussion about the salaries of public schoolteachers. If most of the salaries are similar, then it doesn't matter much whether you choose the mean or the median, because they'll be very similar numbers. If one or two teachers earn very high salaries, and you want to convince others that teachers are overpaid, then you may report the mean salary, because it will be higher than the median. If you want to convince people that teachers are underpaid, you may choose the median salary.

Table 5.1 Teachers' salaries

Salary	# Of Teachers Earning This Salary
$38,000	1
$39,000	4
$40,000	9
$40,300	4
$41,000	5
$80,000	1
$81,000	1

Here's a specific example. If most teachers at Bishop Elementary earn $40,000, plus or minus a few thousand, but two teachers have somehow managed to earn $80,000, then the mean and median will be significantly different. Table 5.1 gives the data set.

These data give a mean salary of $43,248. If we want teachers to look better off, we could report that the mean salary of teachers at Bishop Elementary is $43,248. If we want to suggest that teachers are less well paid, we could report that the median salary of teachers at Bishop Elementary is only $40,000. (If you list each of the salaries individually, so that you see all 25, you'll see that $40,000 is the median.) Just by selecting which number to report, we can "change" the teachers' salaries by over 8 percent. By cleverly choosing how we present salary data we may be able to influence state legislators regarding teacher pay raises.

How to frame an argument is partially an ethical decision, which you can make only when you understand what the numbers mean, how they are derived, and how they can be used to inform, or misinform, an argument. If you really wish to be accurate in your examination of data, you should use the number that most accurately describes the sample. The ethical choice is to give the most accurate description, regardless of the implications.

5.2   Practical Exercise

What is the median of these standing broad jump scores?

3 feet 6 inches

3 feet 9 inches

3 feet 9 inches

4 feet 0 inches

4 feet 6 inches

Mode

The **mode** is the most frequently occurring score. We find it simply by counting how many times each score appears in the data. If there is a tie, then the data set is called "multimodal." For example, each of the numbers shows up as often as the other numbers.

1, 2, 3, 4, 5

mode = 1, 2, 3, 4, 5 (multimodal)

However, if the distribution were 1, 2, 3, 3, 5, the mode would be 3. The mode is more useful for large sets of data. For example, if you are giving the Athletic Training Certification Exam, you might be interested in knowing the most common score. If most people are scoring barely above a failing score, you might be concerned.

In the next section, we'll examine the "normal" or standard curve, and we'll see that this curve has only one mode, which is exactly in the middle (median) of the group of scores which is identical to the mean. This suggests that we can use the mode, the median, and the mean to help us judge how close a group of scores is to being "normally" distributed—which is a very useful thing to know.

5.3   Practical Exercise

What is the mode of these standing broad jump scores?

3 feet 6 inches

3 feet 9 inches

3 feet 9 inches

4 feet 0 inches

4 feet 6 inches

Distributions: Normal Distributions and the Normal Curve

Any group of values or scores can be organized into a frequency distribution. A **frequency distribution** is organizing scores to show how often a particular score appears. To create a frequency distribution, we simply list the scores from top to bottom, in order. This will show how often each number appears. Table 5.2 shows a group of push-up scores to illustrate this concept.

If we create a graph with the number of push-ups (scores) on the *x* axis and the number of participants who did that many push-ups (frequency) on the *y* axis, we will see a rough approximation of a common distribution known as the **standard distribution** (also called a normal distribution). (See Figure 5.1.) As stated earlier, the mode helps us to judge whether a group of scores is "normally" distributed. Figure 5.1 is a frequency distribution: the vertical (*y*) axis shows how many times a given score was

Table 5.2 Sample push-up scores

2
10
10
11
12
12
13
13
13
15
15
17
17
17
17
17
18
18
18
18
19
19
19
19
19
19
20
20
20
20
21
21
21
22
22
23
24
24
25
25
26
30

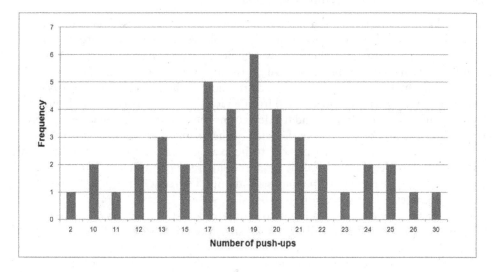

Figure 5.1 Normally distributed data

achieved. We can see that only one person (frequency = 1) scored 2, but two people (frequency = 2) scored 10. For a normal distribution, the mode lies right in the middle (along with the mean and median).

If we had hundreds of scores, the curve in our graph would appear closer to the ideal "bell" shape shown in Figure 5.2. The normal curve (also called a "Gaussian" or "bell" curve) is very valuable, as we will see in the next section. The **normal curve** is a symmetrical curve with all scores clustered around the curve's midpoint and with all measures of central tendency—the mean, median, and mode—falling in the exact same location, right in the middle of the curve.

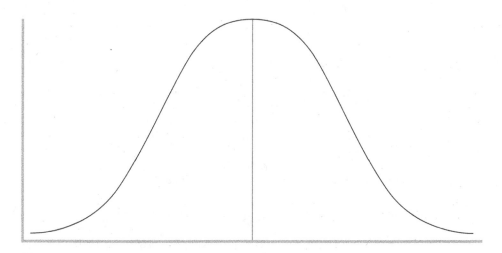

Figure 5.2 A normal curve with mean, median, and mode exactly in the middle

Measures of Dispersion: Standard Deviation

The standard deviation (SD) is a measure of how data are dispersed (spread) around the mean. The **standard deviation** is a very useful measure of variability in a distribution of scores, because it shows how individual scores vary from the mean and permits us to calculate the percentage of scores that are distributed at different intervals in the normal curve. Looking at SD in relation to the normal curve allows us to make predictions about the population from which the sample was drawn. Figure 5.3 shows the normal curve with standard deviations measured along the baseline. If we go out one standard deviation to either side of the mean score, we have encompassed 34 percent on each side (34.13 percent to be exact), or a total of about 68 percent of the whole sample. If the sample is large enough and is representative of the entire population, then we have also encompassed about 68 percent of the population. If we go out another standard deviation to either side, we get 13 percent more in each part (13.59 percent to be exact), meaning two standard deviations give us 68.26 percent + 13.59 percent on the left side and 13.59 percent on the right side, or about 95 percent of the total sample.

The third standard deviation encompasses only about 2 percent (2.145 percent to be exact) on each end. You may be wondering why each standard deviation encompasses less and less of the sample, from 34 percent for the first one to only 2 percent for the third. If you look at the curve, you will see that the farther you get from the mean, the fewer people make a given score, so fewer get included in the standard deviation segment of the curve. Another way of saying this is that most people score near the average; very few get extremely low or extremely high scores.

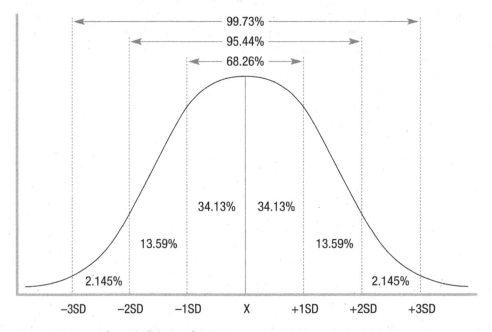

Figure 5.3 Normal curve showing the SD

Think of the standard deviation as a number that tells us how closely clustered or how widely scattered a group of scores is. The SD establishes the value of a unit of measure, which we'll discuss later.

5.4 Practical Exercise

Without looking at the figure in your text, draw a graph of a normal curve. Show each of the first three SDs around the mean, and show the approximate percent of scores encompassed by each SD. Now draw in the median and the mode.

Compare your drawing with the figure in the text. How did you do? Having a good idea of the shape of the normal curve and the percentage of the scores encompassed by each SD will help you when you begin doing statistical tests of data to evaluate validity.

Calculating the SD

The standard deviation is a *deviation,* meaning that it indicates a *difference* (deviation) from the average. The first step in calculating the SD, therefore, is to find the difference between each score and the mean.

Let's try this with a very simple data set: 1, 2, 3, 4, 5. We calculate that the mean of this distribution is 3. Now, let's subtract the mean from each score. Here are the subtractions:

$$1 - 3 = -2$$
$$2 - 3 = -1$$
$$3 - 3 = 0$$
$$4 - 3 = 1$$
$$5 - 3 = 2$$

If we total these, we find that $-2 + -1 + 0 + 1 + 2 = 0$. In fact, if we calculate the mean and do the subtractions correctly, the deviations from the mean will *always* add up to zero. This is *always* true—you can make up several data sets to demonstrate it to yourself.

5.5 Practical Exercise

Calculate the mean, the deviation from the mean for each number, and the sum of these deviations for the following two data sets:

(continued)

(continued)

Data Set A	Data Set B
4	22
7	86
12	94
13	103
18	117
22	191
26	245
34	262

When we calculate the deviation from the mean for each number, half of them are negative numbers. However, we aren't interested in whether the deviation is positive or negative, only how large it is. To eliminate the minus signs, we square each deviation (multiply it times itself). If we square –2, we get –2 * –2 = +4. If we square –1, it is –1 * –1 = +1. By squaring each deviation from the mean, we change the minus signs to plus signs. After doing this, we can add up the deviations, and we no longer get zero:

$$(-2 * -2) + (-1 * -1) + (0 * 0) + (+1 * +1) + (+2 * +2) = 4 + 1 + 0 + 1 + 4 = 10$$

The larger the sample, the larger this sum will be. Large samples will tend to give large sums, and small samples will likely give smaller sums. However, we are not very interested in the sum itself; what we want to know is the *average* deviation, which will tell us how spread out the group is. Therefore, we need to calculate the average deviation. To do this we simply divide the sum that we just calculated by the sample size (the number of scores). At this point, we have calculated the **variance**, which is another measure of the dispersion of data away from the mean. To finish the job and find the standard deviation, we need to "un-square" the number that we squared earlier, by taking the square root of it. The SD is the square root of the variance.

Using the data given above, the *sum of squares* is 10. We divide 10 by 5 (the sample size, or number of observations in our sample) and get 2. Dividing the squared deviations by the sample size gives the "average" of the squared deviations. This is the variance. Calculating the square root of 2, we get 1.41, which is the SD for these data.

Excel will calculate square roots. The function "SQRT" is found under the "Formulas" tab, under "Math & Trig," or you can simply type SQRT into the function cell and then click on the cell with the number whose square root you want.

By following this procedure, you can calculate the SD for any set of data. The example above was a very easy one. Imagine if you had physical education classes with 140 students and that the mean of the scores worked out to be 77.5. You would have to subtract 77.5 from each score and then square all 140 of those numbers, including the ones ending in 0.5. What a mess! Later, you will learn a way to rearrange the SD equation so that it is much easier to calculate with a calculator or by hand. However, with a spreadsheet on a personal computer, you can calculate the SD for 140 scores in about 15 seconds, once they are all entered. With a spreadsheet, you can also go back and correct an error in the data, and the spreadsheet will automatically recalculate the SD.

Adjusting for Sample Size

We need to make one more adjustment. Remember, we are dealing with a sample that we hope represents some larger population of interest. We typically represent the sample size with the symbol n. The sample is a good representation of the entire population if it is *fairly selected* (without bias) and if the sample is *large enough*. When the sample size, n, is small, the SD of the sample tends to be considerably smaller than the *population SD* that we are trying to estimate. Therefore, we must increase the estimate of the population SD when the sample size is small, but this adjustment does not need to be as great when the sample size gets bigger (and thus becomes more representative of the entire population). We can increase the estimate of the population SD by dividing the sum of squares (the sum of the squared differences between each score and the mean score) by $n - 1$, instead of n. By making the divisor $(n - 1)$ smaller, we are making the calculated SD larger, because we are dividing by a smaller number. If n is small, then subtracting 1 from it makes a large adjustment, but as n gets larger, subtracting 1 makes a smaller and smaller adjustment. For example, with a data set of only five numbers, subtracting 1 makes the divisor 4 instead of 5, which will raise the SD by 20 percent (one fifth). On the other hand, if we had a data sample consisting of 1,000 different scores, subtracting 1 changes the divisor to 999, so instead of dividing by 1,000, we divide by 999, which only raises the SD by 0.1 percent (one thousandth). Therefore, you should *always* divide by $n - 1$ instead of n, because it gives you the best accuracy with very few disadvantages.

Let's look again at the example from above, adjusting for the fact that now we are considering it as a sample and we want to estimate the SD for the population. First, we calculate the sum of the squared differences, just as before:

    $1 - 3 = -2$, squared $= 4$

    $2 - 3 = -1$, squared $= 1$

    $3 - 3 = 0$, squared $= 0$

    $4 - 3 = 1$, squared $= 1$

    $5 - 3 = 2$, squared $= 4$

This gives us the sum of $4 + 1 + 1 + 4 = 10$. Instead of dividing by 5, we divide by $5 - 1$ $(n - 1)$ so we have:

    $10 / 4 = 2.5$

Next, we take the square root of 2.5, and we get 1.58. Thus, if we use the sample SD formula, we get an SD of 1.58 instead of the SD of 1.41 we found earlier. This SD of 1.58 will be a better estimate of the population based on the small sample of only five observations. That is, 1.58 represents a better estimation of the true population SD than 1.41 does.

Manually Calculating the SD

If you need to calculate the SD by hand, use the following formula (Σ = summation):

$$SD = \sqrt{(\Sigma X^2 - ((\Sigma X)^2 / n)) / (n - 1)}$$

Remember that there is an important difference between Σx^2 and $(\Sigma x)^2$. Σx^2 is the sum of the squared scores—that is, we add up all the squares of the scores. This is very different from $(\Sigma x)^2$, which means that we add up the (unsquared) scores and then square the result. For the data set 1, 2, 3, 4, 5, the calculation by hand would go as follows:

First, we square each of the scores:

1 squared = 1

2 squared = 4

3 squared = 9

4 squared = 16

5 squared = 25

Next, we find the sum of the squared scores:

$1 + 4 + 9 + 16 + 25 = 55$

Next, we calculate $(\Sigma x)^2$:

$1 + 2 + 3 + 4 + 5 = 15$

$15 * 15 = 225$

To finish the calculation:

$n - 1 = 5 - 1 = 4$

$SD = \sqrt{(55 - (225/5))/4}$

$SD = \sqrt{(55 - 45)/4} = \sqrt{10/4}$

$SD = \sqrt{2.5} = 1.58$

Fortunately, as stated earlier, Excel in seconds can calculate the SD for a set of data (see Appendix 5.A).

5.6   Practical Exercise

Calculate the SD for the following data by hand. You may use a calculator to do the arithmetic.

2, 4, 5, 6, 8, 10

Now perform the same calculation using Excel. Did you get the same answer?

Concluding Thoughts

Descriptive statistics are useful in providing basic information about a set of data. One of their most important uses is evaluating a set of data to see if it is "normally" distributed. A normal distribution is handy because it allows us to predict what percentage will fall between a set of scores.

Application Questions

1 How would you recognize data that are normally distributed? What characteristics would you look for?
2 Give examples of how knowing the mean and SD would allow you to make predictions about the entire population.
3 If a measure is normally distributed, approximately what percentage of the sample would fall within one SD of the mean? What percentage would fall within two SDs of the mean? What percentage would lie more than two SDs from the mean?

Appendix 5.A: Computing Standard Deviation with Excel

1 Open Excel, enter the sample data. Each score should be entered in a separate cell, with the scores in a column. Save your data.
2 Pick a cell at the bottom of the column of data, and click on it.
3 Go to the "Formulas" tab, pull it down, and select "More Functions" and then "Statistical."
4 In the list of functions, scroll down to STDEV.S and click on it. A "function arguments" box will open, asking you to indicate which cells to use. It will automatically specify the cells above the cell where you have clicked. Make sure that it is indicating the correct cells, and make changes if necessary. Click "OK." The SD will appear in the cell.

(Note that Excel's STDEV.S function calculates the SD for the sample as an estimate of the population's SD. This is the one I recommend.)

6 Evaluating Validity
t-Tests and Correlations

Abstract

Criterion validity lends itself to statistical analyses. If a new measurement method is developed, and there exists a criterion measure, the two measurements can be compared by computing a paired t-test of means, and also examining the correlation between the scores. Both statistics are needed to evaluate the validity, and a large p and r are seen in strong validity.

Keywords: sample, population, inferential statistics, paired t-test, Pearson Product-Moment Correlation, trendline, correlation coefficient, R^2, p value

This chapter will demonstrate a method to measure and evaluate validity for norm-referenced and criterion-referenced measurements. We will evaluate criterion validity because it is the simplest type of validity to evaluate and it provides a strong basis for evaluating the degree of validity of a measurement. The skills you learn here will be valuable in many situations.

When we evaluate criterion validity, we begin with a criterion measurement and a new measurement technique that we wish to evaluate. We may have chosen a new measurement technique because it is faster, easier, or cheaper. Regardless of why we developed the new measurement technique, we *must* have a criterion measurement, or we cannot evaluate criterion validity. Recall that a criterion measurement is a measurement that we know, or mutually agree, to be valid. That is, we agree that the error in the criterion measurement is acceptably small. (Don't confuse criterion validity with criterion-referenced tests!)

Evaluating Criterion Validity for Continuous Measures

To measure and evaluate criterion validity for continuous measurements, you may employ several different methods: comparison of group means (t-tests), correlations (Pearson Product-Moment Correlations), and error analysis (Bland-Altman analysis). Recall that continuous measurements are only limited by the precision of the measurement device.

Comparing Mean Scores: t-Tests

The first method for evaluating the criterion validity of continuous measurements is to compare mean scores. Suppose we have two measurements: a criterion measurement and a new measurement technique for measuring the same underlying constructs. For example, it has been suggested that the distance run in 12 minutes may be a good measure of aerobic fitness, since good distance runners have high aerobic fitness. Since we can obtain a criterion measure of aerobic fitness ($\dot{V}O_2$max measured in the laboratory), we can try to validate the new measurement technique, the distance run in 12 minutes. To do this, we collect data on a group of students. First, in the lab, we measure their $\dot{V}O_2$max. Then, on the track, we measure their 12-minute run distance. This gives us a criterion measure of $\dot{V}O_2$max (aerobic fitness) and running distances to the nearest 100 meters for a group of fit students (including two cross-country team members).

Preparing the Data for Evaluation

Because the data we collected involve two measurements, we have two groups of continuous numbers (see Table 6.1). The numbers in the first column, for $\dot{V}O_2$max measured in a laboratory, are expressed in mL • kg^{-1} • min^{-1}, or milliliters of oxygen per kilogram of body weight per minute, as indicated in the column head. The numbers in the second column, for the 12-minute run distances, are not expressed in mL • kg^{-1} • min^{-1}, but rather in meters. At this point, we don't know how to compare

Table 6.1 Data collected for criterion measurements of $\dot{V}O_2$max in the laboratory and measurements of 12-minute run distances

Measured $\dot{V}O_2$max (mL • kg⁻¹ • min⁻¹)	Meters run in 12 minutes (m)
65.2	3400
61.1	3300
61.0	3000
59.8	3400
59.1	3000
57.6	2800
55.2	3000
53.5	2900
51.2	3200
49.3	2700
47.8	2100
46.3	2500
45.8	1900
45.1	2500
43.8	2800
42.7	2400
41.9	2400
41.3	2400
40.4	1900
39.0	2300
38.2	2300
37.3	2800
37.1	2100
35.2	1800
33.5	1400
31.8	1900
29.2	1500
27.6	1600
26.0	1900
23.3	1300
21.9	1400
19.9	1800
19.5	1300
19.2	1300

the $\dot{V}O_2$max expressed as mL • kg^{-1} • min^{-1} and distances run in 12 minutes expressed in meters. We need to use an equation to predict the $\dot{V}O_2$max from the 12-minute run distance so that we can see if the run distance is a valid way to predict $\dot{V}O_2$max. This is criterion validity, because we have the laboratory $\dot{V}O_2$max measurements to serve as the criterion for comparison with the 12-minute run data.

Using one measure to predict another. Given one measurement (distance completed), we may be able to predict another measurement ($\dot{V}O_2$max) because of the relationship between the two measurements. We are able to make this prediction because the characteristics associated with a high $\dot{V}O_2$max are also associated with fast distance-running ability. A person who has a large heart and muscle fibers that process oxygen well will tend to have both a high $\dot{V}O_2$max and good running ability.

The Cooper 12-Min Run/Walk Test (Cooper, 1968) uses the following equation to predict $\dot{V}O_2$max from distance run:

$$\dot{V}O_2\text{max} = ((\text{meters run} / 1609.3) - 0.3138) / 0.0278$$

Fortunately, with spreadsheet software, the calculations won't be difficult. To do this, the first task is to enter the data into the spreadsheet. (For instructions on setting up the spreadsheet see Appendix 6.A.) The great advantage of performing calculations using a spreadsheet is that as long as the entries are accurate, the math will be accurate. Another advantage is that if the data and spreadsheet are organized properly, when we find an error and correct it, the calculations will automatically be corrected as well. With spreadsheet software, it is very easy to keep a backup copy of our work. When you make backup copies, be sure to date everything to ensure you are working on the most recent version.

After all of the data are entered in a spreadsheet, we set up the formula to calculate the predicted $\dot{V}O_2$max from the distance run. We also calculate the averages for each column of data (see Table 6.2). The next task is to reduce this large group of numbers to a more manageable one. We have several options for doing so. That is, we can describe this group of data in several different ways.

Deciding how to describe the data. To describe the data, we could compare the mean, the median, or the mode between the measurements, but what would that tell us?

We know that the mean for the measured $\dot{V}O_2$max was 41.4 mL • kg^{-1} • min^{-1}, the mean distance was 2,303 meters, and the mean for the predicted $\dot{V}O_2$max using the 12-minute run distances was 40.2 mL • kg^{-1} • min^{-1}. When we look at the median score, we see that the median score for measured $\dot{V}O_2$max was 41.6 mL • kg^{-1} • min^{-1}, for meters run in 12 minutes was 2,400 m, and for predicted $\dot{V}O_2$max was 42.4 mL • kg^{-1} • min^{-1}. Finally, when we look at the mode scores, we find that measured $\dot{V}O_2$max was bimodal, since two scores occurred more often than any others. For meters run in 12 minutes, the mode was 2,400 m, and for predicted $\dot{V}O_2$max the modes were 17.8 and 42.4 mL • kg^{-1} • min^{-1}.

The question is, which of these descriptors—mean, median, or mode—is the best descriptor of the data? We can eliminate the mode score, because neither 17.8 mL • kg^{-1} • min^{-1} nor 42.5 for the predicted $\dot{V}O_2$max is very representative of the data set, in this case. The median might be an appropriate descriptor. If we didn't have as many

Table 6.2 Predicted $\dot{V}O_2$max from run distance in meters

	E36		▼		f_x	=AVERAGE(E2:E35)	
	A	B	C	D	E	F	
			Measured $\dot{V}O_2$max	Meters run in 12 min	Predicted $\dot{V}O_2$max		
1							
2			65.2	3400	64.7		
3			61.1	3300	62.5		
4			61.0	3000	55.8		
5			59.8	3400	64.7		
6			59.1	3000	55.8		
7			57.6	2800	51.3		
8			55.2	3000	55.8		
9			53.5	2900	53.5		
10			51.2	3200	60.2		
11			49.3	2700	49.1		
12			47.8	2100	35.7		
13			46.3	2500	44.6		
14			45.8	1900	31.2		
15			45.1	2500	44.6		
16			43.8	2800	51.3		
17			42.7	2400	42.4		
18			41.9	2400	42.4		
19			41.3	2400	42.4		
20			40.4	1900	31.2		
21			39.0	2300	40.1		
22			38.2	2300	40.1		
23			37.3	2800	51.3		
24			37.1	2100	35.7		
25			35.2	1800	28.9		
26			33.5	1400	20.0		
27			31.8	1900	31.2		
28			29.2	1500	22.2		
29			27.6	1600	24.5		
30			26.0	1900	31.2		
31			23.3	1300	17.8		
32			21.9	1400	20.0		
33			19.9	1800	28.9		
34			19.5	1300	17.8		
35			19.2	1300	17.8		
36		AVERAGE	41.4	2302.9	40.2		

scores as we do, or if we had any scores that were very unusual, the median would be a better representation than the mean. The mean, however, has one great advantage for us: it can be statistically compared with other means, because it is derived from all of the data. The comparison of means is called a *statistical test of means*.

The mean for measured $\dot{V}O_2$max was 41.4 mL • kg^{-1} • min^{-1}, and the mean for predicted $\dot{V}O_2$max using 12-minute run distances was 40.2 mL • kg^{-1} • min^{-1}. You may be looking at these two means and thinking, anybody can see that 41.4 is different from 40.2! But consider this: If the fastest or the slowest runners had been absent when we made the measurement, how would that have changed things?

If you follow the procedures above and simply delete the first person's scores you will obtain the following means:

Measured $\dot{V}O_2$max		Meters run in 12 min	Predicted $\dot{V}O_2$max
AVERAGE	40.7	2272.7	39.5

Compare this with the means obtained with all the data:

Measured $\dot{V}O_2$max		Meters run in 12 min	Predicted $\dot{V}O_2$max
AVERAGE	41.4	2302.9	40.2

The means have changed. They are still different, but the point is that if the right two or three people had been absent, or the right two or three had shown up, then the difference could have been 0. What we have here is a *sample*. We aren't terribly interested in exactly how this particular group did, we are interested in how valid the 12-minute run might be for the population sampled. If we had a different group of runners, we would have a different distribution of scores and a different outcome. Hence, we have to consider the issues of samples and populations.

Designating a population and sample. In measurement, a **population** is all of a designated group that we wish to measure. For example, "all Division I American football players" comprise a population. "All college students" is another population and a much bigger one. "All athletes" is a population, and "all the clients of a fitness club" is another population. Most populations that we might be interested in are far too large to measure directly, because there are too many people, the people are scattered widely, and it would take too much time and money to measure them all. To overcome this problem, we typically study a representative *sample* of a population. If the sample is properly chosen and large enough, it will do a good job of representing the population from which it was taken. The data we have been analyzing so far represent a sample from a student population. We could have picked the sample from any population of interest. How we choose the sample is important, because the validity of the equation that we are testing will pertain only to the population from which we drew the sample. For example, if we choose a sample from competitors in a regional cross-country meet, we would see very different data. For certain, we would not have found a $\dot{V}O_2$max of 19 or a 12-minute run distance of only 1,300 meters. The equation we used to convert meters to mL • kg^{-1} • min^{-1} may *not* apply to cross-country runners. Similarly, if we had selected a sample from the local senior citizens center, the data would also look quite different. Not only would the data look different, but also the outcome of our study would be externally valid only for older people. We could validate the 12-minute run by a measure of fitness for older folks, for high school students, or for cross-country runners, but each validation would require a different sample, because each represents a population that differs in running ability and $\dot{V}O_2$max.

We can use **inferential statistics** to infer, or generalize, things about a population based on what we learn about the sample. Here, we will use an inferential statistic called a *paired t-test* (also called a *dependent t-test*) to make inferences about the population from the sample. "Paired" means that this is a test for paired data: Each person has two scores, one from the distance run and one from the laboratory test. The term "t-test" means that we are comparing the two means. If the two means are very different, this suggests that the laboratory test and the running test are measuring different constructs; therefore, the t-test would find that the 12-minute run as a measure of aerobic fitness is invalid. In general, a **t-test** is a test designed to compare two sample means so that we can determine whether the difference between means is probably from luck, or really in the population. The good news is that we can do a paired t-test with the tools and equipment we already have.

Types of t-Tests

Before doing a t-test, we have to determine the kind of t-test that is appropriate: paired or independent, and one-tailed or two-tailed.

Paired vs. independent t-tests. In the example of comparing a $\dot{V}O_2$max lab test with a running test, we are doing two tests with *one* group. We call this a "dependent," "paired," "single sample," or "repeated measures" test. Excel calls this test a paired t-test. These names imply that two tests are being performed on the same group of test subjects, as opposed to two different groups of test subjects. For example, if we are examining the effects of caffeine on running performance, we would probably use a paired test. We would test all of the research subjects twice: Once after they have taken caffeine and another time after they have taken a placebo (a "false" treatment; that does nothing, but allows the researchers to run a "blind" test by preventing the subjects from knowing whether or not they have received the treatment). These two tests on the same subjects are considered to be "paired" with each other, hence the name **paired t-test**. We could also call it a repeated-measures test, since the test is repeated.

In some situations, we need to compare data between two different (independent) groups. We do this using an **independent t-test,** also called a "two-sample" t-test. For example, we might compare running performances between two groups, one of which has done one type of training all season and the other a different type of training. Because the groups are independent of each other, this is an "independent" t-test.

One-tailed vs. two-tailed t-tests. To illustrate the difference between a one-tailed test and a two-tailed test, let's consider an example from athletic training. Suppose we have developed a new method of assessing a concussion, and we believe that the new method is better than the old one. However, the new method is more difficult to administer and it is more expensive than the old one, so the new method will not be adopted unless it is substantially better at detecting concussions than the old one. In this case, we are only interested in knowing whether the new method is superior to the old one. If the new test is only equal to, or worse than the old, we will just keep the old one. Hence, we would use a one-tailed test, because we are only interested in determining whether the new method is better, not equal to, or worse, than the old one.

Now let's consider a different situation, from American football. Suppose we want to compare a new method of coaching blocking that has some advantages but also some disadvantages compared to the old one. Coaches might use one method or the other, depending on the situation. In this case, we want to know whether the new coaching method is *better or worse* than the old one. If it is substantially worse, then coaches would not be likely to adopt it. If the new method is substantially better, then they probably would adopt it. If the two methods are equal overall, then coaches would simply pick the one that they think works best for a particular situation. Since we need to know if one method is better *or worse* than the old one, we have to look in two directions—that is, at both (two) "tails."

In our attempt to show whether the 12-minute run is a good test of fitness, it does not matter if the $\dot{V}O_2$max predicted from the 12-minute run is larger or smaller than the criterion, but it does matter if it is *different*. Hence, for our evaluation of validity, we want a *two*-tailed test. One tail will tell us whether the measured $\dot{V}O_2$max mean is higher than the predicted $\dot{V}O_2$max mean, and the other tail will tell whether the measured mean is lower than the predicted mean.

A **one-tailed t-test** indicates whether the mean of one test is higher than the mean of another. A **two-tailed t-test** indicates whether the first mean is *higher or lower* than the second mean. A one-tailed test makes it twice as easy to find a difference, because we only look at one end of the distribution. In other words, we can detect the difference between two means that are closer together with a one-tailed, as opposed to a two-tailed, t-test.

With a two-sample test, in addition to determining the kind of t-test to run, we also need to determine whether the two samples have equal variances or unequal variances. For our purposes, we need to determine this simply because Excel requires us to choose one or the other, and the choice will affect how Excel calculates the results. Our $\dot{V}O_2$max example is a one-sample test, but let's pretend for a few minutes that it is a two-sample data set (that is, we used two different groups of students for the two tests). We need to determine if the variances for the two data columns (in Table 6.3 columns C and E) are equal or unequal. Remember, a variance is simply the square of the standard deviation. (Or, the standard deviation is the square root of the variance.)

Table 6.3 Computations of SDs for the measured VO_2 max and predicted VO_2 max

E38		f_x	=STDEV(E3:E36)	
A	B	C	D	E
1				
2		Measured VO_2max	Meters run in 12 min	Predicted VO_2max
3		65.2	3400	64.7
4		61.1	3300	62.5
		⋮	⋮	⋮
36		19.2	1300	17.8
37	AVERAGE	41.4	2302.9	40.2
38	STDEV	13.3	652.5	14.6

Using Excel, let's compute the SD for the two measurements: measured $\dot{V}O_2max$, 12-minute run distance, and predicted $\dot{V}O_2max$. Table 6.3 shows the results. The standard deviation for the $\dot{V}O_2max$ predicted from 12-minute run distance is 14.6 ml/kg, and the square is 212.7 ml^2/kg^2. The standard deviation for the measured $\dot{V}O_2max$ is 13.3 ml/kg, and the square is 176.4 ml^2/kg^2. Hence, the variances are unequal simply by comparison.

Excel will test the equality of the variances with the FTEST function. To do this, find the cell where you want to display the result, then select the function FTEST and highlight the two columns of data. Excel will display the *probability* that the two variances are *not different*—that is, the probability that they are equal. If the value Excel gives is greater than 0.05, then you should assume the variances are equal and use the "equal variances" type (type 2). If Excel's FTEST value is 0.05 or less, then the variances are unequal, and you should use type 3 for unequal variances.

Performing a t-Test

After you have determined the type of t-test you want to run, you are ready to perform it to see how the sample means compare. Let's go back to the data set and work from there to establish the validity of the 12-minute run measurement by comparing group means. This section will be most useful if you read it with a personal computer and a spreadsheet right in front of you. Table 6.4 shows the results. Appendix 6.B shows how to run a t-test with Excel.

Interpreting the t-Test

In Table 6.4, cell C39 displays the t-test results. This is the probability that the two means would be as different as they are *by chance alone*. The probability that two means are different only by chance is called a **p value**. In this case, the p-value is 0.30, which

Table 6.4 Results of the t-test for the $\dot{V}O_2max$-12-minute run distance example

C39			f_x	=TTEST(C3:C36,E3:E36,2,1)		
	A	B	C	D	E	F
1						
2			Measured VO_2max	Meters run in 12 min	Predicted VO_2max	
3			65.2	3400	64.7	
4			61.1	3300	62.5	
			⋮	⋮	⋮	
36			19.2	1300	17.8	
37		AVERAGE	41.4	2302.9	40.2	
38		STDEV	13.3	652.5	14.6	
39		TTEST	0.3			

Table 6.5 Example of data with large positive and negative errors that cancel each other

	A	B	C	D	E
	D17	▼	f_x	=STDEV(D3:D15)	
1					
2		Method 1	Method 2	Difference (meth1-meth2)	
3		99	81	18	
4		93	79	14	
5		90	72	18	
6		82	93	-11	
7		80	57	23	
8		79	71	8	
9		75	62	13	
10		74	90	-16	
11		73	89	-16	
12		70	82	-12	
13		65	98	-33	
14		60	42	18	
15		55	79	-24	
16		76.5	76.5	0	difference
17				19.1	STDEV

means there is a 30 percent chance of finding a difference this size by luck alone. (We would find a difference of this size 30 times out of 100, just by luck.) This tells us that the probability that these two means are really different is somewhat small. Therefore, we conclude that there is *no statistically significant difference* between the mean obtained by the laboratory measure and the one obtained from the 12-minute run estimation. So far, the test is looking valid, but we can't conclude yet.

We have not yet established criterion validity. After all, we might come up with identical means even though the individual predictions were inaccurate. This could occur because the large positive errors could cancel the large and negative ones. Table 6.5 provides an example of this effect. Both methods gave the same mean, yet the differences between the scores were very large, and the SD for the differences is 19! Just by looking at the scores, you can see that the two methods must be measuring different constructs. Clearly, a t-test would find no difference between the means. Therefore, we need an additional method for evaluating the validity of our test: correlations.

6.1   Practical Exercise

Calculate the one-tailed and two-tailed probabilities for a paired t-test with the data given in Table 6.3. Why is the one-tailed t-test result half the result of the two-tailed t-test?

Correlations: Pearson Product-Moment Correlation

We can't learn everything we need to know just from a t-test comparison of means. Therefore, we need to compare the individual differences in the $\dot{V}O_2$max scores obtained in the lab and by prediction. To determine the **correlation,** the measure of the strength of the relationship between two variables, we calculate a statistic called the **Pearson Product-Moment Correlation,** a statistic used to compare individual scores on two methods of continuous measurement. Like the SD, the Pearson Correlation is very useful for lots of applications.

Before performing a Pearson Correlation, however, the first step in evaluating the validity of measurements through correlation is to examine the nature of the data. First, we look at a graphical depiction of the data to discover any patterns. For example, do the data result in a graph that is long and skinny like a stick, or round like a basketball? If the graph is like a stick, is it straight or curved? By looking at the data we can discover important information that will help us determine what type of correlation we may have and help keep us from making errors.

Visually Examining the Data

Before we calculate a correlation, it is important to look at a visual representation of the data, by constructing a *scatter plot.* This chart can be created within the spreadsheet we have already compiled in Excel. Appendix 6.C gives instructions, and Figure 6.1 presents the results.

After constructing the chart shown in Figure 6.1, we look at the data to see if any patterns stand out. This brings us to a very important skill: reading and understanding figures (charts), including scatter plots. This is crucial, because trends in data sometimes are best expressed and understood in pictures.

Among the first steps when you look at a figure is to try to grasp what the figure is supposed to show. A title or the figure legend should tell you this. Study the labels of the x and y axes to see what the two axes represent. In Figure 6.1, the y axis is the predicted $\dot{V}O_2$max, and the x axis is the measured $\dot{V}O_2$max.

Now look at the overall shape of the chart. First, notice in Figure 6.1 that the data appear to be fairly linear—that is, the points fall roughly in a line. This chart is only "fairly" linear because the shape is more spread out than a line. The closer the data are to a thin, straight line at a 45-degree angle, the stronger the correlation. If the data were round like a ball, then the correlation would be very weak. If the data were U-shaped (right-side-up or inverted), or if they made a curve, then we may have a strong relationship, just not a linear relationship. For data that have a strong nonlinear relationship, a Pearson (linear) correlation may not be high, despite the strong relationship.

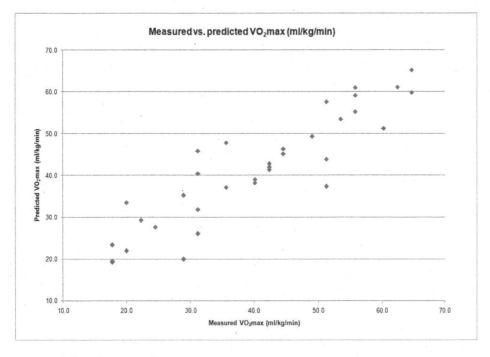

Figure 6.1 Sample scatter plot

The closer the data are to a straight line, the stronger the linear correlation. But the more the data look like a ball, the weaker the correlation. Before calculating the correlation, we want to ensure that the data make a line rather than a curve. If the data are curved, then there is some factor that we may need to examine and correct. For example, the data may make a straight, slanted line up to some point and then suddenly "plateau" into a line that is almost flat (see Figure 6.2). This "bent" line might mean that there is a "ceiling effect" in the data, such that no one scores above a particular score. If we gave a written test of snow-skiing knowledge to a large group of middle school students from across the United States, we would probably find that a group of students scored 0, another group scored somewhere between 0 and 100, and a third group earned a perfect score of 100. If we related the written test score to the students' skiing experience, we would find that those scoring 0 mostly lived in parts of the country with no snow skiing and those scoring very high were regular skiers, with those in between having varying degrees of experience. The correlation between experience and knowledge would be much weaker than it should be because of the nature of our sample: it included a large number of skilled skiers who all scored very high, and the test was too easy for skilled skiers. A large portion of the sample scored 100. That is, a lot of students got the same score (100), even though *among those with perfect scores,* some students had much more experience than others. The fact that students could have different levels of experience but still get the same score (100) hurts the correlation. This would be evident when we looked at the figure.

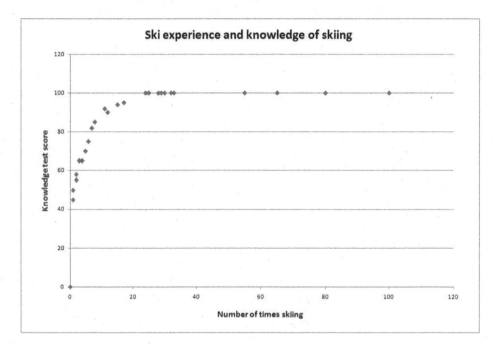

Figure 6.2 Example of ceiling effect

Check to see if the data are offset, either higher or lower than a 45-degree imaginary line. If they are consistently offset, then examine the data to see if this is an error or if the measurement can be improved. We will discuss this further later. Finally, notice how the data points are distributed. We generally expect to see data points clustered in the middle of the chart and just a few points at the extremes, because most scores are close to the average. If a lot of data appears near the extremes (very high or very low), then this data may not accurately portray the population, and you should know that in advance. When a lot of data appears at the extremes, this will artificially increase the correlation.

Performing a Pearson Product-Moment Correlation

Now that we have looked at a scatter plot of the data, we are ready to calculate the Pearson Correlation. Once again, Excel makes the calculation easy. Appendix 6.D gives instructions, and Table 6.6 shows the results for our data.

Evaluating the Correlation

What does the correlation presented in Table 6.6 tell us? To evaluate a correlation, we can examine it in several ways, including assessing the r value, the trendline, and the R^2 for the data.

r value. The correlation is expressed in terms of an **r value**, also called the correlation coefficient. The **correlation coefficient** is a statistical expression of the relationship

Table 6.6 Results of the Pearson Product-Moment Correlation for the V̇O₂max-12-minute distance example

	C40	▼	f_x	=CORREL(C3:C36,E3:E36)	
	A	B	C	D	E
1					
2			Measured VO₂max	Meters run in 12 min	Predicted VO₂max
3			65.2	3400	64.7
4			61.1	3300	62.5
36			19.2	1300	17.8
37		AVERAGE	41.4	2302.9	40.2
38		STDEV	13.3	652.5	14.6
39		TTEST	0.3		
40		CORREL	0.9		

between the two variables. It can range between 0 (no relationship) and +1 or –1 (perfect relationships). A perfect correlation, where one variable increases in exact proportion to another, has an r value of 1.0. A perfect inverse correlation has an r value of –1.0. An inverse (or negative) correlation is one where a variable *decreases* in exact proportion to the increase in the other variable.

There are some situations where a negative correlation is acceptable for a validity study where one variable decreases proportionately as the other goes up. We'll look at an example of that later.

Table 6.7 provides some general guidelines for interpreting Pearson Correlations. Whether the correlation is negative or positive doesn't matter when we are considering the strength of the relationship.

In Table 6.6 the value of 0.9 indicates a very strong correlation between our two measurements.

Trendline. In addition to evaluating the r value, you can gain additional information about a correlation by examining the calculated slope of the **trendline** for the data.

Table 6.7 Guidelines for interpreting Pearson Product-Moment Correlations (applicable for both positive and negative correlations)

r = .80 to 1.0 is considered a very strong relationship.
r = .60 to .79 is considered a strong relationship.
r = .40 to .59 is considered a moderate relationship.
r = .20 to .39 is considered a weak relationship.
r = less than .20 is considered a very weak relationship.

The *trendline* is the line that best fits all the data points; the "best" fit is defined as the smallest total distance between all the points and the line. You can easily determine the trendline from the scatter plot you have already created. Appendix 6.E provides instructions for creating the line and calculating its slope. Figure 6.3 shows the results.

The slope of a line is defined as the change in *y* value per unit change in *x* value and is used in the following equation for a straight line:

y value = the slope * the *x* value + the *y* intercept (point where *y* = 0)

This is the same as saying

$y = mx + b$

We selected "Display equation on chart" when we created the chart, so you should see the equation of the trendline next to the chart. For our data, the first equation appearing in Figure 6.3 includes the calculated slope of the trendline: 0.823. The *y* value goes up .82 units of the *y* axis for every unit of *x*. What this tells us is that we can compute the predicted value of $\dot{V}O_2$max by multiplying the measured $\dot{V}O_2$max by .82 and adding 8.28. How accurate is the prediction? If we look at the data points in the figure, we see that they are all fairly close to the trendline. The closer the points of the scatter plot are to the trendline, the higher the r value and the more accurate the prediction.

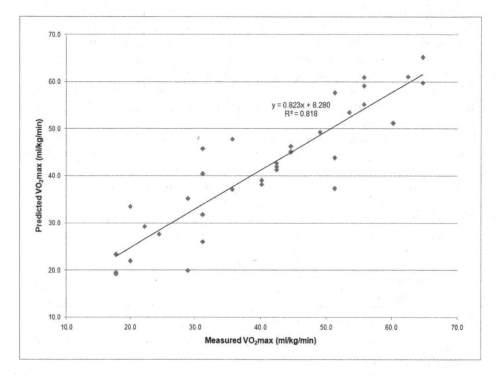

Figure 6.3 Scatter plot showing trendline with displayed equations for slope and R^2 for measured and predicted $\dot{V}O_2$max data

R^2. If we square the correlation coefficient, we get the **coefficient of determination** (R^2). The coefficient of determination tells us the amount of variability in one variable (e.g., predicted $\dot{V}O_2$max from 12-minute run distance) that is explainable by the other variable (e.g., measured $\dot{V}O_2$max). In our example, $\dot{V}O_2$max and predicted $\dot{V}O_2$max from 12-minute run distance are related with a correlation coefficient of r = .90. The coefficient of determination is as follows:

$$R^2 = 0.90 * 0.90 = 0.81 = 81\%$$

So the coefficient of determination tells us that 81 percent of the variability in the predicted $\dot{V}O_2$max from the 12-minute run distance is attributable to $\dot{V}O_2$max. Hence, the other 19 percent of the variability in predicted $\dot{V}O_2$max is attributable to other factors that affected the 12-minute run distance, such as proper pacing, effort given, and so forth. Sometimes, being able to express the relationship as a "percent of variability in performance accounted for" helps us better understand the relationship.

Now look back at Figure 6.3. Note that the R^2 value appears in the second line next to the scatter plot. Whenever you create a scatter plot, if you check the "Display R-squared value on chart" box, Excel will calculate the coefficient of determination. Note, that if you want to calculate the correlation coefficient (r) itself in Excel, you can simply type the R^2 value in a cell and use the SQRT function.

A high coefficient of determination can be useful when what you want to measure is difficult to measure directly. If what you want to measure is strongly correlated to something that is easy to measure, then you can simply measure the easy thing and predict the hard one. For example, measuring aerobic fitness is challenging. As in our example, the criterion measure is maximal oxygen uptake, which is typically measured with expensive laboratory equipment. The measurement involves high stress for the person being tested and requires skill and time for the testers. If we have to measure many people, and we don't have a well-equipped lab, a 12-minute run, which is at least moderately correlated to aerobic fitness, will be easier, faster, and cheaper than the measurement of maximal oxygen uptake.

If the correlation coefficient is r = .80 or higher, we generally feel that the measurement is valid. However, this is not always the case. For example, suppose that the measurement device was defective and multiplied all measurements by ten. The results for the example we have been discussing are displayed in Figure 6.4. Compare Figure 6.4 to Figure 6.3, created from the original data. What's different? Although the coefficient of determination is the same, indicating we still have the same correlation coefficient, the data are now in a straight line that is offset, and the y-intercept is now 10 times larger than in the original data.

The differences between the two figures are important. Because the predicted $\dot{V}O_2$max has an error that is very consistent, the correlation coefficient and coefficient of determination are still extremely high (close to 1.0). In contrast, the intercept and position of the data points suggest that there is low validity. The occurrence of these discrepancies explains why we always need to compare the means between the criterion and the new method of measuring, to be sure that we are seeing a true correlation. If we reran the t-test, we would find that the means now are very different.

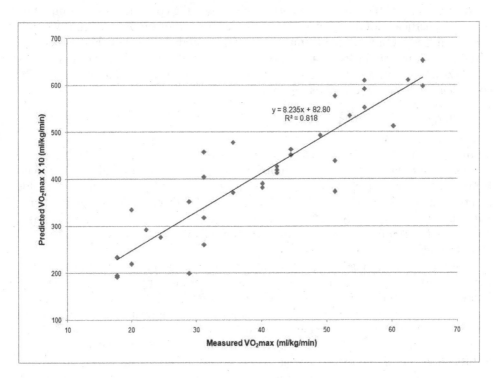

Figure 6.4 Example of an offset line

6.2   Practical Exercise

Using the data in your Excel spreadsheet, multiply each value of the predicted $\dot{V}O_2$max data by ten. Now run a t-test (two-tailed, paired) to obtain the p value, the probability of a difference this large between the two means happening by chance alone. How does this p value compare to the original p value?

In Practical Exercise 6.2, you should have calculated a p value of .00000000000000007. That is, the odds are extremely small that these two numbers are the same. (There is only a tiny chance that the difference is due to luck alone.) In other words, the mean for the measured and for the predicted $\dot{V}O_2$max are definitely different, so we must be measuring two different constructs. Our prediction of $\dot{V}O_2$max from 12-minute run distance in this case would *not* be valid.

Quick Review

CORRELATION COEFFICIENT, R VALUE. We always have to use good judgment in measurement. If something is important to measure, but extremely hard to measure, and a simple and inexpensive new measurement technique is available, we might accept a slightly lower r value. In addition, even if the r value is low, it is still necessary to examine and evaluate a visual depiction of the data. Good judgment is indispensable in measurement.

Additional Practical Exercises

6.3 Practical Exercise

Using Excel, perform the following tasks using the data set given below.

Weight (pounds)	Height (inches)
191	69
160	68
157	70
191	72
141	65
185	69
210	72
149	65
169	70
173	68
150	68
144	69
146	60
155	61.3
183	64.5

r = .70

a   Convert the weights from pounds to kilograms (1 kg = 2.205 lbs).
b   Convert the heights from inches to centimeters (1 in = 2.54 cm).
c   Calculate the Pearson Correlation between height and weight, using centimeters and kilograms.
d   Calculate the Pearson Correlation between height and weight, using inches and kilograms.
e   Calculate the Pearson Correlation between height and weight, using centimeters and pounds.
f   Compare these correlations. What would you conclude?
g   Using the "create chart" option, create a scatter plot of these data and insert a trendline. By examining the trendline, what would you predict to be the weight of a person who is 67 inches tall? Just by looking at the graph, how close do you think your prediction is?

6.4   Practical Exercise

For the following paired data, evaluate the validity of the new measure using a t-test, a Pearson Correlation, and a Bland-Altman analysis. Was the new measure valid for this sample?

Criterion Measure	New Measure
56	53
55	53
51	47
49	45
49	44
49	44
45	45
44	46
41	39
40	40
37	33
36	36
32	30
30	26
28	29
26	22
22	19
18	13
18	12

6.5   Practical Exercise

Using the following ordinal data, calculate the correlation.

Racquetball skills test score	Tournament finish place
89	1
93	2
83	3
83	4
83	5
86	6
89	7
77	8
80	9
73	10
70	11
68	12
69	13
65	14
50	15

Application Questions

1   Why is it important to visually inspect data before running a correlation on it?
2   Why are the results of inferential tests, such as t-tests, expressed as probabilities?
3   Why might an evaluator deliberately try to test a group of volunteers who represent the extremes of whatever characteristic is being measured? For example, if someone were evaluating a test of golf ability, why might they deliberately choose very experienced golfers and those who had never played, with very few golfers of intermediate ability? What is the problem with this approach?

Reference

Cooper, K. H. A means of assessing maximal oxygen intake. *Journal of the American Medical Association* 203: 201–204, 1968.

Appendix 6.A: Predicting $\dot{V}O_2$max (mL • kg^{-1} • min^{-1}) from Meters Run, Using Excel

1   Open an Excel file.
2   Click cell C1 and type "Measured $\dot{V}O_2$max". In D1, type "Meters run in 12 min". In E1, type "Predicted $\dot{V}O_2$max".
3   Format the cells in Column C as number cells with one decimal place. To do this, click on the cell with the "C" in it to highlight the column. Then click on the "Home" tab and look for the "Number" area. We select one decimal because that reflects how precisely we can measure the two $\dot{V}O_2$maxs. For Column D, since we can only measure meters run to the nearest 100, highlight that column and set it to 0 decimals.
4   Go to C2 and type the first piece of data, in this case, "65.2". Press Enter.
5   In D2, input the first distance: 3400.
6   Now, here is the good part. In E2, type the Cooper equation for predicting $\dot{V}O_2$max from distance run, "=((D2/1609.3)-0.3138)/0.0278" and press Enter. This command tells Excel to divide the number in cell D2 by 1609.3 and subtract 0.3138 from that, then divide this amount by 0.0278. Note the = sign, which *must* be used to start all equations! The only other thing you need to remember is that Excel will solve an equation by first doing the multiplication and divisions in it, then the additions and subtractions, all from left to right. If you need a calculation done in another order, then enclose in parentheses the operations that need to be done first. Calculations in parentheses are always completed first. Many errors arise from not paying attention to the order in which Excel does its mathematical calculations. I put sub-calculations in parentheses whether I need to or not, simply because it's easier for me to stay organized and avoid errors that way. If you make a mistake in an equation, sometimes Excel will recognize the error and recommend a correction. When Excel does not catch the error, you will have to catch it yourself. The best way to identify errors is to have a good idea of what the answer should be *before* you do the calculation. For example, the prediction of $\dot{V}O_2$max should be reasonably close to the measured value.

Measured	Meters run in	Predicted
$\dot{V}O_2$max	12 min	$\dot{V}O_2$max
65.2	3400	64.7

7 Before you do anything else, look at the computation to see if the number is approximately correct. In E2, you should expect to see something close to 65. If everything is correct, E2 will display 64.7, if the cell is formatted to show one decimal place. Note that cells can be formatted to show additional decimal places as desired, but in our case, we selected one place.

8 Once everything is set up and calculating correctly, you can input all of the measured $\dot{V}O_2$maxs in Column C and the distances in Column D.

9 Here's another helpful feature of Excel. Click on E2 and then put your cursor on the small box in the lower right corner of the cell. Holding down the left mouse button, drag straight down Column E. Stop when you get to the last row with data, and release the mouse button. The calculation will be repeated all the way down. Look at E3. Is it correct? It should display 62.5 (or 62.47, possibly with some additional decimal places).

10 We can do one more thing, just to make life a little easier. Go to the first open box under Column C, and click on it. Now go to the "Formula" tab and click on "More Functions." Click on "Statistical," then select "AVERAGE" from the list. Click OK. The average for Column C, 41.4, should appear.

11 In Column B, just to the left of the average you just calculated, type "AVERAGE" to remind you what this number is.

12 As in Step 9, you can drag the cell with the "average" function in it across the bottom of the columns to get the averages for Columns D and E. Easy, isn't it?

13 This brings us to an important rule for all spreadsheets: Always look at the answer to make sure it makes sense! Anytime you drag an equation or function, or use copy and paste, the spreadsheet makes a guess as to what it thinks you want. You have to double-check to make sure it guessed correctly.

14 The last step is to save the file by either clicking on the disk icon or clicking on the Office button and then the "Save" command.

Appendix 6.B: Running a t-Test with Excel

1 Select a cell below the bottom of Column C and click on it.

2 Click on the "Formulas" tab and "More Functions" and select "Statistical," just like before.

3 Scroll down to TTEST, and click on it. A function arguments box will open.

4 For "Array 1," select all the data in column C (just the data itself). (An array is simply a list of data that you want to use for a calculation.)

5 For "Array 2," select all the data in Column E (just the data itself).

6 For "Tails," type the number "2" to specify a two-tailed t-test.

7 For "Type," type the number "1" to specify a one-sample (paired or dependent) t-test.

8 Now, click OK. The cell should display 0.3 if the cell is formatted to show one decimal place.

Appendix 6.C: Creating a Scatter Plot with Excel before Calculating Correlations

1   With data already in the spreadsheet, creating a figure is easy. We will create the plot on a new Excel sheet. First, highlight Columns C, D, and E, click on the "Home" tab, and then click on the "Copy" command.

2   Now, click on "Sheet 2," at the bottom of the screen. Click on Column C, then click on "Home" and select the "Paste" command.

3   Before you create the plot, the data must be arranged so the two variables you plot, measured $\dot{V}O_2$max and predicted $\dot{V}O_2$max, are side by side. Click Column E so that it is highlighted and then click the "Home" tab, then the "Insert" command list, then "Insert Sheet Columns." A blank column, which now becomes Column E, should appear to the left of the predicted $\dot{V}O_2$max column (now Column F). Next, highlight the entire measured $\dot{V}O_2$max column, including the heading. Then click the "Home" tab and select the "Copy" command. A blinking box should appear around all the data and heading that you selected. Now click in blank Column E, click on the "Home" tab, and select the "Paste" command. A duplicate of Column C should appear. Double-check to make sure it is the right data and that the data are complete.

4   Now highlight the two columns of data, Columns E and F. Highlight only the data, not the headings or calculations. The convention is to show the new method on the y axis and the criterion method as the x axis. With the measured $\dot{V}O_2$max data in Column E, Excel will see it first and make it the X values.

5   Now, with the data highlighted, click on the "Insert" tab and then select "Scatter" in the Chart section. Choose the type without any lines. The chart should appear in a box beside the data.

6   Now, the rest is mostly window-dressing. When you click on the chart, chart option tabs will appear at the top of the screen. You can add titles and labels, modify the type of chart, change the layout, and so forth.

7   Now save the file and savor your accomplishment.

Appendix 6.D: Calculating Correlations with Excel

1   Have your Excel file open to the sheet with the data.

2   Choose a blank cell where you want the correlation value to appear.

3   Click on the "Formulas" tab and then on "More Functions." Under "Statistical," select "CORREL," which is the Pearson Product-Moment Correlation.

4   For "Array 1," highlight the measured $\dot{V}O_2$max data. For "Array 2," highlight the predicted $\dot{V}O_2$max data. Click "OK." The correlation coefficient will appear. Easy, right?

5   You should have calculated a correlation of .9 (possibly with some extra decimal places), which is a strong correlation.

You can view the formulas by clicking on the cells and looking under the "Formula" tab.

7   Evaluating Validity for Ordinal Measures, and Error Analysis

Abstract

Ranked (ordinal) data must be analyzed using different statistics than continuous (interval or ratio) data. This is true for validity, reliability, and objectivity, and also true for research applications. Although there are non-parametric tests of the difference in ordinal means, for our purposes, we will only consider the Spearman's rho to quantify the relationship between an ordinal variable and another variable. The Bland-Altman error analysis allows simple evaluation of continuous measures by evaluating the error between measurements. It also provides information on how the new measurement might be improved. It is a bit simpler than the t-test and correlation and gives us more information, so is a good way to assess validity.

Keywords: ordinal data, Spearman's rho, phi, Bland-Altman Analysis, error analysis, regression line

Evaluating validity for ranked data requires its own set of techniques. Ranked data are simply a set of scores arranged in order (ordinal numbers), as in the rankings of sports teams. The first- and second-place teams may be separated by a small difference or by a large amount. The numbers "1," "2," "3," and so on simply show the order of the teams in the rankings; hence, they are called *ordinal* (meaning "ordered") numbers. *Ordinal numbers* give the place in line, but no information about the distance between the performances which have been ranked. Ordinal numbers contrast with *interval numbers* (also called *scalar numbers,* because they derive from a scale), which are separated by equal intervals. Ordinal numbers are NOT normally distributed, and require their own special inferential statistics.

Because ordinal numbers are only "placeholders," it doesn't usually make sense to add, subtract, multiply, or divide ordinal numbers, except in a few situations. If you were to beat me in a footrace by ten places, the rankings do not tell how badly you beat me, just that you beat me. In a few sports, such as cross-country running, we do add ordinal numbers to determine the winning team.

Spearman's Correlation for Ordinal Numbers

In physical education and sports, we sometimes have to establish the validity of ordinal measurements. For example, I was part of a research team that examined the validity of urine color as an indicator of hydration status. The urine color chart provides an example of ordinal numbers, because the urine color is arranged in order (rank) of darkness, but the "distance" between two colors is not specified. The urine color scale we used was an ordinal scale, with the lightest color at the top, scored as a 0, and the darkest at the bottom, scored as 8 (Armstrong et al., 1994). Scores of "1" and "2" on the chart may not be the same distance apart as scores of "3" and "4," and a score of "3" isn't necessarily three times as dark as a "1."

In those cases where one of the variables is ordinal, we can use a special correlation called the **Spearman's rho** (Greek letter rho). Excel does not calculate Spearman's rho, but there are some websites that will calculate it, such as www.wessa.net/rankcorr.wasp.

It didn't make sense to compare the means of the two measures of hydration, because the criterion method was a ratio measurement and the color scale had no units, only ordinal numbers. So, when we ran the Spearman's rho correlation between data for weight loss and data for urine color, we found the correlation to be $-.25$. The correlation is negative because as the person's weight decreased (he or she became more dehydrated), the color score increased. (Had we correlated dehydration with urine color, both measurements would have increased, and the sign would have been positive.) The negative sign was expected in this case; the only issue was the magnitude of the correlation. When our subjects rehydrated with an electrolyte beverage, the correlation between body weight change and urine color became 0.005. In two other trials with water and an electrolyte with more rapid rehydration, we found correlation coefficients of $r = .12$ and $r = .11$. These very weak correlations suggested that there was no useful relationship between urine color and hydration status. Hence, from our data, we concluded that the current practice of judging hydration status based on urine color is invalid under the conditions we tested.

7.1 Practical Exercise

The following sample data show fitness test scores and placement in an all-around athlete contest. Try entering the data at the website for Spearman's rho (www.wessa.net/rankcorr.wasp) and run the calculation.

Fitness test score	All-around athlete place
64	15
63	14
70	13
70	12
68	11
75	10
77	9
80	8
85	7
82	6
90	5
93	4
90	3
96	2
94	1

In Practical Exercise 7.1, you should find the Spearman's rho to be −.97, which is a very strong negative relationship. That is, as fitness scores increased, the number indicating place decreased. If you were to do a Pearson Correlation on the same data, the results would not be too far off, but they would still be incorrect. Remember, with ranked data, it is improper to use a Pearson Correlation.

Bland-Altman Error Analysis

In addition to running a t-test and a Pearson Correlation, we can evaluate validity using a simpler method that gives us additional useful information. Martin Bland and Douglas Altman, developed the **Bland-Altman Analysis** approach to evaluating criterion validity (Altman and Bland, 1983). They noted that correlations between two measures taken from an abnormally diverse group of subjects will show an artificially high correlation. Their error analysis also may give us suggestions as to how to improve the new measurement.

In Figure 7.1 we see data which display a group of very diverse subjects who probably represent a non-normal distribution. In a normal distribution, most of the data are grouped close to the mean, and the farther you get away from the mean, the fewer data points you see. In a non-normal distribution, little of the data are grouped around the mean, and large amounts of data fall far from the mean. Figure 7.2 shows more normal data, while the data in Figure 7.1 are non-normal. The standard deviation of

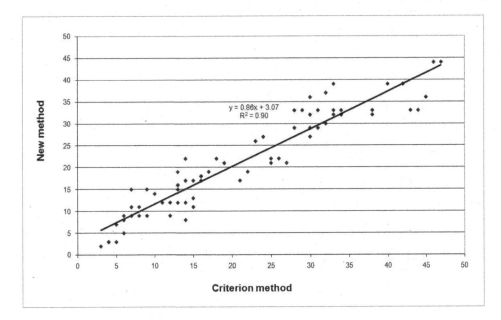

Figure 7.1 Non-normal data

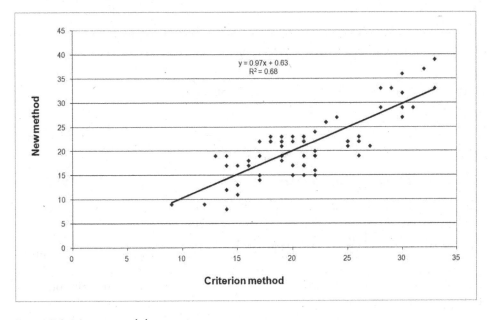

Figure 7.2 More normal data

the more normal data in Figure 7.2 is a less than half that of Figure 7.1. The coefficient of determination is also much lower in Figure 7.2 ($R^2 = .68$ in Figure 7.2 vs. .90 in Figure 7.1). From this example, we can see that non-normally distributed data can inflate the true Pearson Correlations.

Table 7.1 Spreadsheet for a Bland-Altman analysis

	A	B	C	D	E	F	G	H	I	J
2										
3			Predicted VO$_2$max	Measured VO$_2$max	Averages	Differences				
4			64.7	65.2	65.0	0.5				
5			62.5	61.1	61.8	-1.4				
6			55.8	61.0	58.4	5.2				
7			64.7	59.8	62.3	-4.9				
8			55.8	59.1	57.4	3.3				
9			51.3	57.6	54.4	6.3				
10			55.8	55.2	55.5	-0.5				
11			53.5	53.5	53.5	0.0				
12			60.2	51.2	55.7	-9.0				
13			49.1	49.3	49.2	0.3				
14			35.7	47.8	41.7	12.1				
15			44.6	46.3	45.5	1.7				
16			31.2	45.8	38.5	14.6				
17			44.6	45.1	44.8	0.5				
18			51.3	43.8	47.5	-7.5				
19			42.4	42.7	42.5	0.3				
20			42.4	41.9	42.1	-0.5				
21			42.4	41.3	41.8	-1.0				
22			31.2	40.4	35.8	9.2				
23			40.1	39.0	39.6	-1.1				
24			40.1	38.2	39.2	-1.9				
25			51.3	37.3	44.3	-14.0				
26			35.7	37.1	36.4	1.4				
27			28.9	35.2	32.1	6.3				
28			20.0	33.5	26.7	13.5				
29			31.2	31.8	31.5	0.7				
30			22.2	29.2	25.7	7.0				
31			24.5	27.6	26.0	3.1				
32			31.2	26.0	28.6	-5.2				
33			17.8	23.3	20.5	5.5				
34			20.0	21.9	20.9	1.9				
35			28.9	19.9	24.4	-9.0				
36			17.8	19.5	18.6	1.7				
37			17.8	19.2	18.5	1.4				
38						1.19	AVERAGE			
39						6.22	STDEV	Upper limit	13.37	7.40
40						12.18	STDEV × 1.96	Lower limit	-11.00	-5.03

Performing a Bland-Altman Analysis

Instead of running the t-test and correlation, the Bland-Altman focuses attention on the error scores. Appendix 7.A gives instructions for performing the Bland-Altman analysis, and Table 7.1 and Figure 7.3 show the results.

Interpretation of the results of the Bland-Altman analysis depends on a good understanding of the normal curve, and how the SD relates to normal distribution. If you do not feel confident that you understand these concepts, review the description of the normal curve and the SD.

Interpreting Trends in Errors

The trendline from the Bland-Altman analysis depicted in Figure 7.3 represents the trend in errors. That is, the trendline tells us how the errors (differences between measured and predicted VO$_2$max) change as the VO$_2$max goes up. First, look at the R^2,

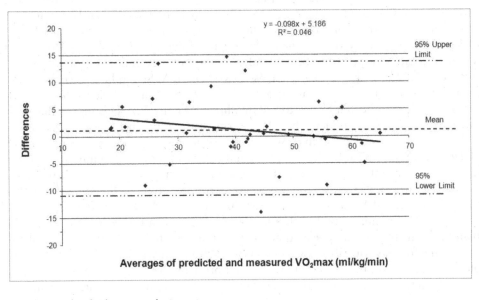

Figure 7.3 Bland-Altman analysis

which is 0.046. Just like the R^2 of a Pearson Correlation, the R^2 of a Bland-Altman analysis indicates the strength of relationship between the score and the errors. If the measurement we are trying to validate is a good representation of the criterion measurement, then the errors should be random, *not* fitting a line well (low R^2).

A strong relationship between the errors and the score, as indicated by a high R^2, would indicate that there is some relationship between the error and the score. It could be, for example, that the error is greater for people scoring higher. This would tell us that there is an error in the prediction equation. We might be able to change the equation to improve the accuracy of the predictions and thereby reduce the error.

In our case, the correlation coefficient is $r = .21$, so the relationship between the error and the mean score is weak. The equation for the line is $y = -0.098x + 5.2$. The slope is negative, which just means that as $\dot{V}O_2$max increases, the error decreases. Also, the slope is very flat (.098). A slope of 0 would be ideal, because that would mean there is no trend in the differences. The intercept is the last number in the equation (5.186), and it tells us that if the $\dot{V}O_2$max were 0 mL • kg^{-1} • min^{-1} (not physiologically possible since $\dot{V}O_2$max = 0 is dead) the correction would be 5.2 mL • kg^{-1} • min^{-1}.

A steep slope in the trendline would tell us that the ability of the test measure to predict $\dot{V}O_2$max is different depending on whether $\dot{V}O_2$max is low or high. For example, the measure may predict well at low $\dot{V}O_2$max, but not at high $\dot{V}O_2$max, or vice versa. This information might be especially valuable if we had to measure mostly people at the low or high end of $\dot{V}O_2$max.

It is possible to have a trendline that is curved. If we find a curved trendline, we might have to choose another trendline shape in Excel besides linear, such as logarithmic or polynomial line fits. The one with the highest coefficient of determination would be the best fit.

Figure 7.3 allows us to see the disagreement between the criterion measurement and the prediction based on our new method ($\dot{V}O_2$max predicted from 12-minute run distance). The mean error (recall that the mean error is measured minus predicted) of 1.19 indicated by the dotted line in the middle of Figure 7.3 tells us that predicted $\dot{V}O_2$max could be expected to be 1.19 mL • kg^{-1} • min^{-1} too high. One SD of the differences is 6.22 mL • kg^{-1} • min^{-1}. We used two SDs (1.96 SD, to be exact) above and below the mean error to give us approximately 95 percent confidence limits. Two SDs is 12.18, as indicated by the top dotted line on Figure 7.3. This means that with our data, we can be confident that 95 percent of the differences between predicted $\dot{V}O_2$max and measured $\dot{V}O_2$max will lie between the mean difference plus 12.18 (1.19 + 12.18 = 13.37 mL • kg^{-1} • min^{-1}) and the mean difference minus 12.18 mL • kg^{-1} • min^{-1} (–11 mL • kg^{-1} • min^{-1}). If a person ran the appropriate number of meters to score 40 mL • kg^{-1} • min^{-1} on the 12-minute run, we could be 95 percent sure that this person's actual $\dot{V}O_2$max lies between 40 + 13.37 and 40 – 11, that is, between 53.4 mL • kg^{-1} • min^{-1} and 29 mL • kg^{-1} • min^{-1}. This is a pretty big spread. By the Bland-Altman analysis, it appears that our 12-minute run test for this sample would be useful only for very roughly classifying our test subjects. If we were just screening people for basic fitness, the 12-minute run would probably be fine, but if we were doing research on techniques to improve $\dot{V}O_2$max, then it would not be accurate enough.

Quick Review

Validity is always a question of degree. In our efforts to establish the validity of the 12-minute run test, the test of means gave us some confidence that the means were the same. The correlation looked pretty good with a correlation coefficient of .90. The Bland-Altman analysis was not as supportive. Now, we have to use good judgment. If we are using the 12-minute run to motivate and give people an idea of their general fitness, then it is pretty good. If we are thinking of using the 12-minute run to test the effects of a short exercise training program, it is not valid enough.

Application Questions

Explain how the Bland-Altman method of evaluating validity differs from the t-test and the correlation approach.

References

Altman, D. G., and Bland, J. M. Measurements in medicine: The analysis of method comparison studies. *The Statistician* 32: 307–317, 1983.

Armstrong, L. E., Maresh, C. M., Castellani, J. W., Bergeron, M. F., Kenefick, R. W., LaGasse, K. E., and Riebe, D. Urinary indices of hydration status. *International Journal of Sports Nutrition* 4: 265–279, 1994.

Wessa.net, Spearman Rank Correlation – Free Statistics Software (Calculator), available at www.wessa.net/rankcorr.wasp.

Appendix 7.A: Creating a Trendline in Excel

1   After creating a scatter plot, click on the plot and then on the "Layout" tab at the top of the screen. Click on "Trendline" and then on "Linear Trendline." You should now see the trendline on the plot.

2   Now, click on "Layout" and "Trendline" again. This time, choose "More Trendline Options." Check "Display Equation on chart" and "Display Rsquared value on chart" and close the box. You should now see the equation and the R^2 value.

3   Save your work.

Appendix 7.B: Evaluating Criterion Validity with a Bland-Altman Analysis Using Excel

1   Open a worksheet and enter (or copy and paste) the data for the predicted $\dot{V}O_2$max in column C beginning at row 4 and the criterion measure, measured $\dot{V}O_2$max, starting in D4. If you want to copy the predicted $\dot{V}O_2$max numbers, you will have to use a special copying method, because these are computed values. Select the column of numbers and choose "Copy" under the "Home" tab. Then click on cell C4 in the new worksheet, click on the "Home" tab, and choose "Paste" and then "Paste Special." Select "Values" and click "OK." The resulting numbers should match the calculated values you copied.

2   Now you need to compute the differences between predicted $\dot{V}O_2$max and measured $\dot{V}O_2$max. To do this, click on cell F4 (not E4) and type "=D4-C4". Look at the values in cells C4, D4, and F4 to check the calculation.

3   To compute the differences for all of the data, click on cell F4, grab the corner box, and drag it down the column.

4   In column E, you will compute the average of the predicted and measured $\dot{V}O_2$max. Highlight cell E4 and type "=(C4+D4)/2". You must use the parentheses, because otherwise the computer would divide first and then add C4 to D4/2. Verify that the resulting number is between the values in cells C4 and D4. To compute the averages for all of the data, click on cell E4, grab the corner box, and drag it down the column.

5   Now, calculate the mean for the difference column by first clicking on the blank cell at the bottom of the column (cell F38). Click the "Formulas" tab, then "More Functions" and "Statistical." Choose AVERAGE. Highlight the data and then click "OK." Your result should be 1.2 (or 1.19, possibly, with extra decimal places).

6   Now, compute the standard deviation of the differences by first clicking in a blank cell at the bottom of the column (cell F39). Go to the list of statistical functions (using the steps given before) and select "STDEV." Select the data in the differences column and close the box. Your result should be 6.22.

7   The next step is to calculate 2 SDs by multiplying the standard deviation by 1.96. Click on the blank cell at the bottom of Column F (cell F40) and enter "=F39*1.96". You should see 12.18.

8   Now you are ready to create the chart. Highlight Column E and Column F, and click on the "Insert" tab, then "Scatter." Choose the type without any lines.

9   Now, in cell H39 type in the words "upper limit", and in cell H40 type in "lower limit".

10   To compute the upper limit, you need the mean of the differences *minus* the STDEV * 1.96 you calculated in cell F40. Type in "=F38+F40". You should get 13.37.

11 To compute the lower limit, you need the mean of the differences *plus* the doubled STDEV you calculated in cell F40. Type in "=F38-F40". You should get −11.00.

12 Now, you will add the mean value and the upper and lower limits to the plot. You will have to draw these on the plot "by hand." To do this, click on the chart and then on the "Layout" tab. Under "Shapes," choose the straight line with no arrows. Now, on the plot, click on the y axis as close as you can to the value 1.19. Holding down the left mouse button, draw the line across the plot. At the right side, release the mouse button.

13 Repeat the same procedure to draw the upper and lower limits. You can choose a different type of line for the limits (a dashed line works well).

14 Finally, plot the trendline. You did that earlier by simply clicking on the chart, then clicking on the "Layout" tab and selecting "Trendline," then selecting "Linear Trendline." Don't forget to go back under "More Trendline Options" to add the equation and the R^2 value.

8 Evaluating the Validity of Criterion-Referenced Measures

Abstract

Criterion-referenced measures provide results in the form of passed-failed, and so do not lend themselves to inferential statistical testing. To test validity we look for consistency with the criterion criterion-referenced score in terms of passed-failed. Phi, which is bit more complex and might be thought of as a sort of correlation for criterion-referenced scores can also be calculated.

Keywords: criterion-referenced, phi

With criterion-referenced tests, the results are usually given as either "passed" or "not passed." In this case, we cannot calculate the mean or a correlation to evaluate validity, because the scores are not numerical. To evaluate criterion validity in this case, we

Table 8.1 Comparison between true classifications and new-measurement classifications to estimate the validity of a criterion-referenced measurement

		True classifications	
		Competent	*Not competent*
New measurement classifications	*Competent*	CR	NCW
	Not competent	CW	NCR
CR = Competent and classified right (correctly) by new measurement			
NCW = Not competent and wrongly classified by the new measurement			
CW = Competent but wrongly classified by the new measurement			
NCR = Not competent and classified right (correct) by new measurement			

have to know the true classification for each person, based on a known valid measurement, so we can compare these true classifications to the classifications resulting from our new measurement technique.

Criterion Measure

The CR and NCR classifications in Table 8.1 specify when the new measurement got the classifications correct, and the NCW and CW classifications specify when the new method got it wrong. When the two "correct" categories include a large proportion of our sample measurements, then we have a criterion-referenced measure with good validity. When the two "wrong" categories have a large proportion of our sample measurements, then the criterion-referenced measure has poor validity.

To evaluate the categories, we simply divide the number of correct measurements by the total number of measurements we made to determine the **validity ratio,** the ratio of the number of scores classified correctly to the total number of scores. Mathematically, we can write this ratio as follows:

Validity ratio = (CR + NCR) / (CR + NCW + CW + NCR)

As always, the level of validity that we demand will depend on both the situation and how badly we need a new measurement method. Generally, a validity ratio of .80 or better would be acceptable. If the ratio is only 0.5, we could do just as well if we classified scores at random, without even measuring. There are only two outcomes, so about 50 percent of the time we would guess correctly just by luck.

Here's an example of calculating a validity ratio. Suppose we were interested in determining whether a new test to certify lifeguards is valid. First, we find a valid measurement that we can use as a criterion. Next, we measure 50 people using the criterion measurement. Suppose, for simplicity, we got 25 who were competent lifeguards and 25 who were not competent lifeguards.

Then we measure these same 50 people using our new experimental lifeguard evaluation technique. The results might look like those in Table 8.2.

Our new lifeguard test actually identified the competent lifeguards 84 percent of the time. Because lives are at stake, the new test would not be a good one.

Balance between Competent and Not Competent

In evaluating validity for criterion-referenced measurements, it is important that the proportion of competent and not-competent people in the sample be as nearly equal as possible. If, for example, the sample included only competent people, we would not be able to evaluate how well the new measurement method is able to recognize when people are incompetent. It is even possible that the test did not measure anything at all, it just indicated (wrongly) that every person was competent. To show that a test like this is invalid, we must have both competent and not-competent people in the sample.

Another Statistic for Evaluating Validity for Criterion-Referenced Tests

To evaluate the validity of criterion-referenced tests, we may also use phi, a calculation that is somewhat equivalent to a correlation. It looks like this:

Phi=   ((CR*NCR)–(NCW*CW))

SQRT ((CR+NCW) (CW+NCR)(CR+CW)(NCW+NCR)

This is the product of the correct cells, minus the product of the incorrect cells, divided by the square root of the paired combinations of all the outcomes. The phi is interpreted just like a correlation, with a phi close to 1.0 being very high and a phi close to 0 being very low. A negative phi would be very bad indeed.

Let's calculate the phi for the lifeguard test data in Table 8.2.

$$phi = \frac{((CR * NCR) - (NCW * CW))}{\sqrt{((CR + NCW) (CW + NCR) (CR + CW) (NCW + NCR))}}$$

$$phi = ((22 * 20) - (5 * 3)) / \sqrt{((22 + 5) (3 + 20) (22 + 3) (5 + 20))}$$

$$phi = (440 - 15) / \sqrt{(27 * 23 * 25 * 25)} = 425 / \sqrt{388125} = .68$$

Phi can vary between +1 and –1, but the nature of the variables is such that it is very hard to get as high a correlation as we do with a Pearson Correlation or with a

Table 8.2 Example diagram for evaluating the validity of a criterion-referenced measurement

		True classifications	
		Competent	*Not competent*
New measurement classifications	*Competent*	CR = 22	NCW = 5
	Not competent	CW = 3	NCR = 20

Note that the sum of the "competent" count is 25, and the sum of the "not competent" count is also 25, which confirms the fact that 25 of the subjects are competent lifeguards.
validity ratio = (CR + NCR)/(CR + NCW + CW + NCR)
= (22 + 20)/(22 + 5 + 3 + 20) = 42/50 = 0.84 = 84% correctly identified

Spearman's rho. We can't demand a correlation of .8 for a phi, but we can hope for a correlation above .5, and it must be positive, because a negative relationship would indicate that those designated as competent on the new test would have consistently been designated as *not* competent on the criterion test.

Concluding Thoughts

Statistical evaluation of criterion validity for norm-referenced measurements involves comparison of the means of the new measure and the criterion measure, evaluation of the figure showing the data, and calculation of the appropriate correlation coefficient (Pearson or Spearman). For criterion-referenced measurements, a different approach is needed, but a percentage accuracy can be calculated, as well as a type of correlation (phi).

Don't be distracted by all these calculations. Most of our effort in this chapter has been devoted to establishing the validity of the measurement, but never forget that this is only half of the concept of validity. Validity means that we have an acceptably accurate measurement, that we are truly measuring what we intend to measure, and *also* that we are interpreting and applying the measurement appropriately.

Application Questions

1   Why can't we calculate correlations with criterion-referenced measurements?
2   Describe a situation wherein you could be comparing a new measure to a criterion measure and have a very high correlation but significantly different mean scores for the two measures.
3   Describe what we can learn from visually inspecting data for a criterion validity evaluation.
4   What are the advantages of statistical tests of criterion validity compared to judgments of content validity?

Practical Exercise

8.1   Practical Exercise

Using the following data, calculate the criterion-referenced validity ratio.

True classifications:	Competent = 23
	Not competent = 20
New measurement classifications:	Competent correctly classified (CR) = 20
	Not competent correctly classified (NCR) = 18
	Not competent wrongly classified (NCW) = 2
	Competent wrongly classified (CW) = 3

9 Understanding, Calculating, and Evaluating Reliability

Abstract

To be a valid measurement, it MUST be reliable and objective, though the reverse is not true. Reliability and objectivity can be statistically examined and when there is no criterion measure, they may be taken as evidence (not proof) of validity. Test–retest is the strongest assessment of reliability, but since that requires two independent administrations of the test, additional split-half methods have been devised, such as Cronbach's alpha. Other factors such as fatigue or learning may hurt reliability and must be considered.

Keywords: reliability, split-half reliability, intraclass correlation, Cronbach's alpha

Earlier, we discussed that *reliability* refers to the consistency of measurement and *objectivity* refers to the degree to which a measurement is free from a variable influence resulting from the person or people doing the measuring. In terms of error, a measurement with good reliability has consistent error and a measurement with good objectivity has acceptably small error originating from the measurer. If a measurement is valid, then it will be both reliable and objective. That is, if a measurement is not reliable (that is, if it is inconsistent), it cannot be valid. If a measurement is not objective (if the score changes depending upon who is doing the measuring), then, likewise, it cannot be valid. The reverse is not true, however. It is possible for a measurement to be reliable but not valid (the error may be consistent and, therefore, reliable, but the error may be unacceptably large). A measurement may also be objective, because the error arising from the measurers is very small, but invalid because the error arising from other sources is unacceptably large. For some measurements, it is very difficult to establish validity. In many interesting measurements, especially those without a criterion measurement available, the best we can do is establish that the measurement is reliable and objective and use those attributes as evidence (not proof) of validity.

In this chapter we will examine some ways to evaluate reliability. As with validity, we can seldom gain absolute knowledge of reliability or objectivity, but rather we can observe degrees of these qualities. How much reliability and objectivity we demand depends on the difficulty of measuring and the importance and application of the measurement.

Evaluating Reliability

The most rigorous way to evaluate the reliability of a measurement is to perform the measurement one time and then administer it again to the same group. Many measurements require considerable time and energy. To perform the measurement twice to evaluate *test–retest reliability* might be impractical. Consequently, less rigorous but faster evaluations have been developed, in which we treat a single measurement administration as a test–retest by dividing the measurement into two parts. In the following sections we will consider the various tools for evaluating reliability.

Test–Retest Method

The most straightforward way to determine reliability is simply to do a **test–retest** evaluation. For a test–retest, we simply give a test, allow the test takers to rest and fully recover, and then give the test again. If the test is new to the test takers, then they may gain some skill the first time they take the test; consequently, their second score may improve simply because of the experience they gained by taking the test the first time. This situation can be avoided by allowing the test takers to practice the task before they take the test the first time, so that they become thoroughly familiar with it. For example, if students take a test of archery skill, the first few arrows they shoot will show great improvement as they get a feel for archery. After several days of archery training, there shouldn't be much difference, after warm-up, between two tests of their shooting skill with sufficient recovery between tests.

Estimates of test–retest reliability assume that there are no major changes in the construct being measured between the two measurements. For example, if we gave a knowledge test, and the test takers were allowed to study before the retest, then the construct being measured—knowledge—would change, so the retest results would change because of the test takers' increased knowledge of the test questions and the subject matter. Or, if we gave a test of muscular fatigue to fully rested athletes and then gave it again immediately, the fatigue status would have changed.

The amount of time elapsed between repeat measures is critical. Generally, the shorter the delay between tests, the better the reliability; the longer the time elapsed, the lower the reliability. In terms of physical performance, however, it's not that simple. If a test is fatiguing, such as a measure of muscular endurance or cardiovascular endurance, then we must allow test subjects to recover before the second test. On the other hand, many physical changes can occur between tests if the recovery duration is very long. Training or detraining can occur if tests are several weeks apart. More troublesome is the fact that sleeping changes, eating differences, or weather changes between tests may affect test performance, even if the key underlying constructs don't change. So, generally speaking, the closer the test and retest, the better, assuming sufficient recovery from fatigue.

The practical question is, how do we evaluate the degree to which a measurement has reliability? As with validity, reliability is a matter of degree rather than an absolute determination.

Evaluating Test–Retest Reliability

Test–retest stability gives strong evidence for reliability, but it is time consuming and laborious. As with evaluations of validity, statistical techniques are available for evaluating test–retest reliability, and one of these techniques is a correlation. In the case of evaluating reliability, we compute the **reliability coefficient**, a ratio that shows the relationship between two measurements, indicating the consistency (reliability) between the two measurements. For test–retest reliability, we obtain the two measurements simply by measuring the same students, athletes, or volunteers twice, making sure nothing affects the scores between measurements. For example, we wouldn't want to do relevant teaching or training between the tests, because that would affect the retest.

When we compare the scores from the test and retest, we follow a procedure very similar to the one for validity. We first compare the means between the tests using a paired, two-tailed t-test. This can be conveniently done with Excel or another spreadsheet, as described earlier.

As with validity, a good correlation means good reliability. Although it seems we could use a Pearson Correlation to evaluate the relationship between the test and retest results, one of the statistical assumptions required for using a Pearson Correlation is that there be two *independent* measures. In the case of the validity study described earlier, we used two different types of measurements: the criterion measure and the new measure. In test–retest reliability evaluations, however, the measurements cannot be considered independent, since the same individuals are being measured twice using the same measurement. For this special situation, we must use a special type of correlation called an *intraclass correlation*.

The **intraclass correlation** is a statistical technique for computing the reliability coefficient to assess the relationship between measures "of the same class" (i.e., measures of the same thing and same people), as in a test–retest study. Intraclass correlation is common in measurement and research, and is sometimes abbreviated as ICCR or as $r_{x,x}$ Here, r is the standard symbol for correlations, and the x,x shows that the two measurements are not independent but are the same measurement made twice. (The symbol for a Pearson Correlation is $r_{x,y}$ indicating that there are two different measurements; e.g., predicted vs. criterion, or height vs. weight).

Appendix 9.A gives instructions for calculating the intraclass correlation with Excel. As with all correlations, the maximum intraclass correlation is 1.0.

Alternative calculation of intraclass correlations

A simple-to-use intraclass correlation program is available at www.obg.cuhk.edu.hk/ResearchSupport/StatTools/IntraclassCorrelation_Pgm.php. Try using this website with the data from the example above. The website gives a mean $r = .976$ for each of the three possible models available on the site. Each of these models approaches the computation of intraclass r slightly differently, but for our purposes, the correlations are all about the same. This confirms that we have a good correlation and good reliability.

Although the website might seem like the easiest way to calculate the correlation, once you set up an Excel spreadsheet, it's just as easy to paste in new data. You may have to move the calculations at the bottom to make room for large data sets, but that is not difficult.

In some situations, a test–retest reliability test is not feasible because of the lack of time or other resources. Because a test–retest reliability evaluation isn't always practical, some alternative approaches have been developed for evaluating reliability.

9.1   Practical Exercise

With the data provided in the previous section, use the website www.obg.cuhk.edu.hk/ResearchSupport/StatTools/IntraclassCorrelation_Pgm.php to compute the intraclass correlation. Did you get the same answer as with Excel? If not, what caused the discrepancy?

Single Test Administration Methods

An alternative method of evaluating reliability is to estimate the consistency of results across items *within* a test. With a single test administration, we may estimate **split-half reliability** by comparing one half of the test with the other half, or we may compute the **internal consistency reliability** by averaging all possible split-half estimates. The major advantage of these estimates of reliability is that they require only a single administration of the measurement; however, these approaches are practical only for a test with a large number of items. As a result, they are not useful for most physical performance tests.

Split-Half Reliability

To calculate split-half reliability for an exam on tennis knowledge, for example, we would give the entire instrument to some test takers. Suppose the test has a total of 30 questions. We could treat the first 15 questions as one test, and the second 15 as a second test, and compare the scores on the first 15 with the second 15. Even better, we could compare the even-numbered questions with the odd-numbered questions. In fact, there are several ways we could divide the questions, including odd–even, every other pair, and so forth.

After calculating the score for each of the two halves, we then evaluate the reliability of the halves simply by determining the correlation between the two sets of scores. One drawback of the split-half method is that the correlation between the two halves depends on the method that is used to divide the items. That is, we may obtain a different correlation for each possible way of dividing the 30 questions. Which would we use?

Table 9.1 Sample scores for evaluating split-half reliability

Odds	Evens
43	47
44	50
38	35
40	38
40	33
45	47
37	39
30	37
42	45
35	38
50	42
40	45
43	49
44	48
36	34

Despite the fact that the correlation will vary depending on how the test is divided, it does provide a fairly accurate measure of the reliability of our exam. If the two halves are highly correlated, then they are probably measuring the same constructs, and the score for one half would predict that of the other. If we find very high reliability, we might even be tempted to discard half of the test questions, because it shouldn't impact the grades.

For an example of calculating the split-half reliability, let's consider hypothetical scores from a tennis knowledge test. The test consists of 30 questions given to 15 students. The odd questions were scored separately on a 50-point basis, and the even scores were scored the same way, giving each test taker two scores. Table 9.1 presents the 30 scores.

To find the split-half reliability, we simply calculate the correlation between the two groups of scores.

Pearson Correlation

We could calculate the Pearson Correlation to evaluate the split-half reliability. In this case, we are able to run a Pearson Product-Moment Correlation to compute the reliability coefficient because the two halves are technically independent, similar to comparison of two different measurements. The Pearson Correlation between the two sets of scores is $r = .63$. Although it is always somewhat arbitrary, we hope to see a correlation coefficient of at least .70, and an even better result would be around .90 (see Table 9.2). Remember, the degree of validity and reliability required is always specific to the situation. For crucial measurements we need better validity and reliability than for less important measurements.

Several factors may influence the reliability. For instance, in the above example, most of the test takers scored in the upper 30s and 40s. If their scores had shown more variety (been less homogeneous), the correlation would likely have been stronger. Again, the more the two variables vary, the easier it is to see a relationship. A longer test would have helped, too. The more times you measure something, the higher the reliability of the composite score.

Spearman-Brown Prophecy Formula

The **Spearman-Brown Prophecy Formula** is a way to estimate the impact on reliability of increasing test length. The formula is:

predicted reliability $= kr/[1 + r(k-1)]$

Here, k is the number by which we are multiplying the test length (that is, if we double the test, $k = 2$; if we triple it, $k = 3$, and so forth). r is the original correlation. If the tennis test were doubled in length, from 30 to 60 test questions, the calculation would be as follows:

$k = 2, r = .63$

predicted reliability $= kr/[1 + r(k-1)]$

$= 2 * .63/[1 + 0.63(2-1)] = 0.77$

By doubling the length of the test, we would improve the correlation coefficient. As in all measurement, we have to evaluate various factors to determine whether changing the test is worth the trouble.

Internal Consistency Reliability

When we compute the split-half reliability, this represents just one possible way to divide up the test items. In the example above, we compared the odd question scores with the even-question scores. There are many more ways we could divide the test into two parts, and the more items there are, the more possibilities. By averaging all of the possible split-half estimates, we estimate internal consistency reliability.

Cronbach's Alpha

By using a statistic called **Cronbach's alpha,** we can find the average of all the possible split-half estimates without calculating each one. Alpha is simply the name given to the product of the computation. To see how to calculate Cronbach's alpha, let's return to the tennis test with 30 items. Because all of the test takers completed all of the 30 items, we can use a computer program to generate and analyze all of the subsets of items and compute the resulting correlations.

Typically, Cronbach's alpha is calculated with a statistical program such as the Statistical Package for the Social Sciences (SPSS) or the Statistical Analysis System (SAS). Here's how it would look in SPSS:

Let's say we have 30 test items in a test battery. We will call the test items t1, t2, t3, and so on up to t30. We give the test to 50 people. We would use the RELIABILITY command as follows:

RELIABILITY

/VARIABLES = t1, t2, t3, t4, t5, . . . t30.

The expected SPSS output would be as follows:

R E L I A B I L I T Y A N A L Y S I S -S C A L E (A L L)

Reliability Coefficients

N of Cases = 50.0   N of Items = 30

Alpha = .xx

The .xx would be the output alpha value.

In SAS, for computing coefficient alpha or Cronbach's alpha, we would use the PROC CORR procedure. For a WORK data set called ONE, to obtain the internal consistency or coefficient alpha or Cronbach's alpha for variables t1 through t30, the commands would be:

PROC CORR DATA = WORK.ONE ALPHA;

VAR t1–t30;

RUN;

The output will list an alpha.

Evaluating the Reliability of Criterion-Referenced Measurements

A criterion-referenced measurement, as you will recall, yields results of a "pass" or "not pass." To evaluate its reliability, we calculate percentage agreement between a test and a retest.

The diagram that we used for establishing validity is useful here as well. We only have to change the headings from "True" and "New" to "Trial 1" and "Trial 2." Table 9.2 shows how it would look.

To estimate the reliability, we could calculate the percentage of agreement by using the following equation:

percentage of agreement = [(Cboth + NCboth)/(total number tested] * 100

The divisor of the fraction in the equation should equal *n*, since every person who takes both tests should fall into one of the categories. Essentially, we are calculating the ratio

Table 9.2 Comparison between Trial 1 and Trial 2 to estimate the reliability of a criterion-referenced measurement

| | | Trial 1 classifications | |
		Competent	Not competent
Trial 2 classifications	*Competent: Not Competent*	Cboth C:NC	NC:C NCboth
Cboth = people scored as competent in both trials			
NCboth = people scored as not competent in both trials			
NC:C = people scored as not competent on Trial 1 but competent in Trial 2			
C:NC = people scored as competent on Trial 1 but not competent in Trial 2			

of the number of people who were rated the same on both trials to the number in the total group. Table 9.3 shows a calculation using 50 people (total of 100 scores).

It can be argued that some of the agreement we see between the two tests is a product of chance. In other words, since only four options are available, some of the agreement happened just by luck. To see how this could happen, imagine flipping a coin, with heads representing competent and tails representing not competent. If you flipped the coin 50 times on each of two days, you would find some agreement between the two trials. That's just the nature of criterion-referenced measurement. If we recognize that the reliability number gets some boost from luck, we can just set our standards a little higher. Again, the degree of reliability that we should require depends on the context. If the measurement is a very important one, or if we cannot evaluate the validity, we will want a very high correlation. If the measurement is very difficult to make and if we can tolerate a higher error, we can accept lower reliability.

Table 9.3 Example diagram for evaluating the reliability of a criterion-referenced measurement

		Trial 1 classifications	
		Competent	*Not competent*
	Competent	Cboth = 23	NC/C = 4
Trial 2 classifications	*Not competent*	C/NC = 3	NCboth h = 20

percentage of agreement = [(Cboth + NCboth)/(Number of people taking test)] * 100
= [(23 + 20) (23 + 4 + 3 + 20)] * 100 = (43/50) * 100 = 86%

Why Is Reliability Important?

1 How does reliability relate to validity?
2 Give an example of a measurement that is reliable yet not valid.
3 Explain why the Spearman-Brown Prophecy Formula might underestimate the reliability of a full test.
4 Why is it important to determine if the mean score from the first test is different from the mean score on the second test? Even if the means are not different, why is it important to examine the correlation between the first test and the second test?
5 Why do we use a special correlation for a test–retest reliability evaluation? What is this correlation called? What is the significance of this name?

Additional Practical Exercises

9.2 Practical Exercise

For the data below, calculate the intraclass correlation on a spreadsheet. Fourteen individuals were each measured twice (28 observations).

Trial 1	Trial 2
50	50
45	40
41	47
38	30
32	40
34	32
30	29
29	37
23	39
25	30
25	32
22	22
20	27
19	24

How would you evaluate the reliability based on the intraclass correlation?

9.3 Practical Exercise

Using the data in Practical Exercise 9.2, use an appropriate t-test to compare the means for the two trials.

9.4 Practical Exercise

Use the Spearman-Brown Prophecy Formula to estimate the reliability if we were to triple the length of a test. Assume that the reliability coefficient at the present length is .67.

9.5 Practical Exercise

For the following data from a criterion-referenced measurement of 100 people performing two trials each, calculate the percentage of agreement.

Trial 1 classifications: competent = 63; not competent = 37

Trial 2 classifications: competent = 68; not competent = 32

Would you consider this criterion-referenced measurement reliable?

Appendix 9.A: Calculating the Intraclass Correlation Using Excel

1 Input the data provided in Table 9.1, with the first data item in cell C4 and each column labeled correctly. Count to ensure that you have 15 data points for each trial and 30 for the two trials.

2 Skip down to cell E21 and type the number of data points, "15". In cell D21, type "n". In cell E22 enter the number of trials, "2", and in cell D22, type "k". Now these numbers are easily available for the calculation.

3 In Column E we will calculate the total for each person. In cell E4, type the label "T". In cell E4, type "=C4+D4". Press Enter. The cell should display the sum, 130.

4 To copy the formula down the column, click on cell E4 and drag the little box down to the last row of data.

5 In cell E19, type "=SUM(C4:D18)". This is the sum of all the scores, which is ΣX. Label it "ΣX" in cell D19. (To type the Σ, click on the "Insert" tab, then on "Symbol." Select the "Symbols" tab. Scroll down until you see the "Σ" symbol, and click on it. Then click the Insert button, then close.) Since we will be needing $(\Sigma X)^2$, in cell E20 type the function "=POWER(E19,2)". This raises the value in cell E19 to the second power. Label it "$(\Sigma X)^2$" in cell D20. (To make the 2 a superscript, highlight it with the cursor, then click on the "Home" tab and open the "Font" menu. Check the superscript box and click OK.)

6 Next, we need to square each score and sum the results. Label Column F "Trial 1 Squared" and label Column G "Trial 2 Squared". In cell F4 type the function "=POWER(C4,2)" to raise cell C4 to the second power. Cell F4 should display the number 3969.

7 Copy the formula in cell F4 down the column.

8 Copy cell F4 into cell G4. The formula will automatically change so that it squares cell D4. It should display the number 4489. Copy the formula down the column.

9 In cell G19, type "=SUM(F4:G18)" to display the sum of all the squared scores for both trials. Label it by typing "X^2" in cell F19.

10 In cell H3, type the heading "T Squared". Copy the formula from cell G4 into cell H4, and then copy it down the column. The formula will again automatically change so that it squares cell E4.

11 In cell G20, type "=SUM(H4:H18)" to sum all the T-squareds. This displays the sum of all the squared totals. Label it in cell G21 "ΣT^2".

12 Now we can calculate SSa. You will find it useful to type the equation (as a line of text, not a formula) at the bottom of the calculations so you can refer to it easily. Put it in cell C25. Then, in cell F25, enter the following formula: "=(G20/E22)–(E20/(E21*E22))". This simply translates the equation into an Excel formula that refers to the correct cells. The cell should display the number 3306. If not, check to see if you have made any mistakes.

13 To calculate SSw, type the equation for SSw in cell C27. Then in cell F27, enter the formula "=G19-(G20/E22)". The cell should display 83.5.

14 Type the equation for intraclass reliability in cell C29. In cell I29, type the Excel formula (see if you can figure this one out on your own). If you have done everything correctly, when you hit Enter you should see the intraclass correlation of .976428. Format the cell to show two decimal places, to give 0.98.

10 Understanding, Calculating, and Evaluating Objectivity

Abstract

Evaluating objectivity is helpful when criterion validity cannot be established, and may be useful in improving validity because it may help you identify error. Intraclass correlations can be used for assessing objectivity for continuous measurements, and ratios can be computed for criterion-referenced measures.

Keywords: objectivity, inter-rater reliability

Evaluating Objectivity

Objectivity, as you recall, is the degree to which different raters give consistent measurements of the same performance. Objectivity reflects the degree of error due to the measurers. Before using any test, we need to establish that we have good objectivity, to make sure that different test takers or observers are not getting different results for similar performances. This is important, for example, when many different test administrators are giving a physical or cognitive abilities test for employment or special training, such as for referees, teachers, firefighters, or law enforcement. If objectivity is low, then we must adjust the measurement technique or improve the training for the test givers. If the measurement technique is being used for a long period of time, it is necessary to re-examine the objectivity periodically to ensure that the test administrators are staying consistent. You should be able to see why clear, complete, detailed instructions for test givers are so important for high objectivity.

To estimate objectivity, two methods are commonly used, depending on whether the measure is continuous or discrete.

Calculating Objectivity for Continuous Measures

To estimate objectivity in a situation where the measure is continuous (that is, there is the possibility of any score between a maximum and minimum), we can calculate the intraclass correlation between the scores, just as we did for reliability. In fact, it is reasonable to consider objectivity just a special case of reliability, called *inter-rater reliability*. When you visited the website for calculating the intraclass correlation, you may have noticed that the columns could be for trials or raters. To evaluate reliability we compare trials, but when we are evaluating objectivity we compare raters.

For example, if *one* judge viewed a videotape and scored a single gymnastics routine performed by several gymnasts, and then sometime later the same judge rescored the same routine, we could evaluate the *reliability* for that judge using an intraclass correlation. Or, if two different judges scored a single gymnastics routine performed by several gymnasts, we could evaluate their *objectivity* (inter-rater reliability), just as we did for reliability using an intraclass correlation.

Calculating Objectivity for Discrete Measures

If the measurement consists of discrete categories in which the test administrators are categorizing each observation, we can calculate the percent agreement between the administrators. This is similar to what we did for evaluating the reliability of criterion-referenced measures. For example, suppose we had 50 observations of students, and these observations were being rated by two different graders. For each observation, the rater could select one of five rating categories. Imagine that on 42 of the 50 observations, the graders gave the same rating. In this case, the percent of agreement would be 42/50 or 84 percent. This simple approach is useful regardless of the number of rating categories. When there are multiple possible scores, we must decide "how close" is close enough to count as the same score. We can use it for any pair of graders, but this approach is especially useful for comparing a new rater with an experienced or very knowledgeable rater. This is because we assume that the more experienced rater has greater validity (a more tolerable amount of error) than the novice. We are really measuring the objectivity of the novice against a more trustworthy (but not quite criterion) standard, the ratings of the experienced judge.

For example, if we were training new gymnastics judges, we could compare each of them against an experienced, certified gymnastics judge. We might establish a minimum percentage of agreement and certify only those trainees reaching this standard level of agreement. Or, if several good judges were available, we could use the mean score of this group as the standard for evaluating the new judges' objectivity.

Concluding Thoughts

Reliability and objectivity are very similar concepts. In fact, objectivity may be considered a special case of reliability. Hence, most of the techniques that we use in evaluating reliability can also be used to evaluate objectivity. It is possible to have high reliability or objectivity without high validity, as illustrated previously. On the other hand, good reliability or objectivity will always be present with a valid measurement. Sometimes we cannot evaluate validity directly. In these difficult situations, our only clues about a measurement's validity may come from assessment of reliability and objectivity. Again, good reliability and objectivity do not establish good validity, they simply suggest that the measurement *may* be valid. As always, the required degree of reliability and objectivity is determined by the context.

Application Question

1   Explain why objectivity may be considered a special case of reliability.

Practical Exercise

10.1   Practical Exercise

Based on the following hypothetical information, answer the questions below:

A group of researchers from your university is evaluating the reliability and objectivity of a push-up test for determining 1RM strength and has obtained the following results:

a   Test–retest reliability via intraclass correlation of a push-up test for determining 1RM strength is $r = .93$.
b   Objectivity determined using intraclass correlation for four different scorers for push-ups averages $r = .92$, with lowest being $r = .88$.

1   Is this a reliable test? Give all the reasons why you reached your conclusion.
2   Is this an objective test? Give all the reasons why you reached your conclusion.
3   Is this a valid test? Give all the reasons why you reached your conclusion.

Now, go back and reread the information about the test. Is this really a valid test? Is the application valid?

11 Devising Measurements

Abstract

Developing any new measurement requires about seven steps: defining, researching, developing, scoring, pilot testing, modifying, and establishing norms. Each step of this process is crucial in developing a valid, reliable, and objective measurement.

Keywords: pilot testing, norms

Physical educators, coaches, and athletic trainers are among the best qualified professionals to develop tests of physical abilities, and you may develop tests as part of your work. In this chapter we will establish a general pattern for developing physical, cognitive, and affective (related to emotions and feelings) measurements.

This pattern of test development can serve as a guide regardless of the type of test you are developing.

Here are a few examples of the kinds of situations where you may find yourself devising tests:

- A friend wants a test to measure physical abilities for College ROTC cadets to compare with US Army troops to guide the students' physical training.
- An Exercise Scientist needs to design tests of clothing and equipment to keep Law Enforcement personnel cooler in hot environments.

The chief goal of this chapter is to give you practical hands-on experience with devising tests to maximize validity, reliability, and objectivity. You will gain insight into the basic process of test development and evaluation and consider validity, reliability, and objectivity not just in theory, but also in practice.

The Process of Devising a Test

It's one thing to talk about measurement theory, but quite another to design and perform measurements. Devising a new test of physical ability requires that we begin to think about measurement issues in a practical way.

Let's start with an example based on a real need: When astronauts go on an extra-vehicular activity (EVA or "spacewalk"), they must wear pressurized spacesuits. One of the key problems of EVA is that astronauts must close their gloved hands against the pressure of the suit. The astronauts must grip against the pressure of the glove, which quickly fatigues their forearms. NASA needs to train astronauts to improve their grip strength and endurance. The first step in this process is to develop tests to measure the astronaut's grip strength and endurance.

Developing a new test has seven steps:

1 Defining what to measure.
2 Researching relevant information.
3 Establishing testing procedures.
4 Determining scoring for the test.
5 Pilot-testing the test, scoring system, and instructions.
6 Evaluating, modifying, and retesting the pilot test.
7 Developing norms.

Step 1: Defining What to Measure

The first step in developing a test is to develop an operational definition that describes exactly what we want to measure. For the present task, measuring hand grip strength, we need only define hand strength. Strength is generally defined as the maximal force one can exert. Hand strength would be the maximal force exerted one time—this is often called a one-repetition maximum, or 1RM. This is a good general definition, but we need to be more specific. For the purpose of developing NASA training, we will probably be interested in one-handed strength, and we are probably thinking of the dominant hand. Therefore, we will define hand strength as: *the greatest force a person can produce using only the dominant hand.*

But let's consider other ways hand strength could be defined, depending on the anticipated applications of the test. We could define strength as a person's maximal average force produced on three separate maximal effort trials. We could define hand grip strength as the sum of the best of three hand squeezes with the left hand added to the same measure for the right hand. Or we could define it as the maximal score on three trials for the nondominant hand. This last definition has particular interest in measurement. We might choose to test the nondominant hand because it is less "skilled" than the dominant hand, so measures of this hand would reduce the element of "skill" in performing the test. Removing the element of "skill" might allow a "purer" measurement of hand strength.

So, we can define hand strength using the dominant or the nondominant hand. The hand we choose will depend on the situation. Either choice may be correct or incorrect, or it may not matter. A thoughtful and knowledgeable measurement expert, such as you are becoming, will make an appropriate choice.

The definition we choose for measurement purposes is important because the definition specifies the constructs. To establish validity, we will need to ensure that we are measuring the correct constructs. If our measurement tests the constructs of the definition we chose, then we should find acceptable validity.

Step 2: Researching

Now that we have chosen a definition, the next step is to start to think of a way to measure the strength as defined. A little research can help us get started. We might discover an existing test that measures what we want to measure. Even if we don't find a test that we can use practically in our situation, we may find a test that we can modify for our application. We may also discover something that could cause us to adjust the definition of the characteristic we want to measure. For example, as we see the definitions or techniques that others have used, we might decide to redefine hand strength using information we have encountered.

To find tests, we can contact experts, look for information in books, look for published research articles, and search the Internet. If we find a published test, we must be aware of copyright restrictions and intellectual property rights. Someone may own the rights to a given test, which means we can't just use it as we desire. We may have to get permission from the publisher to use the test, or we may have to purchase the test or the rights to use it. Fortunately, some published tests are in the public domain, which means anyone is free to use them. For example, the Physical Activity Readiness Questionnaire (PAR-Q) is a free survey. Be careful, however, not to assume that a test or questionnaire is free for use.

11.1   Practical Exercise

Research tests for hand grip strength in books, in published articles, and on the Internet. Compile a list of tests and their sources, and indicate whether each test is copyrighted or in the public domain.

Based on what we found in our research, we decide what to do next. If we found a test that looks good for our situation, we can use it as is. We may have found a test that is almost ideal. If we make a few changes, it may work even better. However, we may have concluded that there is no existing test that we can use. In this case, we will have to develop a test from start to finish. We will have to do a great deal of work in creating, modifying, and validating a new test.

Step 3: Establishing Testing Procedures

Let's say we have found a test that will work with some modifications. We choose to base our new test on an existing one that uses a hand grip dynamometer, a squeezable device that registers squeezing force (see Figure 11.1). We have access to a hand grip dynamometer, so we can think about how to employ this dynamometer in our test. The most straightforward approach would simply be to have the test subject pick up the dynamometer and squeeze away. But before adopting this approach, we want to think a bit more.

Could the size of the hand grip part of the dynamometer influence the score? Research, or a bit of experimenting with a dynamometer, would show that grip size does indeed influence scores. We need an adjustable dynamometer and some means for fitting the dynamometer to the test takers' hands. The test has to be practical, so we must devise a simple procedure for accurately fitting the dynamometer to each subject's hand.

One simple approach is to have the test taker open her hand. We will place the dynamometer snugly against the web at the base of the thumb and then adjust the grip size so that the front edge of the grip just reaches the second joint of the index finger. Notice that this instruction is simple but specific. Remember, we will need to write procedures down. Because the objectivity of the test will depend on other test givers' understanding of how to give the test correctly, they will need clear and precise written instructions. We may be able to come up with an even better method for sizing the dynamometer to the test takers' hands, so consider any approach that seems accurate and practical.

Figure 11.1 Example hand grip dynamometer for use in hand grip strength measurement

Besides the grip size, could other factors influence hand grip? Again, if we research a bit and experiment with the procedure, we may discover other factors that might influence scores. If a person swings his or her arm or snaps his or her hand down, for example, this could influence scores. Perhaps the arm's angle with the body or the lower arm's angle with the upper arm could influence scores. Anything that we decide is important, we must specify in the test procedures. And remember to keep things practical: the specifications must be clear and easily followed.

11.2   Practical Exercise

Using a hand grip dynamometer, follow the hand grip size measurement procedures just above Figure 11.1. Based on your experience, what modifications would we make to the directions?

Step 4: Determining Scoring for the Test

The fourth step is to decide how to score the test. We could have the person do just one trial, which would be simple and quick. Requiring only one trial does present problems. A test taker's grip might slip. A test taker might not be able to give his or her best squeeze on the first try, since the task may be unfamiliar. We could, on the other hand, have the test taker do 20 trials. A large number of trials presents problems too. First, it may be very fatiguing for the subject, and it would take a long time to test a single person. If we have to test a whole team of baseball players, or a school class, it may take too long. So, we might experiment and decide that two, three, or four trials are enough. To determine how many trials we will need, we must make an informed, evaluative judgment. We have to be practical, but we also must ensure that we have a reliable measurement. If we put these two aspects together it implies that we should do enough trials to assure reliability, but no more.

In general, it's probably best to start with three trials and then evaluate the reliability. To do this, we would follow the procedures and record the best of three trials as the score. After a sufficient recovery period, repeat the exact procedure and record the best of three trials again. Then, find the intraclass correlation, and if it is acceptable for our purposes, then we can either accept the procedure or try it with the best of the first two trials to see whether two would be sufficient. If the correlation is too low, then we will add another trial, since adding more trials often increases reliability.

Suppose we decide to require three trials. How will we record the grip strength, which is a single number, if we have scores from three trials? We could use the best of three, but this is not the only way. We could average the scores. Averaging scores is usually a good idea, because it helps to cancel the error of scores that have positive error (they are too high) with scores that have negative error (they are too low).

Earlier we described every score as a true score plus or minus some error. That principle applies to these scores. Averaging is usually a good procedure, but it may not be in this situation of measuring hand grip strength. To see why, look back at the definition for hand grip strength. We defined hand strength as "the greatest force a person can produce using only the dominant hand." So, for this test at least, strength is defined as the *maximal* force, not the *average* force. If we average the scores, in most cases the average will be less than the maximum. We could choose to average the scores and simply change the definition—that is, redefine strength in terms of the test. But if we want to adhere to the original definition and be in agreement with the most common conceptions of strength, we should choose to consider the strength score as the highest (maximal) score attained in the specified number of trials.

Assuming the best of three trials is the optimum procedure for this test, let's consider reasons why we might select a different alternative. First, depending on the purpose of the testing, we might believe that a definition of strength *other* than the common one of maximal force is appropriate in our case. If we have good reasons for changing the definition, we should be able to convince other people that the new definition is legitimate. Second, if some measurement were extremely important, we might use a longer or more thorough measurement. We might repeat the measurements over multiple days and then choose a mean or a maximal score. This approach would be very time consuming and impractical for many applications; but, there may be situations where that would be the most valid way to measure.

For example, suppose a person had a very serious disease where deadly blood clots were likely. In using a pharmaceutical to control blood clotting, health professionals would need to make sure that the blood wasn't clotting too readily (which could cause a stroke) or not readily enough (which could cause the person to bleed to death). They could test the blood clotting numerous times over several days and then calculate the mean blood clotting time. This would be considered the measurement of the blood clotting time. They would be justified in using this time-consuming measure because this measurement is life or death, and it does vary slightly day to day.

Step 5: Pilot-Testing the Test, Scoring System, and Instructions

Our first test of a newly developed measure is called a **pilot test**. The purpose of a pilot test is to identify any problems or errors in the measurement procedures. To pilot-test our hand grip strength test, we will need several volunteers to perform the test and give us feedback. The volunteers should help answer certain questions about the test: Is it practical? Is it dangerous? Is it painful to perform? Is there a way to "cheat"?

To answer this last question, we can encourage the pilot test subjects to try to figure out ways to "cheat." Because any error resulting from a subject's cheating will add to the error in the scores and reduce the test's validity, we may need to add instructions to prevent any methods of cheating. We will also be looking for ways to make the test easier, faster, and better.

The pilot test is also our best opportunity to have others look at the written instructions to help we make sure they are complete, clear, and understandable. Why so much concern for the test instructions? Instructions are important because, as we discussed, to have an objective test, each person administering the test must understand exactly what is to be done and must be willing and able to administer the test according to the instructions. Writing good test instructions can be very challenging. Generally, we should assume that anything that can be misunderstood *will* be misunderstood. Pay close attention to detail—it is better to have too much detail than too little.

Step 6: Evaluating, Modifying, and Retesting the Pilot Test

After we have given at least one trial run (pilot test), we are ready for one of the most important steps: to evaluate and modify the test in order to improve it. In fact, we will need to repeat steps five (pilot testing) and six (test evaluation and modification) until the test is ready for use. Even after we begin to use the test, we can still modify it to make it better, but the test should be as good as we can make it before we begin to measure.

The key qualities of a test are its validity, reliability, and objectivity. Hence, our efforts during this step should focus on evaluating these characteristics, along with practical aspects of the test. As discussed earlier, to evaluate the validity of a newly developed measurement, we hope that some criterion measure is available. In many cases, it is not that simple, and we must employ less direct measures to establish validity. We may recruit experts to help evaluate the measurement's content validity, and we may evaluate reliability by running test–retest trials and objectivity by having more than one administrator give the test.

It is also necessary to evaluate the practical aspects of the new test. This mainly involves reviewing its administration procedures. If we can administer the test in a reasonable period of time, by ourselves or with a reasonable amount of help, with available equipment, then the test seems practical. Any changes that make the test simpler, faster, and easier (both for the test takers and the test administrators) will increase its practicality.

Step 7: Developing Norms

It is often useful to measure the performance of an individual and compare it to the performance of a group of similar individuals. To do this comparison, we need tables that show how different groups have scored. A **norm table** provides criteria for identifying a good score, an average score, and a poor score. Earlier, we learned how to use a spreadsheet program to calculate the standard deviation, which, along with the mean score, can be used to establish the norms. For example, if we found a mean hand grip score of 46 and an SD of 11, we could use z-tables to set percentiles for that population.

As the size of the sample gets close to the size of the population, obviously it becomes a better and better representation of the population, but it also becomes less and less practical as a sample because of all the measurements that must be taken.

Once we have developed norms, then we must keep in mind that any change to the test will alter the norms. For example, suppose we created a table of norms for hand grip strength using procedures which specified that test takers should be seated. Then, we change the procedures to allow test takers to stand and move their arm downward as they grip. This might raise the scores, and our norms would no longer be applicable. We would have to develop new norms, based on the scores using the new procedures.

As an alternative to developing norm tables, we could make the test criterion-referenced. It may be that astronauts only need a specified minimum grip strength. If we know what that minimum grip strength is, we can make our test pass/not-pass, instead of making it norm-referenced. A criterion-referenced test will be simpler to score, because we need only compare the subject's score to the criterion score. But, a criterion-referenced test requires that we identify an appropriate score to pass.

Quick Review

DEVELOPING A TEST. In general, we follow these steps to develop a measurement instrument or test:

1 Define what we want to measure.
2 Research to find any existing tests.
3 Modify or develop a test procedure with instructions designed to measure what we have defined.
4 Determine an appropriate scoring system.
5 Pilot-test the test, scoring system, and instructions.
6 Evaluate, modify, and retest the pilot test to make it as valid, reliable, objective, and practical as possible.
7 Develop norms.

Additional Practical Exercises

11.3 Practical Exercise

This exercise will allow you to experience valid, reliable, and objective measurement firsthand. Student groups of four to eight students will design and test a strength measurement procedure and present their protocol to the other groups. The other groups will critique the test for validity, reliability, and objectivity. Then, each group will repeat the process for endurance, which is more difficult to measure.

Equipment required:

hand grip dynamometer for each group

stopwatch or metronome (optional)

Tasks:

1 Determine what is being measured. What is a practical definition of hand grip strength?
2 Decide what tools you will need.
3 Use these tools to design the hand grip strength measure.
4 Write out detailed instructions for the hand grip strength measurement (see Practical Exercise 11.2).
5 Test the new strength measurement technique on others in your group or class.
6 First evaluation: Does your test agree with your definition?

(continued)

(continued)

7   Redesign the test if necessary to make sure it matches your definition.
8   Second evaluation: How does your test differentiate among different popula-tions? How should rock climbers perform on your test? How should bigger athletes do? Why? To be valid, the test must be able to discriminate among people of different abilities.
9   What should happen to scores after people become fatigued?
10 How enjoyable is your test for your subjects? How do you know? How could you find this out in a systematic manner? Could your test be modified to make it easier to administer and more accurate?
11 Write up a survey to determine your subjects' ideas, complaints, and sugges-tions about the test.
12 After your subjects have rested, retest them.
13 Make an official record of all data.
14 Have another group administer your test. Does the test appear to be objec-tive? Are the results the same no matter who administers the test?
15 Give your test instructions to another group of students and see if they can administer the test correctly without further explanation. If they make errors, rewrite your instructions to make them more clear and detailed.
16 Based on your evaluation of your test, how would you rate its validity, reliabil-ity, and objectivity? What can be done practically to increase these qualities?
17 Modification phase: Redesign your test, test instructions, and survey. Turn them in to your teacher. Include a brief summary of what you learned in this exercise.
18 Repeat this entire process for a test of hand endurance. It should be more challenging.
19 Combine all the data for all groups for the strength test and devise norm tables based on the combined data. Devise a norm table for the combined endurance data. Use the data to analyze reliability and objectivity statistically.

11.4   Practical Exercise

In designing any measurement instrument, it is necessary to follow certain steps. Choose one of the following tasks:

a   Describe the steps you would take to design a test to measure the fitness of a candidate for a Rescue Emergency Medical Technician to enter the Rescue EMT academy. You should not list specific test items, rather, describe how you would find and choose individual items to make up your test battery. Give examples for your major points.

b   Suppose you have been awarded a $30,000 grant to design a softball skills test for the city of Perth, Australia. Describe in detail the steps you would take (not the specific test items) to devise a good skills test. Be complete.

What test items would you include for either of these skills tests?

11.5 Practical Exercise

Search the Internet for good sources of tests for your specialty area. Record the URLs of helpful sites.

12 Evaluating New Measurements

Abstract

After a new test has been pilot-tested, it is necessary to estimate the validity, reliability, and objectivity of the new measurement. This final evaluation is crucial in finalizing the measurement procedures.

Keywords: validity, reliability, objectivity

Estimating the Validity of a New Measurement

The validity of the new measurement is always of greatest concern. To do a thorough job of estimating the validity of the measurement, we must check the validity in more than one manner.

Construct Validity

The most fundamental approach to estimating validity is to conduct a construct evaluation by examining the underlying qualities that account for good performance. Some people have very high grip strength. Experienced rock climbers, for example, develop good grip strength. Football offensive and defensive linemen also develop good grip strength, as do gymnasts. On the other hand, people who neither engage in strength training nor do any activity that would build grip strength do not, on average, have unusually good grip strength. Generally, we would expect bigger people to have higher grip strength than smaller people. If we gave the test to people who should score well and to people who we would not expect to do well, the test should give appropriate outcomes, if the measurement is valid.

If, on the other hand, we found that everybody scored about the same or that those who ought to have done well scored very low or those with no reason to have done well scored higher than expected, then we should conclude that the new test is not valid.

Criterion Validity

When it is possible, the most direct and simplest method of estimating the validity of a new measurement is to compare it with a criterion measure, if it exists.

Suppose that during our research on hand grip tests, we discover a criterion measure. We might ask, if a criterion measurement exists, why would we develop a new measurement? There are many reasons to devise new measurements. In athletic training, we might find a criterion measure that would not be practical to do on the athletic field or that requires equipment not available at every high-school competition. The criterion measurement might take too long for our application. The new measurement might be quicker, cheaper, or more practical for a desired application. As we can see, there are a number of reasons that a criterion measurement may not be practical in every situation.

If we do find a criterion measurement, we can compare our test with the criterion using the paired t-test and Pearson Correlation or with the Bland-Altman procedure. If we find good agreement, we can make a claim of good validity. If no criterion standard for hand grip strength is available, we can still compare our test with other existing measurements. This would help, since our test is the "new kid on the block," but because these tests themselves may not be valid, comparisons with them will be only "suggest" validity.

Content Validity

The least trustworthy method of estimating validity is by means of content validity. Good content validity would simply mean that the hand grip measurement *seems* logically to be a test of hand grip strength. Since we define strength as the maximal force generated with the dominant hand (with some other specifications), the test looks pretty good. It does measure hand grip, and the scoring system does look like it should measure hand grip strength. If we could find some people with expertise in hand grip measurement, we might ask them for their expert evaluation of our test, and this would support a claim of content validity.

Content validity seems simple, but it is neglected surprisingly often. In many cases, poor content validity arises from imprecise definitions. For example, sometimes tests of muscular endurance (e.g., push-ups) are improperly used to measure strength. A test may intend to measure a concept such as "agility," but agility is difficult to define. Often, a test described as measuring a difficult-to-define attribute such as "agility" actually only measures the test taker's ability to perform that specific test. For example, if the test used a stop-and-go type shuttle run, it may be measuring sprint speed or acceleration more than agility. In even more challenging measurements, say of sportsmanship or motivation, accurately establishing content validity is extremely difficult. Qualities such as these can easily be contaminated by the test taker's desire to "appear" a certain way, and other issues, and it is difficult to judge whether a measurement technique overcomes such subtleties.

Quick Review

EVALUATING THE VALIDITY OF A TEST. Construct validity is fundamental to evaluating validity. Remember also that criterion validation, when it is possible, provides trustworthy evidence. Most often, however, we are simply trying to accumulate enough evidence to give others and ourselves confidence in a newly developed measurement technique. Validity is typically a question of degree.

Estimating Reliability

If we are extremely confident that an application of a measurement is valid, there is no reason to test reliability. If the test is valid, then the error must be small, and the measurement must be reliable. If we are unsure of the degree of validity—and this will often be the case—then we would want to evaluate test–retest reliability.

As stated earlier, the reliability of a measurement increases with increasing numbers of trials. With multiple trials, "accidental" scores—those due, for example, to a slip or a misreading—have less effect on the overall, final score. By administering the test multiple times, we can then examine the agreement of the scores.

It is important to consider factors that could impact the reliability of a measurement. If we were to administer the hand grip strength test to the same subject twice in a row (three trials and then three more trials), it is likely that fatigue from the first three trials will cause error. Another factor to consider is the delayed-onset muscle soreness that will occur about 48 hours after a novel exercise. Administering the hand grip measurement on Monday and then giving the retest on Wednesday is not a good idea.

Each measurement we make will have different factors influencing its reliability and, consequently, our assessment of its validity. Whatever the measurement, we must take into account the factors that hurt reliability and validity. Since these same factors may arise during the actual use of the test, the test instructions should point out these factors.

The same person who administers the first measurement should also give the retest, so that the results cannot be influenced by poor objectivity.

Estimating Objectivity

As with reliability, a measurement that is known to be valid need not be tested for objectivity: If the measurement is valid and administered according to the instructions, the error must be small. However, it is seldom possible to be certain that a measurement is valid. Even if a measurement is valid, if the instructions are not followed very carefully, then the test administrator can invalidate an otherwise valid measurement. This is why we must be careful to draft complete and understandable instructions. If the measurement is modified after pilot testing, the instructions must also be modified.

To ensure objectivity, several people should independently administer the pilot test to the same group of test takers. With only a single test administrator, we would see only this particular administrator's interpretation of the instructions. Other test administrators might interpret the instructions differently, which would hurt the test's objectivity.

Objectivity should be evaluated with the same group of people who will be giving the test. If a measurement is intended to be given by athletic trainers, then the objectivity should be tested with a sample of athletic trainers. If a measurement is to be given by physical educators, then these people should comprise the testing group. Different groups use different terminology and may interpret test instructions differently. Clearly, we want to test objectivity with the people most likely to utilize the test.

Additional Real-World Measurement and Evaluation Applications

Hand Grip Endurance

The problem that NASA faces with regard to astronauts' grip includes not only hand grip strength, but also hand grip endurance. So NASA needs to measure both capacities. As we begin developing a hand grip endurance measurement, we will discover there are several different ways to define muscular endurance. The basic definition for endurance is the ability to repeat a movement over and over. For example, lifting a 50-lb (22.7 kg) crate from the floor to a truck over and over for eight hours requires good endurance. Bicycling 100 miles (161 km) requires the repeated application of force to the pedals and requires very good endurance.

Endurance may also be defined in other ways. It may be defined in terms of what is considered "absolute" (as opposed to relative) endurance. Absolute endurance is the ability to exert a specified fixed force repeatedly, such as in lifting a 50-lb crate. To measure absolute hand grip endurance, we could have subjects pull the dynamometer at a certain force, say 30 pounds (13.6 kg). Every pull would have to be at 30 pounds of force, and we would count the number of successful repetitions in a given time period.

Relative endurance is expressed relative to some other measure. For example, to measure relative hand grip endurance, we might require the subjects to hold some percentage of their maximum grip strength score. We could require them to hold or pull 50 percent of their maximum strength, so that a person who scored 60 pounds of force on the maximum hand grip strength measurement would be required to squeeze to 30 pounds. We could choose any percentage of the maximum, depending on the application. The lower the percentage, the longer each trial will take, so this could be a practical issue.

Whether to choose a relative or an absolute measurement depends on the application. The choice will influence the practicality of the measurement. A relative endurance definition that depends on strength will require that we measure the subject's hand grip strength first. This may not present a problem if strength is being measured anyway, but if not, the extra step will make the measurement process longer.

Both absolute and relative endurance have two types: static (no motion) and dynamic (with motion). To measure static hand grip endurance, we would have a person squeeze once and hold a certain force (30 pounds, for example) as long as possible. The duration of the hold is timed to yield the static absolute endurance score. To measure dynamic endurance, we would assess the subject's ability to squeeze a certain amount of force repeatedly.

The choice of a static or dynamic endurance definition will depend on the application. If NASA is concerned with an astronaut's hand grip endurance while the astronaut is wearing a pressurized suit and working with tools, we might choose dynamic hand endurance. If NASA is concerned with the ability to hold on to something continuously, we might choose a static endurance definition. The measurement definition we choose must be clear, and it must be specified in the instructions since it will guide the development of the measurement.

During pilot testing of the endurance measurement, time will often become a significant factor. With a relative dynamic or static test, the endurance time may be impractically long if the relative contraction level (percent of maximum strength) is too low. For example, if the relative endurance were based on only 10 percent of maximum strength, it might take a long time to tire out the test takers who have good endurance. In contrast, with an absolute test, if the fixed (specific) absolute level were set too high, then the endurance test will be very short for a weaker test taker, but longer for a stronger test taker. If the measurement is too short for a particular test taker, then it will not be a satisfactory test of endurance, because the time will be so short as to not be a practical reflection of the person's endurance. On the other hand, if a measurement takes too long to administer, testing a very large group may be impractical. It may be necessary to adjust the test to ensure that it will be practical to administer.

As you can see, the definition step of test development is extremely important.

Concluding Thoughts

Developing a new test is a big task, but the steps are similar for every measurement tool we develop. The first step is to define what we are trying to measure. This is important because the definition will guide the development of the test. We then conduct research with the hope of finding a ready-made measurement that will save us the trouble of developing a new one. If no practical and valid technique matches our application, perhaps one can be modified to fit our needs. Whether modifying an existing measurement or developing a new one, we must follow certain steps, including pilot testing, modifying, and, ultimately, evaluating the test's validity, reliability, objectivity, and practicality. We repeat the steps of evaluation and modification until the new test is satisfactory, or until we run out of time or money.

Ultimately, what we want is a test that is useful in our situation, and that we are confident is valid. Our highest priority is to develop a valid test, and secondarily we want to develop the simplest, fastest, and easiest test possible.

Skill in developing and evaluating measurements is likely to be useful in many teaching, coaching, and therapeutic situations. By practicing this skill, you will become a more capable and versatile professional.

Application Questions

1   Explain, in detail, how you would establish the validity, reliability, and objectivity of the hand grip strength test discussed in the chapter.
2   Find a published test or test battery and evaluate its validity, reliability, and objectivity.
3   Give an example of how you would establish the validity, reliability, and objectivity of a test item consisting of a 40-yd. sprint. Be detailed.
4   List some real-world situations that require job applicants to pass a test.
5   Explain why it is important that employment and other qualification tests be valid, reliable, and objective.
6   What is the most important quality to establish the legitimacy of an employment qualification test?

13 Numbers and Statistics in Measurement

Abstract

In exercise and physical education, athletic training and other specialties we encounter different *kinds* of numbers with different qualities. These types of numbers require different analyses. We also encounter distributions of data with differing characteristics. The most common, and useful distribution is the standard or normal distribution. Standard distributions are useful in establish the "value" of a unit and in making predictions. Recognizing other, non-normal, distributions is valuable.

Keywords: nominal, ordinal, interval (scalar), ratio numbers, normal (standard) distributions, dispersion, range, standard error of the estimate

Understanding Numbers in Measurement

Numbers are an important part of modern life for any profession. Therapists need to know strength ratios between muscle groups, average performance values for older non-athletes, progress rates, and expected outcomes. Athletic trainers need to know about environmental temperatures, injury rates, hemoglobin levels, body temperatures, and numerical settings on therapeutic modalities. Coaches need to know weight lifted; 40-yard, 100-meter, or mile run times; and lots more. Physical Education teachers need to know scores, duration of moderate to vigorous physical activity, grades, and improvement.

This chapter covers the fundamentals of numbers, and probability distributions.

Introduction to Numbers

Types of Numbers

All numbers are *not* created equal. You already know this: you have a student identification number, a social security number, a telephone number, and a credit card number. These numbers are quite different from those such as your weekly salary, or your savings, or your bills. This first type of number is for identification—really just a substitute for your name. The Latin word for "name" is "nomen," so we call these **nominal numbers**. It doesn't make any sense to add, subtract, multiply, or divide these numbers.

If you look at the rankings for sports teams, you can see a different type of number, that doesn't name anything. These numbers simply show the order of teams in the rankings; hence, they are called *ordinal numbers*. Again, it doesn't make sense to add, subtract, multiply, or divide ordinal numbers, except in a few odd situations. For example, cross-country running scores are added to obtain the team score. However, because of the nature of ordinal numbers, the team's finish order doesn't tell us anything about the *size* of the difference between teams. That is, the first-place team may have beaten the second-place team badly, but you cannot tell from the ordinal scores.

The third type of number is *interval* (also called *scalar*) numbers—these are numbers that are separated by equal intervals (i.e., they form a scale). The Fahrenheit degree scale is scalar, because each degree represents the same amount of heat. In Fahrenheit, 0 °F is not true "zero" since there is still some heat at this scale reading. As you know from temperatures, interval levels of measurement can record scores below zero (e.g., –30 °F). With scalar numbers, ratios are not literally true, in that 50 °F isn't really "half" as hot as 100 °F. Be careful though, as many scales, such as the rating of perceived exertion, noise scales, and so forth, use ordinal numbers because the intervals between scores may vary.

Ratio numbers are numbers that can be divided into each other to form meaningful ratios. This is the type of number that carries the most information. Ratio numbers are superior to all the other types in that all mathematical manipulations make sense with ratio numbers. Fifty dollars is exactly half as much money as one hundred dollars. With ratio numbers, having *zero* dollars really does mean you are broke—you truly have an absence of money. That is, ratio numbers have a true zero. In measurement, the differences between ratio and interval numbers don't usually matter much. However, ratio and interval (scalar) numbers are indeed superior to ordinal and nominal numbers, because they carry more information. Ordinal and nominal numbers must never be treated as if they were ratio numbers.

13.1   Practical Exercise

Identify the proper classification (nominal, ordinal, interval, or ratio) for each of the following number types:

a   Apartment number _____

b   Scholastic Aptitude Test score _____

c   Finish place in a regional volleyball tournament _____

d   Body fatness percent _____

e   Temperature in the gym _____

f   Mean height of the volleyball team _____

g   Rating of physical exertion on a scale from 0 to 10 _____

h   Comfort rating of swimming pool temperature on a scale from 1 to 4 _____

i   Golf scores for a round of golf _____

j   Golf scores expressed in relation to par _____

Significant Digits and Precision

You may remember from a chemistry class that there is much ado in chemistry regarding **significant digits**, the number of digits in a measurement or calculation that have meaning. Significant digits are important, because we trust the values they represent, with only the last one being estimated. For example, if you weigh yourself on a beam-balance scale (a scale, most often seen in a physician's office, on which you slide the weights across the "beams"; see Figure 13.1), you might read 75.2 kg. You can be sure about the 75 kg, and pretty certain about the 0.2 kg because you can read it clearly on the beam, but if you need accuracy to a fourth digit, say 75.25, you would have to estimate the last digit. We would say this weight is accurate to four significant digits. We say four significant digits because we are sure of the 7, the first 5, and the 2, but would have to estimate the second 5. If you happen to weigh 70 kg, the 0 here would certainly be significant, because you know you aren't 69 kg or 71 kg. Therefore, included zeros before the first uncertain digit are significant, if they are to the left of the decimal.

All zeros to the right of the decimal in numbers smaller than 1.0 are *not* considered significant, e.g., 0.00097 kg has only two significant digits (the 9, which we are sure of, and the 7, which we estimated on the measurement device). Zeros which fall to the left of the decimal in a number with no digits to the right of the decimal are typically not considered significant, *unless* the decimal point is placed at the end of the number to indicate otherwise (e.g., "5000." has four significant digits, whereas "5000" has only one). However, common sense must be used. If you are taking a measurement and you know you are precise to four places, but the answer happens to end in three zeros and only the last one is an estimate, then you would say it has five significant

Figure 13.1 Marks on the beam-balance scale illustrate significant digits

digits despite the "rule." If you see a number written 5000.0, you should assume it is accurate to five significant digits, since the last 0 indicates that this was the first estimated digit.

In most athletic training, health, PE, and fitness applications, the biggest danger is implying more precision, i.e., more significant digits, than we actually have (e.g., in the previous example, if we had written 75.254 kg). Problems arise with "over-expression" of significant digits because computers will make calculations with as many digits as you specify, regardless of how many of them may be significant.

Body composition measurements are an example of over-precision. If we obtain a body composition by mathematically combining several different measurements, the answer can be no more precise than the least precise measurement involved. For example, if we compute a body density from skinfold measurements, we measure skinfolds on most skinfold calipers to only three places. We might measure a skinfold at 19.3 mm. Therefore, we should express the resulting body density or body fatness to no more than three places also. Likewise, since body fatness is calculated from body density, then body fatness from skinfolds should never be expressed to more than three places, e.g., 15.2 percent fat. Body density equations that use age in the calculation should be expressed only to two digits, if age is measured only to two digits.

If you have much experience with skinfolds, you probably realize that even giving all the significant digits suggests more confidence than common sense allows. As you may know, skinfolds are accurate only to about four percentage points (i.e., a person estimated at 20 percent fat really lies somewhere between 16 percent and 24 percent). You would probably only give two significant digits, anyway. Again, common sense should prevail.

Normal Vs. Non-Normal (Non-Standard) Distributions

The normal distribution (also called the standard distribution or bell curve) is very common in measurement. Figure 13.2 illustrates the normal curve. Remember that the normal distribution is a set of data wherein the mode and mean are identical to the median, right in the middle of the distribution. For large distributions, the curve of a normal distribution appears bell shaped. Body weight, sprint speed, strength, range of motion, intelligence, and many other common measurements are normally distributed in the general population. However, keep in mind that the distribution and its shape depend on the population and the sample.

A measurement may be expected to be normal if the population is large, if the population is not biased regarding the measurement, and if the sample is fairly selected from the population. Because all of us at times deal with some unusual populations and samples, let's look at some examples of such populations.

If we sampled only basketball players, the mean height of the sample would be much taller than the mean height of the average college student. If the heights are normally distributed, in both cases the mean will fall right in the center. If the Y-axis (vertical axis) represents the frequency (number of persons of a particular height), then the highest point on either curve is the most common (most frequently occurring) height in the sample. As you will recall, the most common score in any distribution is called the mode. If the scores are equally distributed between the left and right halves, then the median or middle score is the same as the mean, falling right in the middle with the median and mode.

If the curve is very narrow because the values are centrally distributed (grouped around the middle), it is not a normal curve. As you can see in Figure 13.3A, the left and right halves of the curve are closer together than in a normal distribution. This is a **leptokurtic distribution** (from "lepto," meaning thin or slender). If the curve is very flat (Figure 13.3B), it is also not a normal curve; the left and right extremes are very far apart because the values are *not* centrally distributed (not grouped around the middle). This is a **platykurtic distribution** (from "platy," meaning flat, as in platypus, or flat-nosed). The data that comprise the leptokurtic curve in Figure 13.3A are more

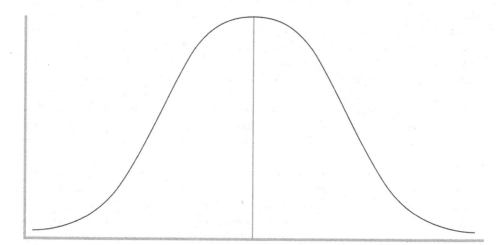

Figure 13.2 Normal curve

homogenous than for a normal curve, meaning all of the data comprising this curve are fairly similar. If, for example, we measure the heights of a representative sample of NCAA Division II basketball players, we might see a distribution similar to the one in Figure 13.3A. If we look at a representative sample of all college students, we should see the curve in Figure 13.2.

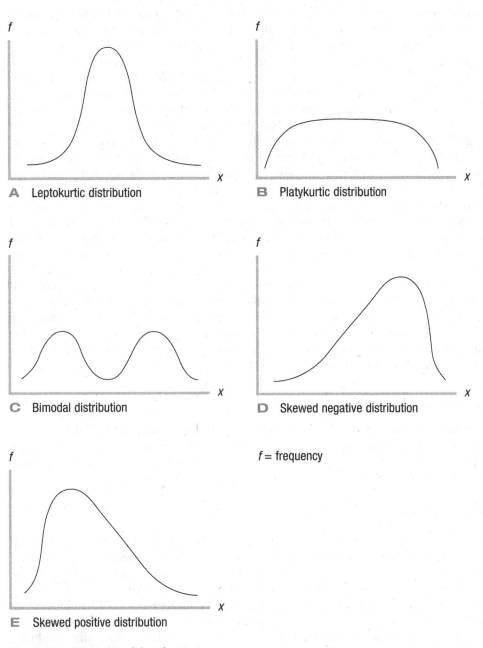

A   Leptokurtic distribution

B   Platykurtic distribution

C   Bimodal distribution

D   Skewed negative distribution

f = frequency

E   Skewed positive distribution

Figure 13.3 Examples of distribution curves

Sometimes a curve will have two peaks. We call this a **bimodal** (two modes) **distribution**. Figure 13.3C is an example. Such distributions may also be called **multimodal** (many modes). For example, a group of athletes that included gymnasts and basketball players might yield one peak at a short height and another at a tall height.

If the peak is not in the middle, the result is a **skewed curve**. This could happen if we tried to sample the heights of people in general, but we collected the sample near the basketball gym shortly after practice. If we sampled basketball players, we would expect a few short people (some point guards, for example), but we would expect the average height (as well as the mode and median height) to be taller than in other samples. The modal height (most common height) would be farther to the right (taller) rather than in the middle, a pattern we call *negatively skewed* (see Figure 13.3D). On the other hand, if we sampled outside the gymnastics practice gym, we would expect the modal height (as well as the average and median height) to be less than for the normal population. The modal height (as well as the average and median height) would be to the left of the middle (shorter) than in the normal sample, and we would describe the resulting curve as *positively skewed* (see Figure 13.3E). A negatively skewed distribution is good when high scores imply better performance (e.g., football, basketball), whereas a positively skewed distribution is good when lower scores imply better performance (e.g., times for track events, golf scores). It is important that you understand the implications of a positively or negatively skewed distribution. Keep in mind that for skewed curves, the usual predictions for standard deviations do not apply. For example, with a non-normal distribution, the first SD above and below the mean will not necessarily encompass 68 percent of the data.

It is not so important that you remember the names of non-normal (nonstandard) curves, but it *is* important that you be able to differentiate between normal and non-normal curves. Recall that in a normal distribution, the mean, median, and mode are identical. You can get a good idea of how close to normal a curve is if you evaluate the measures of central tendency to find out how close the mean, median, and mode scores are to each other, but also note the shape of the curve.

Measures of Dispersion

In addition to the measures of central tendency (mean, median, and mode), in order to describe a distribution of data, we need to know the dispersion. One useful measure of dispersion was the standard deviation, which you will recall from Chapter 5, now let's look at another, the range.

Range

If you look at the point that is farthest to the right in a curve (the highest score recorded) and the point that is farthest to the left (the lowest score recorded), you will get a sense of the **range** of the scores, or how widely they are dispersed (spread out). If you subtract the minimum score from the maximum score and add 1 (i.e., range = (high − low) + 1), you will have the **mathematical range**. The range tells us something about how far apart the extreme scores are and how much **variability** (difference) was in the sample. The range does not depend on whether the distribution is normally distributed or not. On the other hand, any change in the high or low score affects the range. For example, suppose a group of 120 students took an exam on the fundamental concepts of health-related fitness. If the high score was 99 and the low score was 55, then the range on this exam is $99 - 55 = 44 + 1 = 45$. However, if just one student had to do a makeup exam and scored 45, then the range for the whole group becomes $99 - 45 = 54 + 1 = 55$. The range changed by ten, even though only one score was added.

You might wonder why we add one to the difference between the high and the low scores. This is because both the high and low scores are "counted" in the range. Think of it this way: If we calculate the range of the numbers 0 to 10, we get $10 - 0 = 10 + 1 = 11$, because there are 11 numbers encompassed by the whole group of scores. If we calculate the range for 1 to 10, it is $10 - 1 = 9 + 1 = 10$. People sometimes try to simplify by leaving out the addition of one, but to be accurate, it should be included.

Here's another example of computing a range. If the lowest score on a basketball shooting test is 7 and the highest is 50, the range is $50 - 7 = 43 + 1 = 44$. This number can help the coach understand the players' range of skill.

Here's another example. Table 13.1 gives the heights for a nationally ranked university women's gymnastics team. The average height of the general population of

Table 13.1 Sample height data of a university women's gymnastics team and women's basketball team, with computed mean and SD

C19		f_x	=STDEV(C4:C17)
	A	B	C
1			
2		**HEIGHT IN INCHES**	
3		Women's gymnastics	Women's basketball
4		67	76
5		65	76
6		65	75
7		64	74
8		63	73
9		62	72
10		62	71
11		62	70
12		61	70
13		61	70
14		61	69
15		61	68
16		61	
17		60	
18	AVG	62.5	72.0
19	STDEV	2.03	2.76

women is 63.8 ± 2.8 inches (Fryar et al., 2011–2014). As you can see in Table 13.1, these gymnasts are shorter. The shortest gymnast was 60 inches, and the tallest was 67 inches. That makes the range (67 – 60) + 1 = 8 inches. Note also that the mean height is 62.5 inches, with a standard deviation of 2.0 inches. The modal height of this team is 61 inches. Using Table 13.1, contrast the gymnasts' data with the data for the women's basketball team from the same university.

As you can see, the basketball players are taller than the general population of women. The shortest basketball player was 68 inches, and the tallest was 76 inches. That makes the range (76 – 68) + 1 = 9 inches. Also note that the mean height is 72.0 inches, with a standard deviation of 2.8 inches. The modal height of this team is 70 inches. Compared to the women gymnasts, note that the mean height of the basketball team is 9.5 inches taller and the SD is 0.73 inches larger, whereas the range is 1 inch larger for the basketball players. The modal height is 9 inches taller for the basketball players. Now compare the mean heights of these two groups of athletes with women from the general population (63.8 ± 2.8 inches).

Uses for the Standard Deviation

The range gives some idea about the variability of the data. It is not, however, as helpful as the standard deviation.

Using the SD to Establish the Value of a Unit

The SD turns out to be a very important number because the variability of a distribution determines how "valuable" each unit is—that is, how significant it is for two scores to be one measurement unit apart. If the SD is very small, then the scores are tightly grouped around the mean, and a small improvement in a score is important.

Here's an example. If you beat me in a footrace by 3 seconds, is that a photo finish, or did you soundly thrash me? In other words, is that 3-second difference a little or a lot? If you beat me by 1 SD (which might be the SD for 100m), then you beat me pretty badly. On the other hand, if you beat me by 0.001 of a SD (which 3 seconds might be .0001SD for a marathon), then we were very close.

Why is it important to know the value of a unit? In measurement situations in physical education, in fitness, in athletic training, and in physical therapy, you may well encounter measurements you have never seen before. You may even find yourself creating new measurements. For example, in the 1990s, NASA used a specially designed exercise rowing machine for astronauts on the space shuttle. A group of other researchers and I had to create a new measurement for the rower. The machine had a digital output, which counted what we called "Whitmore" units, after the machine's inventor. How many Whitmores are in a workout? If we know the mean and SD in Whitmore units of a fatiguing workout for well-conditioned men and women similar to the astronaut corps, we can easily measure how one astronaut's performance compares to his or her peers'. As you see, once we have a standard deviation and a mean for an appropriate sample, we can give an accurate value to a brand-new unit, the "Whitmore." We can express almost any practical measurement in terms of SDs.

Using the SD for Prediction

Another reason the SD is useful is that, for normally distributed data, it allows us to make predictions about the population from which the sample was drawn. As Figure 13.4 shows, one SD to either side of the mean score encompasses about 34 percent on each side, or a total of about 68 percent of the sample. If we include another standard deviation to either side, we cover a total of about 95 percent of the total sample. The third standard deviation encompasses about 2 percent on each end. These percentages are true only for normal (standard) distributions of scores. The significance of SDs for prediction is that *if* the sample accurately represents the population, then the conclusions we make about the sample, based on the SD and percentages, will also be true of the overall population.

To make the use of SDs for prediction clearer, consider the following examples from exercise and sport. I worked with a team at NASA's Johnson Space Center to design an exercise device that permitted someone to do a full weightlifting workout while remaining in a lying-down posture. NASA wanted this device for research on exercise during the microgravity of space flight. So that the device would fit the test subjects, we needed their mean arm length, but we also needed the SD to determine how much adjustability had to be built into the equipment. Most designers try to accommodate 95 percent of the population, which meant the device should be adjustable to the mean arm length plus or minus about two SDs.

For another example, suppose you want to buy high school football uniforms, to be used by the teams for the next four or five years. If you knew the mean and SD sizes of the football teams over the last several years, you could order the percentage

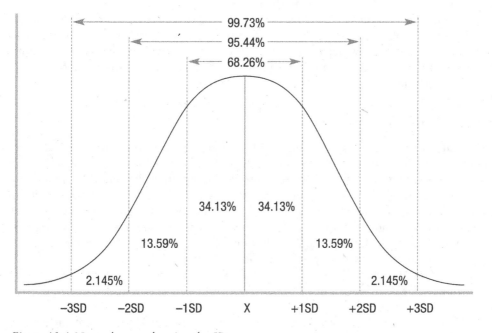

Figure 13.4 Normal curve showing the SDs

of uniforms, helmets, and shoes that would fit future teams. Without this information, you would have to guess.

For a company that manufactures fitness equipment, it would be essential to know how many of each size of equipment to make. If the company produces inventory to fit the average user plus or minus one SD, it would take care of 68 percent of the target population. By producing additional inventory to fit those between one and two SDs above and below the mean, it would cover an additional 27 percent of the population. Equipment made to fit those between two and three SDs above and below the mean would accommodate only another 5 percent of the target population. Covering that 5 percent may cost a lot of money, so the company may have to charge more for that equipment. Pity the people who are more than three SDs taller or shorter, bigger or smaller than the mean, because they will have difficulty finding clothes and equipment to fit them.

Here's a more specific example. Suppose you work for this fitness equipment manufacturer, and you need to make helmets for women's softball. You find data showing that the average female softball player wears a size 7 helmet and that the SD is only 0.5. In this case, you would want to make about 68 percent of each production run between size 6.5 and 7.5. About 13 percent should be sizes 7.5 and 8, and about 13 percent should be sizes 6 and 6.5. Only about 2.5 percent of each production run would be larger than size 8, and about 2.5 percent would be smaller than size 6. It would not be a good idea to make any helmets larger than size 8.5 or smaller than size 5.5, because not many people would want those unusual sizes.

You probably know people who are extremely big or extremely small. Small people often have to shop for shoes and clothes at children's stores, and large people may have a hard time finding clothing at all. This is because manufacturers don't want to make shoes and clothes for such a small fraction of the population. Very few people are more than three SDs bigger than the mean.

It's important to make sure you use recent data, because populations do change over time. In fact, Ford Motor Company, in about 2002, announced it was going to make its auto seats wider to fit the US population, in which obesity has become more common. Populations do change, and old statistics may not apply to fatter and fatter Americans!

Standard Error of the Estimate

The **standard error of the estimate** (SEE) of a prediction is the estimated standard deviation of the error in that prediction. Now that you know how to calculate the standard deviation, you should have no problem computing the standard error. You must have a sample of valid measurements of the variable you are trying to predict. In a spreadsheet, make two columns, one with the valid measurements and one with the predictions based on your equation. Simply compute the differences between the pairs of numbers, and calculate the standard deviation of the differences. This is the standard error of the estimate based on your predictions.

If the data are normally distributed, you can also calculate the 95 percent confidence limits for your predictions.

Upper 95 percent limit = true mean of the sample + (standard error of estimate * 1.96)

Lower 95 percent limit = true mean of the sample − (standard error of estimate * 1.96)

13.2   Practical Exercise

The mean for a particular measurement is 95 cm, and the standard error of the estimate for that measurement has been found to be 10 cm.

a   What is the upper 95 percent limit?
b   What is the lower 95 percent limit?

See if you can use the same information given to calculate the following:

c   The approximate upper 99 percent limit
d   The approximate lower 99 percent limit

Application Questions

1   Why is it important to recognize the difference between nominal, ordinal, scalar, and ratio numbers?
2   Competitions in cross-country running use finish places (ordinal numbers) for final scoring. What might be one advantage to using run times (ratio numbers) instead?
3   Give some examples of scalar numbers that have no "true zero" (that is, where the score of 0 is arbitrary and does not represent the total absence of the quality).
4   From a sport performance standpoint, how precisely would you want to measure a 40-yd sprint? To the nearest second? The nearest tenth of a second? If you were a competitor and you were told that your performance time was accurate to within 0.4 of a second, would you be satisfied?
5   How would you recognize normally distributed data? What characteristics would you expect?
6   Give some examples of how knowing the mean and SD of a sample would allow you to make predictions.
7   How might SDs be used to evaluate monthly attendance at a fitness club?
8   How might SDs be used to establish the adjustability required for rehabilitation equipment?
9   If a measure is normally distributed, approximately what percentage of the sample would fall within one SD of the mean? What percentage would fall within two SDs of the mean? What percentage lies more than two SDs from the mean?

Reference

Fryar, C. D., Gu, Q., Ogden, C. L., and Flegal, K. M. *Anthropometric reference data for children and adults: United States, 2011–2014*. National Center for Health. Statistics, Table 10, available at: www.cdc.gov/nchs/data/series/sr_03/sr03_039.pdf.

14 Standard Scores

Abstract

Standard scores are dimensionless numbers based on the mean and standard deviation. In exercise sciences and physical education, standard scores can be very useful.
Percentile ranks and percentiles are simple and useful, but z-scores are extremely useful
because they allow scores with different units to be accurately combined or compared.

Keywords: percentile rank, percentile, standard error of the estimate, z-score

Sometimes scores are expressed relative to a percentage or other reference. For example, the standard deviation to describe scores is so common and useful that it has

been developed into a system. When a "raw" score has been transformed by use of a reference—a process called *standardization*—the result is called a **standard score**.

Standard scores are useful for combining or comparing scores that are measured in different units. For example, in the heptathlon (a seven-event women's track and field event), some events are measured in meters and others in seconds. We can't add meters to seconds. Sometimes even the same units have different real values. For example, we can't add seconds from a 100-meter dash to seconds from an 800-meter run and get a meaningful sum just because they both happen to be measured in seconds. Perhaps more importantly, we can't add pounds from bench press, squat, and deadlift and get a sum that tells us very much. However, we have to be able to combine the event scores somehow to arrive at an overall score. We can do it by converting "raw" scores to standard scores.

Percent-Based Standard Scores

Percentile Rank

Percentile rank, one of the most common standard scores, tells where a specific score falls within a population that has been tested or measured. The score's **percentile rank** equals the percent of scores that are *lower* or *equal to* the specified score. For example, if you took a college admissions test, you probably were given the results in terms of both a numerical score and a percentile rank. If you scored a percentile rank of 86, then 86 percent of the other people who took the test scored either the same or worse than you scored.

Suppose you scored right on the population mean on some normally distributed measure. Then your percentile rank would be 50 percent, because you scored the same or better than 50 percent of the population. If you scored one SD above the population mean, your percentile would be 84.6, which is 50 plus 1 SD (34.6). You scored the same or better than 84.6 percent of the population.

Percentile rank is a good way to make sense of scores that otherwise would be meaningless. For example, if someone told you that he scored 156 on some new test of fitness, you would have no idea if that was a good or bad score. However, if you learned that 156 was the 99th percentile rank, you would know that this person scored as well or better than 99 percent of the measured population.

Percentile

Similar to percentile rank is a measurement called, simply, "percentile." The **percentile** is a particular *score*, on an ordered list of scores, at or below which a given percent of the other scores fall. (Thus, a *percentile* is a score, but *percentile rank* is the percentage of people or groups or entities with the same or worse scores.) For example, a total score of 520 on the math portion on the Scholastic Aptitude Test (SAT) (an entrance examination for college admission) is the 49th percentile score, meaning that 49 percent of test takers will be expected to score at or below 520. If a person scores 520, then her percentile rank will be 49. Hence, if a person tells you that she scored at the 49th percentile on some test, she is saying that *her math score* was better than or equal to 49 percent of the test-takers (or at least, those from whom the percentiles were derived).

To remember the difference between percentile and percentile rank, think of a "rank" of people—a group of people lined up in order of height. You could count the number of people who are shorter than you and express this number as a percentage (of the number of people) to determine your percentile rank. Once you know your percentile rank, *your height* becomes the percentile at that percentage. Remember: A *percentile* must always be a *score*, but the *percentile rank* will always be a *percentage*.

Z-Scores

Another standard score, the **z-score**, allows us to compare any score to the mean score by expressing it as a fraction of the SD. Z-scores are very useful. Z-scores almost always fall between −3 and +3 (see Figure 14.1). In Figure 14.1, you can see that moving −3 SD away from the mean puts you in the 0.13 percentile rank [50 percent − (34.13 + 13.59 + 2.145 percent) = 0.13 percent], meaning only 13 scores out of 10,000 will be this low. Higher than 3 SDs is above the 99.87 percentile rank, so that only 13 scores in 10,000 will be found there.

Two methods may be used to calculate a z-score. The method to use depends on whether a higher score indicates a better performance (e.g., batting average, free throws, long jump) or a lower score indicates a better performance (e.g., golf scores, swimming times, cholesterol levels, heart rate).

When a High Score Is Better

When a high score is better, to find the z-score we subtract the mean from the score and divide the result by the SD. The equation looks like this:

$$Z_{high\ score\ better} = (score - mean)/SD$$

When you try this equation with real scores, you will notice that the units (meters, seconds, free throws, or whatever the case may be) cancel, leaving the z-score with no units. Once we have calculated the z-scores of two competitors, whoever has the best z-score wins. The difference between the z-scores tells how badly the winner beat the loser.

Here's an example. Suppose the mean score in a cricket league is 200 runs and the SD is 25 runs, and a team scores 225.

$$Z_{high\ score\ better} = (score - mean)/SD$$
$$= (225 - 200)/25$$
$$= 25/25 = 1$$

The z-score is 1. Hence, the score is 34 percent or 1 SD above the mean. Since 50 percent of the scores lie on each side of the mean, the score is higher than the 50 percent of scores that are below the mean plus the 34 percent of scores that are above the mean but below this score. Hence, the score is at the 84th percentile. Only 16 percent of scores would be expected to be higher than this score of 225 runs. Notice that we can discover all of this without knowing anything about cricket!

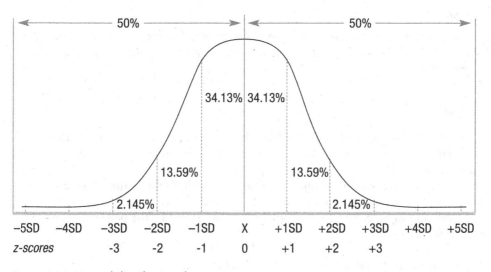

Figure 14.1 Normal distribution showing z-scores

When a Low Score Is Better

When a low score is better, as in golf, swimming, and track and field, you simply subtract the score from the mean rather than the mean from the score:

$$Z_{\text{low score better}} = (\text{mean} - \text{score}) / \text{SD}$$

Let's consider an example using a hypothetical running time of 170 seconds for a male contestant in a 1000-m footrace where the mean for his age group is 150 seconds and the SD is 20 seconds.

$$Z_{\text{low score better}} = (\text{mean} - \text{score}) / \text{SD}$$
$$= (150 - 170) / 20$$
$$= -20 / 20 = -1$$

Note that the z-score simply tells us how many SDs the score falls above or below the mean. Also note that the runner scored below the mean and has a negative z-score because he was slower than the mean time.

Quick Review

STANDARD SCORING. Standard scores are very useful in multiple-event sports such as the heptathlon or decathlon. They allow us to validly combine scores with different units. To determine a winner in the decathlon, we could combine ten different scores, all with different units. The percentile rank is a percentage that tells where a specific

(continued)

(continued)

score falls among the group. A percentile is an actual score—the score that corresponds to a particular percentile rank. A z-score expresses a raw score as a fraction of the SD.

Z-Tables

When we need to know the percentile ranks for certain z-scores for normally distributed data, we use a z-table like the one shown at http://users.stat.ufl.edu/~athienit/Tables/Ztable.pdf.

The **z-table** gives us the percentage of the sample that falls to the *left* of the z-score. From this percentage we can calculate the percentile rank.

Here's an example. For a z-score of 1.23, what would be the percentile rank? Here are the steps to find it:

1   Referring to the table, go down the left side to 1.2.
2   Go over to the 0.03 column.
3   There you find a z of .8907 (89.07 percent). This number is the percentage of z-scores that are smaller than 1.23. Hence, the percentile rank for a z-score of 1.23 is 89.

Here's another example, with a score on the left side of the normal distribution. If the z-score is −1.23, we know that .1093, about 11 percent of the scores are *below* −1.23. Hence, the percentile rank is 11; the z-score of −1.23 is better than almost 11 percent of the sample.

Here's another example. If the z-score is 2, we know the percentile rank should be in the neighborhood of 50 + 34 + 13 = 97. The table shows exactly = 97.72 percentile rank. A positive z-score of 2.55 = 99.29 percentile rank. Thus, we can calculate the exact percentile rank for any z-score down to the hundredth, if we want to do so.

14.1   Practical Exercise

Z-scores can help us understand data better.

Earlier you learned how to interpret figures. Even when we have lots of experience interpreting figures, we can still be fooled. When one of my students presented Figure 14.3, I was badly fooled at first.

The figure shows the Olympic records for two events, beginning with the first modern Olympics in 1896.

- What can you tell from this figure?
- What is the slope for each line? What does the slope tell us?
- Why is the slope for pole vault over four times higher than for high jump?
- What would you predict to happen in the future?

Now, study Figure 14.2 carefully. Can you see why the figure is misleading?

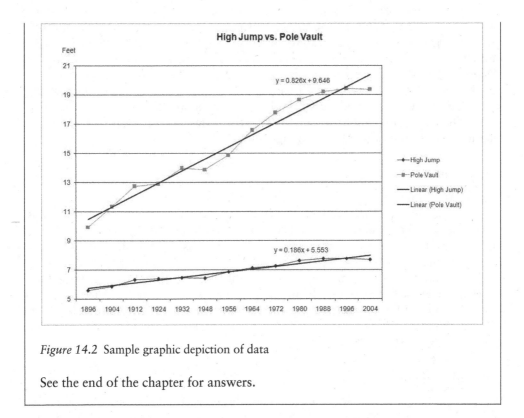

Figure 14.2 Sample graphic depiction of data

See the end of the chapter for answers.

Checking a Measurement Technique

There are several ways to check to be sure that you are using good measurement technique. First, before you begin any calculation, you should think about the problem to get a rough idea of what the answer ought to be. If the result of your calculation is very different from what you expected, consider your estimate and your calculations carefully to find the source of the discrepancy.

When calculating z-scores, rather than trying to remember when to use which formula, you can work out a simple example in your head to see if the end result makes sense. For example, suppose you want to convert raw golf scores to z-scores. If you can't remember the formula, you can work one out logically. If someone shot better (a lower score) than the average score, then the z-score must be positive. Suppose someone shot 71, and suppose the mean is 75 and the SD is 4. Try the formula $Z = (\text{score} - \text{mean})/\text{SD}$. With this formula you would calculate a z-score of -1. Since this person shot *better* than the mean, you know the z-score should be a positive number. So you would reverse the formula to $Z = (\text{mean} - \text{score})/\text{SD}$ and calculate a z-score of 1. This looks correct, so that is the formula you would use for the rest of the scores.

One simple check is to remember that z-scores almost always fall between -3 and $+3$. If a calculation shows something outside of these numbers, you have probably miscalculated.

Another aspect of good measurement is to remember that sometimes the same units have different values, as discussed earlier in the chapter. This is important, because forgetting about it can lead to bad measurement technique. On the Internet, find some powerlifting scores for bench press, squat, and deadlift. Calculate the SDs for a group of those scores in one weight-class, and see how the SDs differ. By making these comparisons, you will see that bench press pounds aren't the same as squat pounds. Although they appear to be the same units, they are not of the same value. The case study will also demonstrate the difference between bad and good measurement techniques in determining value.

One Caveat on Z-Scores

The one disadvantage to z-scores is that you get about half the scores as negatives, and many people aren't accustomed to negative scores. Consequently, the T-score was developed to eliminate negatives. Simply take the z score, multiply by 10 then add 50 to that (so lowest common z of $-3*10=-30$, $T=-30+50=20$ as lowest common T-score). In truth you can manipulate any z-score this way. Since the mean and median z-score=0, you can set the mean to any number by adding that number to the z. The spread of the scores can likewise be determined by multiplying z by whatever spread you want.

For example, if I want my test score mean to be 75 and the high grade to be about 100, I multiply the z by 8, and add 75. So a z-score of 0 on the test= $(0+75=75)$, and a z-score of 3 = $(3*8)+75=99$!

Concluding Thoughts

In earlier chapters we have discussed numbers, distributions of data, standard scoring, and ways to check a measurement technique. The mean, median, and mode are measures of central tendency, which in the normal curve are all equal to one another. The measures of variability, which determine the shape of the curve, are the range and the standard deviation. The standard deviation is particularly useful because it establishes value, it makes predictions possible for normally distributed data, and it indicates how closely clustered around the mean the entire set of scores is. The standard deviation allows us to make a quick estimate of a score's percentile rank, or where the score stands within the group of data. The standard deviation is a key component of z-scores, which can be very useful in transforming or standardizing data whose units have different values. In this chapter we also examined charts and practiced interpreting the data expressed in them.

14.2   Practical Exercise

1   Explain how you could transform a set of grades on a quiz so that the class average would be 75 and the SD would be 10. What equation would you use in a spreadsheet to perform this transformation?
2   What are the key disadvantages of z-scores to someone not used to seeing them?

3   Demonstrate how to convert a z-score to a more acceptable score.
4   Draw a picture of a normal (standard) curve. Label it fully, in great detail. Explain how to use this curve in real-life measurement and evaluation situations.
5   You have 100 students in your physical education (or allied health, or fitness) classes. You give a knowledge test and find that the group has a mean score of 72 with a standard deviation of 5. About how many students would you expect to have scored between 67 and 77? Why?

Answer to Practical Exercise 14.1

- *What can you tell from Figure 14.3?* The high jump performances seem very close to a straight line, and the slope has been about constant since 1896 (the start of the modern Olympic Games). The pole vault data seem to oscillate around a straight line, with a much steeper slope, but the overall improvement seems pretty steady since 1896.
- *What is the slope for each line?* Slope = 0.83 for pole vault and 0.19 for high jump.
- *What does the slope tell us?* It tells us the change in performance with respect to time. That is, from each Olympic competition to the next, on average, the pole vault heights improved more than the high jump performances.
- *Why is the slope for pole vault over four times higher than for high jump?* This could be attributed to the great improvements in pole vault poles and the pole vault pit. True, the high jump pit also improved, but, except for small changes in shoes, there isn't much else to change in the high jump except for technique.
- *What would you predict to happen in the future?* We might predict that continued improvements in pole vault poles will cause a continued more rapid increase in performance.

A Second Look at the Figure

We have all been fooled by the differences in measurement. One inch of pole vault height is not worth nearly as much as one inch of high jump height. The steeper slope for pole vault simply reflects a larger standard deviation for this event. If the data are all converted to z-scores, a very different chart emerges. As you can see in Figure 14.3, the slopes become almost identical when the data are expressed as z-scores.

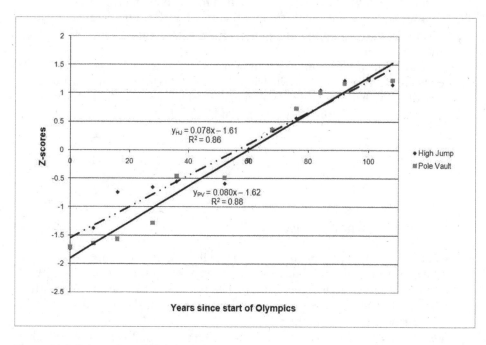

Figure 14.3 Pole vault and high jump in z-scores

Additional Practical Exercise

14.3   Practical Exercise

A multi-event contest between two contestants, A and B, had the following results. Who won and why? Show your work.

Category	A	B	Mean	SD
1 Train pulling (time to 50 m) (Lower is better for train pulling.)	50	45	40	10
2 Refrigerator carrying (# of stairs)	22.5	30	7.5	15
3 Bar bending (maximum diameter in mm)	30	2	15	15

15 Practical Inferential Statistics

Abstract

Inferential statistics are vital to evaluation of validity, reliability and objectivity and to research. Correlations are a means to measure the strength of relationship between two variables, but not cause and effect. A correlation of 0 means no relationship 1 is perfect. The sign (+/−) of the correlation tells whether both variables are increasing, or one is increasing whilst the other decreases. T-tests, both one-sample (dependent) and two-sample (independent) tell us the probability that two means are different by chance alone. Multiple regression is a powerful tool that combines multiple variables to make predictions. To compare more than two means, requires an ANOVA.

Keywords: inferential statistics, correlation, dependent and independent t-tests, probabilities, multiple regression, ANOVA

Inferential statistics is the name of a field of study devoted to using statistical probability tools to help us think about data. These are "inferential" because, data collected on a sample are used to make inferences about the population from which that sample was drawn. In Chapter 6 you already learned a bit about inferential statistics in the discussions of testing the means and correlations of data in evaluating validity. This chapter will introduce you to some additional key practical concepts in inferential statistics. Keep in mind that a population is simply a group of people sharing some characteristics, such as "all soccer players," "all NCAA Division I softball players," or "all college females."

As a health and fitness professional, teacher, trainer, or coach, you will need to understand correlations and tests of group mean differences so that you will be able to evaluate reports on the validity, reliability, and objectivity of different measurement techniques. In order to keep up with the field, you will also want to be able to understand the statistics used in research in your area of interest. Inferential statistics are the calculations used to interpret quantitative research data.

Tests of means between different experimental treatments or groups and correlations are statistics you will frequently encounter when you read research. Keep in mind that most Physical Therapy programs now teach research skills. This chapter will help you become an "informed consumer" of research by giving insight into these useful basic inferential statistics.

Correlations Measure Relationships Between Variables

A *correlation* is a measure of the degree of relationship between two variables (scores that vary). Evaluating validity, reliability and objectivity used calculations of Pearson Correlations for interval and ratio data, and Spearman's rho for ordinal data. Pearson Correlations are appropriate for use when the data for both variables are normally distributed and the variables are independent. You already learned how to perform test–retest reliability evaluations using intraclass correlations.

If the correlation is strong, then the two variables are closely related, and knowing one variable will allow us to predict the other variable. Bear in mind that a correlation establishes the *strength* and *direction* of relationship between two variables. That is, the correlation describes how closely two variables are related and whether they move in the same or opposite directions. A correlation does *not* explain why the two variables move as they do—only *that* they do.

For example, there is a moderate correlation between hand size and intellect in young children. This correlation does not mean that hand size is somehow directly linked to mental abilities. Instead, hand size correlates well with physical maturity and age in young children, and maturity and age correlate with intellectual ability, so hand size is related in this way to intellect. In adults, hand size and intellect—that is, hand size and maturity—are not related, so in adults the correlation is near zero between hand size and intellect. Keeping this example in mind may help you remember that the correlation measures only relationship and not cause and effect.

Suppose you are curious as to the relationship between physical activity and total blood cholesterol. If you can get a good measure of physical activity, perhaps using pedometers, accelerometers, or even a good physical activity questionnaire, half the job is done. Then if you obtain blood cholesterol data from your sample of subjects, you can put the data into a spreadsheet and graph physical activity versus cholesterol. Then you can use the spreadsheet to calculate the Pearson Correlation, which indicates both degree and direction of the relationship between activity and blood cholesterol for your sample.

The size of the correlation indicates the *degree* or strength of the relationship, 0 being no relationship and 1 being a perfect relationship. The sign (positive or negative) of the correlation coefficient indicates the *direction* of the relationship. Muscle size and strength have a positive relationship: as one variable increases, the other variable also increases; however, with physical activity level and cholesterol, you would expect that people who get lots of physical activity would have low blood cholesterol, and people with low activity would have high cholesterol. When an increase in one variable goes along with a decrease in the other variable, this is indirect or negative relationship.

15.1 Practical Exercise

What examples can you give, from the profession in which you are interested, where two variables would have a negative relationship?

Assessing the Correlation Between Two Variables

A correlation coefficient can range between 0 and +1 or −1. A correlation coefficient of 0 indicates no relationship, whereas a perfect correlation has a correlation coefficient of 1.0. That is, if two variables are exactly related to each other, $r = 1.0$. A perfect inverse or negative correlation has a correlation coefficient of −1.0.

Regression from Correlation

When we know the correlation coefficient between two variables, we can develop an equation for the relationship. This equation is called a *regression equation*. When the line that it represents is shown on a chart, this line is called "the line of best fit". The line of best fit is also the straight line that falls as close as possible to all of the data points. The process of finding this line is known as **regression**. When we add a trend-line (or curve) to a scatter plot, that trendline is the line of best fit for those data, and the equation describing that line was the regression equation. As we discussed earlier, straight lines always have an equation in the form of:

y value = the slope * the x value + the y intercept (the point on y where $x = 0$)

This is $y = mx + b$

The great value of regression equations and lines of best fit is that they can be used to make predictions.

15.2 Practical Exercise

Suppose we have the regression equation $y = -1.17x + 30$. Using this equation and the data given below, predict the number of pull-ups from the values for fatness. Here, the number of pull-ups is represented by y and the fatness score is represented by x. Figure 15.1 shows the plotted data and the line of best fit.

(continued)

(continued)

Fatness %	Predicted pull-ups
10	
12	
14	
16	
18	
20	
22	
24	
26	

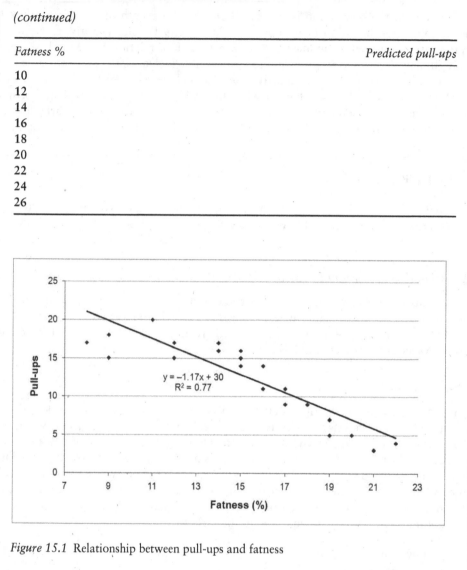

Figure 15.1 Relationship between pull-ups and fatness

Negative Correlations

Whether a correlation is "positive" or "negative" (also called "indirect") has nothing to do with the strength of the correlation. A negative correlation, as mentioned above, is simply one where one variable goes up whenever the other goes down. If fatness is negatively correlated with the ability to do pull-ups, then as fatness increases, the number of pull-ups decreases. Figure 15.2 represents the hypothetical relationship between how much television a person watches and that person's physical fitness score. Each data point represents one individual fitness score and the associated number of television viewing hours per week. You can see that as television viewing increases, fitness decreases, which gives the line of best fit a negative slope. This is a strong, negative correlation. (Keep in mind that these data are hypothetical.) The line fits the data

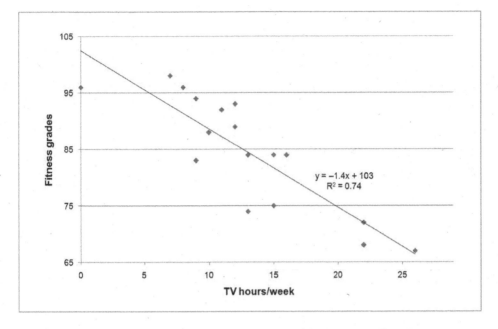

Figure 15.2 Hypothetical data for television viewing and fitness scores illustrating a strong negative correlation

points fairly well, reflecting the fact that the correlation is quite high, at −0.86. The squared correlation which is the coefficient of determination, is 0.74. A weaker negative correlation would have yielded data in a more round shape on the chart, but the slope of the line of best fit would still have been downward.

Remember, a negative correlation does *not* mean there is no relationship. Look at the number itself to see the degree of the relationship, and look at the sign to see whether the relationship is direct or inverse.

Weak Correlation

Figure 15.3 provides an example of a weak correlation. For contrast with a strong correlation, compare it to Figure 15.4. Note that in the weak correlation, the shape of the data is more round, and almost any line would "fit" about as well as any other. If we mathematically fit the best line as shown in Figure 15.3, we find that it slopes downward, indicating a negative correlation. The correlation coefficient is very low, and the coefficient of determination is almost zero.

Multiple Correlation

So far we have been discussing correlations between two variables. However, if we want to make complex predictions, such as a specific American football player's potential in the professional draft, it may be necessary to use the technique of multiple correlation (also called multiple regression).

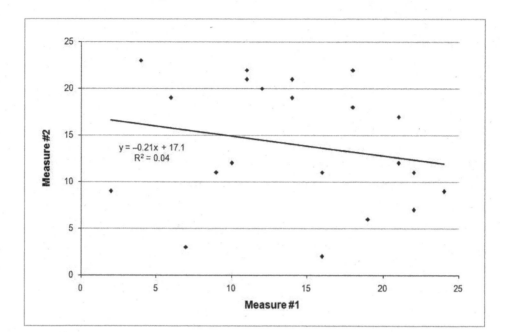

Figure 15.3 A weak correlation

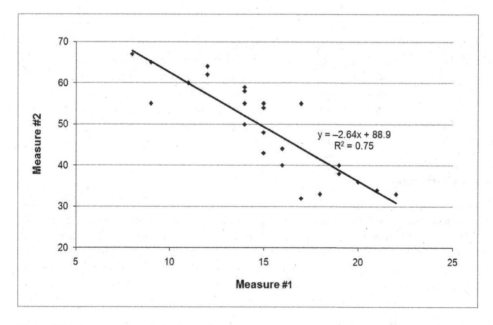

Figure 15.4 A strong correlation

Multiple correlation is the prediction of some variable of interest from several more readily measured variables. For example, with multiple correlation, we can use several independent measures to predict the success of a football player. This is a situation where we *must* consider more than one measure. If a player can run a 40-yard sprint in 4.2 seconds, you might think he's a shoo-in to do well in the NFL. But if I tell you he only weighs 110 pounds, you might change your opinion. To predict the potential of a football player, we must combine size, speed, strength, and other variables to predict playing success. We can then enter all of these data into one large equation. In addition to finding the overall prediction, we can see which variables are contributing the most to the prediction. This is called *modeling,* and it can yield some interesting and useful information. Think about how multiple correlation could be used to predict a player's success in sport.

Complex Comparisons of Group Means

Recall that to assess the validity, reliability, or objectivity of a measurement, we must do more than just look at the correlations. We also must compare the means of our samples, because two measurement methods may be highly correlated yet very different.

Here's an example. Suppose we are making a health and nutrition assessment, and we weigh a large number of people. We have two sets of weighing scales so that we can measure two people at a time in order to speed the process. Both of these scales have been calibrated using known valid weights. In transporting the scales to the measurement site, however, one set of scales is slightly damaged, so that it weighs everyone 10 pounds heavier than they are. If we do a correlation between the two sets of scales, we will see a perfect correlation. See Figure 15.5.

The correlation is 1.0—perfect correlation. However, the damaged scales always weigh 10 pounds too heavy. If we measure the reliability or objectivity of the scales, we will get good results (assuming the testers are well trained and follow directions carefully). The only way to detect the error would be to compare the mean weight from the sample. By looking at the group averages from the two sets of scales, we can detect the 10-pound error. If we fail to compare the group averages, we will never know that one of the scales is off by 10 pounds.

This example might have given the impression that you can simply look at the means and see if they are different. Sometimes this is true, but often the situation is more complicated. That's because most of the time you will be dealing with a sample rather than the entire population. Therefore, you will be making comparisons among samples in order to make inferences about the population. The sample that you happened to choose might have very different statistics than another sample you could have chosen. For this reason, with samples one is always limited to making probability statements about the *likelihood* of differences between population means. For example, we may compare two means and say that statistically, the difference between the two is so large that the probability of a difference that large occurring by chance alone is only one in one thousand (0.001). If the chances are that slim, then we can be fairly confident there is a true difference between the two populations. On the other hand, the results of comparing the means might suggest that a difference this large can occur 60 times out of 100 (0.6). In this case, we cannot be very confident that the means are different. The convention is, that if a difference of this size between sample means can happen more than five times out of 100 just by luck, we generally are unwilling to state that there is a difference in the population.

t-Tests for Independent Data

Earlier you learned that the practical way to determine statistically whether two group means are likely to be different is to do a t-test. The t-test is in fact the best method for

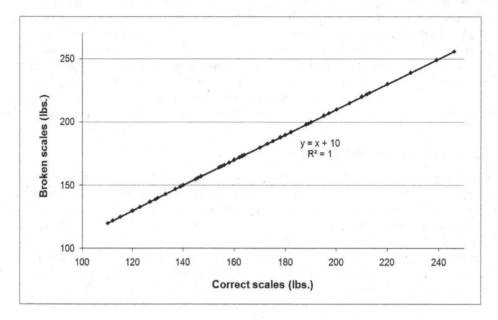

Figure 15.5 Correlation between two sets of scales

carrying out the sample-mean comparisons that we are discussing here. In some cases, you will be comparing two tests with the same group of test takers (as we did for the criterion measurement and new measurement comparison) or looking at test–retest reliability—that is, doing the same test twice with *one* group (this may also be called a "single sample," or, better, a "repeated measures" situation). In these cases, we do a paired t-test, also called a dependent t-test. In other situations, we need to compare the data between two different (independent) groups. We do this with an "independent" t-test, sometimes called a two-sample t-test.

For an independent t-test, we choose either a one-tailed or a two-tailed test, just as we did for a dependent t-test. Recall that the choice depends on how much information we need: Do we need to know only whether the mean of measurement A is larger than that of measurement B, or only if it is smaller, or do we need to know both? That is, for example, if we want to know if mean A is larger than mean B, but we do not care whether A is smaller than B, a one-tailed test is appropriate. If we have to know whether A is larger than B, or B is larger than A, then we are in a two-tailed test situation. Using a one-tailed test makes it twice as easy to find a difference.

For a t-test for independent samples, we may also have to choose between equal or unequal variances. Several statistical tests are available that can absolutely assure us that the variances are equal (e.g., Levene's Test for Equality of Variances), but by looking at the two SDs, we can decide for ourselves whether the difference is large enough to be important. If there is any doubt, we assume unequal variances, because that is always the safest choice. Alternatively, we can follow the same procedure that we used to calculate SD and instead of inserting STDEV, we can use VAR.

Table 15.1 illustrates this method. Here, we are testing two different teaching methods, Method A and Method B. We calculate the STDEV for each of the methods. To

Table 15.1 Calculating variance between two teaching methods

	D29	▼	*fx*	=VAR(D3:D26)	
	A	B	C	D	E
1					
2			Teaching Method A	Teaching Method B	
3			98	98	
4			96	97	
5			95	93	
6			95	93	
7			92	91	
8			90	91	
9			90	88	
10			89	88	
11			85	88	
12			83	86	
13			81	85	
14			81	83	
15			80	81	
16			78	77	
17			77	75	
18			75	75	
19			72	74	
20			72	72	
21			69	70	
22			67	69	
23			66	65	
24			63	64	
25			59	60	
26			42	37	
27		STDEV	13.66	14.06	
28		(STDEV)^2	186.56	197.80	
29		VAR	186.56	197.80	
30					

find the variance, we can then square the SD, or we can use the function VAR to get the same answer.

Testing Three or More Means

As you saw earlier, t-tests are easy to do on a spreadsheet. But they have one very serious limitation. If we only have two measures, A and B, or two samples, t-tests are very useful. However, if we have three or more measures, or samples, we would have to do multiple t-tests. To compare the group means for three teaching methods, A, B, and C, a t-test would let us compare A vs. B, or B vs. C, or A vs. C, but if we need to compare all three, the risk of making a mistake increases. That is, the p value triples as a result of this process. Instead of having a p of .05, for example, the p value increases to 0.15.

This means the risk of mistakenly assuming a difference when one really doesn't exist has increased to 15 times out of 100. This risk of assuming a difference when none really exists—erroneously inferring that a difference exists in a population, based on the test of a sample—is called a **Type I error**. In this case, the value of 0.15 exceeds what we normally would accept.

To make more than one comparison (that is, to compare more than two means at the same time), we must conduct an **analysis of variance** (**ANOVA**). Running an ANOVA can become very complex, which is why major portions of college statistics courses are devoted to this type of analysis. The details of ANOVA won't be covered, but now you know when it is needed.

You may have a hard time imagining yourself running an ANOVA. However, if you want to be an effective professional fitness director, coach, therapist, or teacher, you will need to keep up with the latest discoveries in your specialty area. The latest discoveries are published as research reports, many of which use statistics. You can be an intelligent consumer of published quantitative research only if you have some knowledge of statistics.

Probabilities

To understand inferential statistics, you need to grasp probabilities. Probability is used in statistics just like it is in gambling. If you are betting on a coin flip, there is a 50 percent probability of heads and a 50 percent probability of tails. The higher the probability, the more likely something is to happen, and the lower the probability, the less likely it is to happen.

Means and Probabilities

You already know that the probability that two means are only different by chance, is the p value. It is important to think about the implications of making a mistake as to whether the means are really different, *before* you do the calculations. Sometimes it is very important not to be wrong, sometimes it may be worth taking a risk.

For example, if you are developing a new method for teaching kids to dribble a soccer ball, and your new method gets good results twice as fast as the standard method, you may be willing to risk making a mistake. In this case, you can probably live with a probability value of ten out of 100 ($p = .10$), or even slightly larger, that the improvement you saw happened just by luck and not because you had a better method.

On the other hand, if you have a new method for detecting concussions in athletes, you would want to be very sure that you didn't make a mistake. In this case, you might want the odds of making a mistake due to luck to be very high and perhaps set your p value at one in 100,000 ($p = .00001$). You have to be very careful, because if the new method mistakenly causes a player with a concussion to be sent back in a game, that player could be very badly injured.

Probability and Correlations

Just as we make probability statements when we apply the results of samples to populations, we also have to make probability statements when we measure the correlations of samples and apply those relationships to the population. When we calculate a correlation on a spreadsheet or in a statistical program, we can compute a p value that describes the probability that a real relationship exists in the population. The p value for a correlation is simply the chance that random sampling would result in a correlation coefficient as different from zero (no correlation between x and y in the overall population) as the one we found.

Since we are not normally very interested in correlations that are very low, the p values for correlations usually are not very important, unless we have only a very small sample (fewer than 20 paired-observations). With a small sample, we can obtain a low or possibly even a moderate correlation just by chance, but with a large sample this is highly improbable. Remember, we judge the *strength* of a correlation by the *size* of the correlation (the magnitude of the r). The p value simply gives the probability that the correlation is greater than zero, which we already know if the correlation is very good. Hence, the p value for correlations is usually important only when the sample size is small or when we are interested in very low correlations where the r value may be zero.

Application Questions

1   Draw an illustration of each of the following:

   a   A strong positive correlation
   b   A strong negative correlation
   c   A very weak correlation

2   If one variable increases concurrently with another variable, that is a positive correlation. If one variable decreases while another variable increases, this is a negative correlation. What would you call a situation where one variable decreases as another variable decreases?
3   Describe the general principles of how to use multiple correlation and regression to predict sport performance.
4   Describe in detail a situation in teaching, fitness, coaching, or allied health where correlation might be appropriate and useful. Be specific. Draw a comprehensive illustration of a strong negative relationship.

Additional Practical Exercises

15.4   Practical Exercise

Describe practical physical education, fitness, or coaching situations in which you should use each of these statistical techniques. Give details.

a   Paired t-test
b   Standard deviation
c   Median score
d   Correlation
e   z-score

15.5   Practical Exercise

Choose a sport. What statistics could you use to identify successful athletes in this sport? If you had to devise a statistical system to pick players, how would you do it?

16 Misusing Statistics

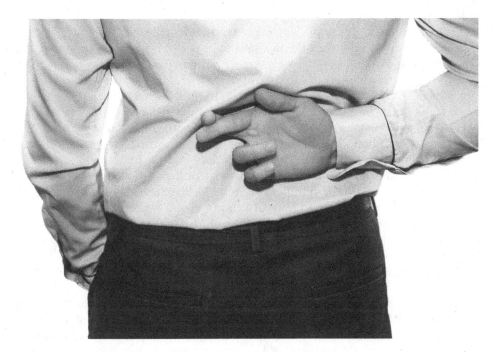

Abstract

Statistics are a tool, but one that can be misused. You are learning to use inferential statistics, and now you are being equipped to use them correctly. Non-normal samples can be misleading with regard to relationships in populations. Type I and Type II errors can result when our analysis of our sample misleads us into thinking we have a difference in means when we don't (Type I) or we don't have a difference when we really do (Type II).

Keywords: non-normal samples, populations, Type I error, Type II error.

Unfortunately, it is easy to mislead others, unintentionally or intentionally, with statistics. As you have learned, statistics can be very useful in making evaluations of measurements. On the other hand, when statistics are misused or misunderstood, serious errors can occur. Misinformation is more dangerous than no information. When we have no information, we know that we are ignorant. When we are mis-informed, we are still ignorant, but we *think* we know, so we aren't aware of our misunderstanding. The real danger is that as coaches, trainers, teachers, or thera-pists, we will pass along the misinformation, which will result in the development of teaching methods, training programs, rehabilitation programs, and so forth that actually cause harm. For now—because the misuse of statistics is an important topic to understand—let's take a quick look at some examples.

Use of Non-Normal Samples

Any statistic can be misused, but one of the most often misused statistics is the Pearson Product-Moment Correlation. As a professional you will often read research studies that use correlation. For example, you might read a research study that tells you there is a strong correlation between the bioimpedance body composition technique and the criterion standard, underwater weighing with simultaneous residual volume. This seems to suggest that bioimpedance is a quicker, easier, and cheaper way to measure body fatness. As an astute student of measurement, however, you notice that the sample is not large. Despite the small sample, the study includes extremely lean and extremely fat subjects, along with a very few average-fat people. Knowing something about normal distributions, you think this is odd. Since most of the subjects in a normal distribution are within one standard deviation of the mean, more subjects in the sample should have been closer to the average rather than at the extremes. You become suspicious, as you should. If a researcher deliberately chooses a sample that has a distorted distribution, with a lot of extreme scores and relatively few average scores, the correlation will be unrealistically high. Recall that we already discussed that this distortion in correlation was one reason that Bland and Altman created an alternative approach to evaluating criterion validity. Whenever you see a situation like this, you must be careful not to be fooled by statistics. Figure 16.1 illustrates a correlation on a non-normal sample.

You can see in Figure 16.1 that there is very little data around the middle of the figure. This is odd, because if the data were normally distributed, about 68 percent of the data points would be within one standard deviation of the mean. Instead, a lot of data seem to be out at the extremes of leanness or fatness, where a normal distribu-tion should have very little data. For a study of a body fatness measurement method, if the data looked like Figure 16.1, your suspicions should be raised. It may well be that the investigators deliberately picked a sample that would yield an artificially high correlation between the experimental method and the criterion method. Notice that the correlation coefficients shown on Figures 16.1 and 16.2 fell (from 0.90 to about 0.68) when the more normal sample was used.

The lesson of this example is that a correlation must be calculated from a repre-sentative sample. That is, the sample used for the correlation should be selected from the population so that it represents the entire population. Deliberately picking some participants or not picking others results in a distorted sample. Bad samples can never give good results, no matter how carefully they are analyzed.

We should have some sympathy for researchers. They want to be sure that the new method works as well for extreme values as it does for average values. Also, col-lecting these data can be costly and time-consuming, and it may be difficult to get a

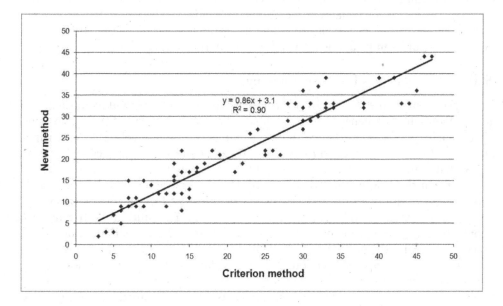

Figure 16.1 Non-normal data

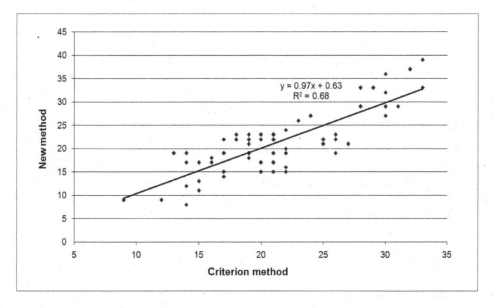

Figure 16.2 More normal data

normal sample. It remains that we must recognize when the data are not representative of the population, and we must know how this will affect the results.

Results can be confidently inferred only to a population that is similar to the one tested. For example, if a research project determines that female weightlifters need four days to fully recover from a total body workout, it would be incorrect to assume that males require the same amount of recovery. The results could only be inferred to females. Further, if the females in the sample were all of college age, the results could not be inferred to older females. In short, the sample determines the population to which the results can be applied depending on external validity.

Substituting Statistics for Clear Thinking

Some people make the mistake of substituting statistics for clear thinking (also known as common sense). Whenever we use statistics of any type, we need to do two things first. One is to look at the data with graphs, tables, or anything else that will help us understand it. We also need to *think* about the data and what it suggests. If the data show that a new method is generating different scores from the criterion method, it may mean the new method is not as valid as the criterion method. However, by looking at the data, we may be able to see a pattern that reveals what is wrong. For example, if a new method has a good correlation but a significantly different mean score from the criterion method, we might be able to make a small addition or subtraction to resolve the problem. Or, if we find a trend in the errors of a Bland-Altman analysis, we may apply a correction, collect new data, and try the correction to see if it works on a new group.

Only after we have looked at the measurements do we use statistics to help us evaluate the data further. Statistics are simply a tool to help us evaluate measurements, and should never replace thinking.

Sometimes it may be of more value to evaluate the answer to a research question by looking at graphs and pictures rather than allowing the statistical values to dictate your thinking. For example, suppose a study shows 40-yd sprint time improves by 0.3 seconds as a result of an ergogenic aid, yet the statistics show a p value of 0.12. The statistics tell us that the difference is not statistically significant, but any track and field athlete or American-football player will tell you that an improvement of 0.3 seconds is terrific!

Concluding Thoughts

Understanding inferential statistics will make you a better teacher, coach, therapist, or fitness professional. Understanding research and where it can go wrong will help you be a more intelligent consumer of the latest professional information and techniques. As professionals, we never stop learning. Continue to learn more about statistics throughout your education and career.

Application Questions

1   Describe Type I and Type II errors.
2   If you were to run an independent (unpaired) t-test to compare the mean height of a group of gymnasts versus a group of basketball players, do you think you would find a significant difference? Based on common sense, you would probably guess yes without even seeing the numbers. How would you go about testing the hypothesis that the two groups are different?
3   Why do statistical errors matter to people who will not be conducting formal research?

Part 3

Measurement and Evaluation Applications

17 Measuring in Quantitative Research

Abstract

Good research requires valid, reliable and objective measurement. It starts with a research question that can be answered with the population and measurements available. There are many ways to go wrong in designing, measuring, and analyzing research. Study this chapter before embarking on your research project.

Keywords: statistical power, ceiling effects, floor effects, regression to the mean, sensitivity of measurement, specificity of measurement, predictive power

Research investigations begin, not with an idea, but with a good research question. To decide whether a research question is a good one, the first thing to determine is, can we make the needed measurements? Consider what it takes to measure well in this area, and whether you will have the resources and skills available to do so. In fact, in most research fields, making the measurements is half the effort of the study.

In research measurements, the essential qualities are the same as in any measurement: validity, reliability, and objectivity. Not only is good measurement essential to good research, but also research is essential to good measurement. In fact, if you wish to be the best possible professional, you must keep up with the latest research findings in your specialty. Attending professional conferences to hear the latest research, as well as reading and discussing research with colleagues, is how most professionals keep up with their field.

Measurement Challenges in Physical Education, Sport, and Exercise Science Research

Research in the disciplines related to sport and exercise presents numerous measurement difficulties. In research on teaching physical education, for example, many variables must be considered. The teacher, the students, the subject matter, the environment, the equipment, and the facilities all interact. Standards instituted by governing bodies, such as local and state school boards, can influence how methods are adapted to local applications, so that even the most effective method may be compromised in its implementation. These standards affect how we make measurements and even whether we can measure in certain educational contexts.

Even measuring outcomes is a challenge, especially when the quality rather than the quantity of a characteristic or performance is measured. How much students really learn is difficult to quantify or qualify. Even when we can assess the learning that took place, it is difficult to draw conclusions from that outcome regarding the effectiveness of a teacher or educational approach. Learning typically depends as much on the student as on the teacher or educational approach or system.

In sport research, replicating sport activity under laboratory or other controlled conditions can be difficult. Sport contests frequently involve over two hours of intense physical activity, making it difficult to replicate these conditions practically, ethically, and safely. For example, traumatic injuries are not uncommon in contact sports such as American football, rugby, and boxing. Studying injuries in the laboratory is difficult because they cannot be ethically or safely replicated, and we cannot delay treatment when injuries occur in competition. This measurement issue is not relevant just to athletic training, but also to sport psychology, sport sociology, and sport biomechanics.

In exercise physiology, measurement difficulties abound. Despite years of research, many aspects of this science remain unknown. Even something that seems to be relatively simple, such as body composition, offers complex measurement challenges. Only recently have exercise scientists been able to divide the body into more than the two components of fat and non-fat tissue. Attempts to account for body water as a third component have been only partly successful. The ultimate goal is to be able to analyze body composition down to the cellular level. Despite progress in the field, this goal is probably a distant one.

Challenges in Quantitative Research

Quantitative research presents unique challenges for the investigator and research reader, including the need to get an overview of the data, the use of non-normally distributed data, the potential confusion of practical versus statistical differences, the need to choose appropriate research subjects, the danger of over-reliance on group means, the need for recognition of ceiling/floor effects and regression to the mean, the problems of measuring the right items and the use of small sample sizes, the risk of drawing wrong conclusions, and equipment issues. Research in the clinical and epidemiological (the study of the causes, prevalence, distribution, and control of diseases and injuries) areas presents additional, unique challenges.

Getting an Overview of the Data

For those engaged in quantitative research, one of the biggest challenges is properly interpreting all the data. It is easy to become distracted by the statistical analyses. Before we begin any data analysis, therefore, we should get an overview of the data. With two variables of interest, we can visually examine the data by using a simple XY (scatter) plot, as you learned to do in Chapter 6. The scatter plot provides useful information in a clear, visual form, such as the outlier data, that is, those data points that vary greatly from the mean. These data may result from error in data collection, data recording, or data entry, or they may be some of the most interesting and valuable data we collect.

Recall that when we construct or examine a figure, we should consider the following key items:

- Is the scale appropriate? Poor choice of the X or Y scale can distort the data and mislead us.
- Are there major outliers that lie too many SDs from the mean? If so, check the data for errors.
- Do the data appear to be normally distributed? If not, why not?
- Does there appear to be any ceiling effect (data are prevented from going as high as they could) or floor effect (data are prevented from going as low as they could)?

Once we have established that the data are as error-free as possible, we should look at the descriptive statistics, such as the mean, median, mode, and SD, and ask the following questions:

- Are the means within the expected range?
- How large is the SD relative to the mean?

These observations are very useful in allowing us to get the "big picture" and helping us better understand the data.

For example, if you were studying athletic injuries in American football, you would want to know the mean and the SD of the number of injuries, the most common type of injury, when the most injuries occurred, and the mean and the SD of the number of plays, practice days, or games missed for a given injury. These simple descriptive statistics will contribute to an overview regarding injuries.

If you were a PE teacher, you might be interested in class means and SDs. You might look at averages from term to term or year to year, by time of day, or by teaching approach. You might study performance means and SDs on fitness tests, motor performance tests, or cognitive tests. These statistics will show you what is occurring in your classes as a whole.

Using Non-Normal Data

Quantitative research requires normally distributed data so that the inferential statistics will be accurate and useful. When data are badly skewed, the assumptions of inferential statistics are violated and inferences will not be accurate. Sometimes research investigators deliberately choose a sample that is not normally distributed. For example, an investigator might choose subjects who represent the extremes of a variable and minimize the number of subjects near the mean. As you have learned, this type of sample will artificially inflate the correlations for the variable.

For example, when investigators are evaluating body composition methods, they sometimes choose subjects who are very lean and subjects who are very fat, but very few subjects who are around the average. You already know that 68 percent of the population is within one SD of the mean for a normally distributed quality like body fatness. What would you predict to be the impact of selecting subjects in this manner? If the goal is to correlate a criterion body composition method with a new method, how will this "stretched" distribution influence the results? Typically ordinal data do not fit a normal distribution, so these data are most properly analyzed using non-parametric statistics (see Bishop and Herron, 2015).

To learn more about non-parametric statistical testing see: http://biostat.mc.vanderbilt.edu/wiki/pub/Main/AnesShortCourse/NonParametrics.pdf.

Confusing Practical Significance and Statistical Significance

Practical significance is a concept often overlooked in quantitative research using inferential statistics. Unfortunately, researchers can become so focused on statistical significance that they ignore important issues such as clear analytical thinking about data. Remember, the purpose of statistics is to *help* us think, not *replace* thinking. The box on the facing page gives an example of a statistical difference that does not have practical significance.

In the scenario described in the box, a difference was statistically but not practically significant. We must also keep in mind that a difference between measurements may be practically significant but statistically insignificant. This happens all the time. For example, in studying legal ergogenic aids (drugs, supplements, foods, beverages, and techniques intended to enhance physical performance), we may find that a few athletes benefit greatly, but most athletes do not benefit at all. In this case, the large number of athletes who did *not* benefit will lead to a finding of no significant difference between the mean performances with and without the ergogenic aid. However, those athletes who benefited greatly *did* have a very helpful and important response, for them.

The problem in this situation is that, unless we can show statistical difference, we can never be sure that if we drew another sample from the population we would find any difference at all. If we accepted, for example, a p value of .5, then 50 percent of the time we would be making a Type I error (believing a difference existed when it really didn't). Hence, if we repeated the experiment, we would have a 50 percent chance of finding a different outcome!

Statistical Difference without Practical Significance

Imagine a hypothetical situation in which research investigators are applying to the Centers for Disease Control and Prevention (CDC) for grant funding. The investigators have the following dialogues with the administrators at the CDC.

Research Investigators: We believe that as one travels north from Mobile, Alabama, the cost of belonging to a fitness club increases. If so, then the CDC should subsidize memberships based on latitude, to encourage more physical fitness and less obesity.

CDC: Sounds reasonable. We'll fund you for three years at 3 million dollars.

Research Investigators: Thanks!

Three years later . . .

Research Investigators: Good news! We surveyed 2 million people and found that there is a high probability (p value of .0001) that for every 100 miles northward you travel, the cost of a fitness membership increases by 0.1 cent! We are certain of these results, since finding a difference this big by luck alone only occurs one time out of 10,000!

CDC: There is only a 0.1 cent difference for every 100 miles?

Research Investigators: Yes, but it is a highly *significant* difference! And, if you let us survey 2 million more folks to raise our total sample to 4 million, we have good reason to believe that we can detect a difference of 0.1 cents at only 50 miles of northward travel!

CDC: Yes, that's the way inferential statistics works . . . but a one-tenth of 1 cent difference is hardly important. Why would anyone care that the difference in fitness center cost between Mobile and Chicago is less than a cent?

Research Investigators: But it was *significant*!

CDC: Yes, but who cares?

In general, we are trying to infer a difference found in a sample to an entire population. To do that, we establish the probability that we might have found a difference as large as we found, from luck alone. If the odds are less than five in 100, we usually feel secure enough to say there is a difference in which we can have confidence. If the odds of finding this big a difference by luck alone are high (i.e., > .05, if we are very conservative), then we cannot declare that any true difference exists at all. It doesn't matter how badly we want to find a difference, we have to play by the rules of probability and logic, plus the rules that have been established in research. By using a larger sample, we improve our ability to find differences (i.e., we can find smaller differences), but eventually the differences will not be of any practical value—as in the example in the box.

Choosing Appropriate Research Subjects

As researchers and consumers of research, we must be aware of who is measured in research studies. Many of the published research studies on physical training have been conducted on untrained subjects. Although untrained subjects are the appropriate group for studying the impact of beginning exercise, most coaches, athletic trainers, and exercise and sport scientists are much more interested in athletes. Moreover, it is easy to make the mistake of applying to athletes the results of research on untrained college students. For example, much of the foundational work on weightlifting was conducted on untrained college students. Although after a few weeks of training, untrained subjects become trained subjects, athletes are quite different from non-athletes in terms of muscle, cardiovascular function, body awareness, pain tolerance, diet, resistance to fatigue, and other qualities. Many athletes have been involved in sports training for many years. The vast majority of them are long past the untrained stage. Hence, it is not appropriate to apply to trained athletes the results of many research studies on physical training.

Suppose we are interested in studying subtle changes in coaching that would help elite athletes improve slightly, just enough to allow them to move from the bronze medal to the gold. If we use novice or mediocre athletes in such a study, we can't expect to succeed. That's similar to applying the results of studies on non-athletes to athletes. This sort of error is very common.

Measuring the Right Variables

Sometimes, even when we have the right subjects, we measure the wrong variables. If we give a treatment for which we hypothesize a certain impact, we need to focus measurements on that variable. For example, if we have a new method of training athletes to improve strength, then we should measure strength and not endurance. If it is a new method for improving children's range of motion, we should focus on that and not on body composition changes. This seems elementary, but simple mistakes like this are not uncommon.

Recognizing Ceiling Effects, Floor Effects, and Regression to the Mean

When evaluating quantitative research for your own use, you should be aware of common pitfalls in interpreting data. The **ceiling effect** sometimes results in misinterpretations of quantitative research data. Suppose someone is proposing a new fitness teaching approach. She designs a research study, using a fitness test to evaluate student improvement, and designates a control group (receiving conventional fitness training) and an experimental group. It turns out that, by chance, almost all of the subjects are already highly fit. Once people are highly fit, it is very difficult to raise their fitness much more. As a result, neither the control nor the experimental training method appears to be effective. This is an example of a ceiling effect. With a ceiling effect, research subjects are near the maximal score and cannot be expected to exceed the "ceiling" value, whatever that ceiling may be.

In athletic training, normal muscle and joint function represents a common ceiling. A trainer would not be expected to rehab a joint beyond its needed range of motion or to rehabilitate athletes to be substantially stronger than they were before their injury.

A **floor effect** is similar to a ceiling effect: It refers to a low value that is very hard or impossible to go below. In body fatness, normal healthy males cannot go below about 4 percent fatness (unless they are extremely muscular). So if we were testing a weight-loss program, and we had male subjects who were very lean, we would expect to find a floor effect: those subjects would be unlikely to become any leaner. If you were studying detraining with unfit subjects, how unfit could you expect them to get? An unfit person's condition represents a floor, below which it would be difficult to go in otherwise healthy subjects.

Regression (which, here, does not mean statistical regression but rather movement) *to the mean* may occur in research and in our own measurements, especially in test–retest reliability measurements. As you learned in Chapter 2, in connection with reliability, if we measure any normally distributed characteristic and find it to be extreme (unusually high or unusually low), and then remeasure it, the probability is that the second measurement will be closer to the mean score. In other words, when the first measure is unusual, the second measurement of the same characteristic will likely "regress," or move closer to the mean for the population.

Suppose a golfer hits 10 out of 12 putts from 14 feet away, with a slight break from left to right, on her first trial. The mean score for golfers of her experience is 7. On the second trial, she would be expected to score closer to the mean. Conversely, if a golfer hit only one putt, the second time she would be expected to do better. You cannot prevent this effect, but you do need to be aware of it and recognize it when it occurs. Do not make the error of assuming an experimental treatment has an effect, when in reality you are only observing regression to the mean.

Over-Relying on Group Means

Another source of erroneous evaluations is over-reliance on group mean values. If treatment of a group of athletes results in half improving and half getting worse by about the same amount, then the mean effect will be close to zero. In this case, the coach should prohibit the treatment for those athletes who got worse and promote it for those who got better. Unfortunately, most published research does not provide the individual measurements. A treatment that could benefit some athletes is not implemented, because the mean effect is close to zero.

Sometimes we are researching populations for which individual results are as important as group means. For example, some athletes might positively benefit from some training technique, whilst others might do worse with that same technique. A coach who recognized this would use this procedure for those who benefitted, and restrict it from those whom it hurt. To be able to identify individual (as opposed to group responses, we devised a statistical test.

In this test the least significant difference is calculated using the group standard deviation, sample size, appropriate tails (one or two), alpha of 0.05, and desired beta weight (probability of finding true differences) of 0.80, using a Power calculator such as that found at www.cs.uiowa.edu/~rlenth/Power/. This least significant difference is used to categorize the individual change scores. If athlete A improves by 15 seconds with some procedure, and the least significant difference is 10 seconds, then she is a POSITIVE responder. If Athlete B gets worse by more than 10 seconds, he is a NEGATIVE responder, and all those athletes whose scores changed by less than 10 seconds were NON-RESPONDERS. Then we can check the reliability of the improvement and then use the new procedure for those who consistently benefit. A description of the technique in use can be seen in Balilionis et al. (2012).

Small Sample Sizes

Many athletic training, physical education, and sports research studies use very small samples of fewer than ten subjects. Small samples are often necessitated by time-consuming and sometimes expensive data collection requirements. Small samples have a big drawback in inferential statistics—the much greater possibility of failing to find a difference that does exist. With a small sample, we must not be so conservative in selecting a p value (to avoid a Type I error, assuming a difference when there is none) that we are likely to miss a difference that is really there (a Type II error). When the sample size is small, Type II errors become more likely, so p values must be higher (.10 may be more appropriate than .05).

You can determine the probability of making a Type II error by running a power analysis of the statistical test for your data. The *power of the test* is the probability that the test will find a statistically significant difference between the measures. When you perform a power analysis, you can select a low probability of making a Type II error. Power analyses used to require using a series of tables, and it was easy to make mistakes. New methods available on the Web make power analyses easy.

Computing Statistical Power

The concept of statistical power is important in research evaluation. You will be a better judge of research if you are able to recognize potential statistical power problems.

Statistical Power Computations on the Internet

As I said earlier, in the past researchers used tables to determine the statistical power in a study. Now several good statistical power calculators are available on the Internet. The website www.cs.uiowa.edu/~rlenth/Power/ provides a statistical power calculator that can be run on the site or downloaded. This calculator allows you to enter all but one piece of data in the statistical power equation and calculate the missing value.

First, select the type of analysis (one-sample or two-sample t-test) from the list in the left-hand box. When the analysis box opens, you can slide the selectors to the values you desire and choose one or two tails.

- sigma = the SD for the variable for which you want to compute power.
- True (mu − mu0) = the difference between means that you expect or that can be detected.
- n = sample size.
- power = the statistical power you want (or that will result from entering the other values).
- alpha = the p value (usually .05).

Suppose you are planning a study of a new method for training athletes. Each subject will require almost 10 hours of study time, and the time and money available will allow you to have only 12 subjects. This gives an "n" of 12. Now, select an alpha level (p value). I suggest starting at 0.05, because this is what most journal reviewers demand. Set the power at 0.8, because you will want to be 80 percent sure of finding true differences that may exist. If the odds of failure are any higher than 20 percent, the experiment is not worth doing. Set the tails at "2" in this case, because you want to know whether the new treatment produces better or worse results than the old one. Sigma is the expected SD of the variable for which you are calculating power. You will have to fill in this value. You can select an appropriate SD from your previous research or from the published literature.

Now the only piece of data remaining is the mean difference. Once you have set all the other values, the smallest mean difference that you can detect statistically will be displayed. This is the smallest difference between means that you can state as being statistically different under the conditions you provided in the power calculator.

For example, if the calculator shows that you can detect a mean difference of five beats per minute of heart rate, you have to decide if a difference of five beats per minute looks unreasonably large. If you do not think it is reasonable to expect the new treatment to give that big of a change, then you must specify a different sample size or a different alpha level and run the power calculation again. You might discover that to be able to find a reasonable difference between means, you would need 20 subjects instead of 12. You now have to decide if you can obtain the time and money to have eight more subjects. If you cannot add the subjects, you must consider whether to do the study at all, since it is unlikely that you will be able to detect statistically significant differences.

Power Errors

As stated earlier, small samples result in low statistical power (low ability to find differences that truly exist in the population). The obvious power error in this situation is a Type II error. A Type II error, again, means failing to find a difference between two groups or treatments that really does exist. A second power error is to make wrong research decisions based on a Type II error. For example, we may have two different small groups, perhaps two different types of athletes. If we test their strength, we might do a t-test and find no difference between the groups. As a result of finding no difference in strength, we might be tempted to combine the two small groups into one large group. If that decision is based on the fact that we didn't find a difference in the t-test, the decision may be flawed due to low statistical power and a Type II statistical error. In other words, we would have made a bad research decision to combine the two groups, based on a Type II error. Basing decisions on errors seldom works out well.

Measurement Challenges in Clinical and Epidemiological Quantitative Research

In many studies in health, athletic training, and physical therapy and in clinical exercise physiology, we are attempting to detect injuries or disease. This is not common knowledge, but very few diagnostic tests are totally trustworthy. For example, an athletic training screening test for concussions will usually be correct, but it will occasionally "detect" a concussion when the person doesn't have one (this is inconvenient, but not usually dangerous). Occasionally it will miss a concussion when the person actually does have one (which could be very dangerous). Because these measurements are not perfect, we have two concepts to describe their quality: sensitivity and specificity. These qualities are expressed as ratios of "true" and "false" measurements of the condition. **Sensitivity** is the probability of a positive test among patients *with this disease*, and **specificity** is the probability of a negative test among people *without* this disease.

sensitivity = (TP/(TP + FN)) * 100

where: TP = number of individuals who both have the disease and receive a positive indicator for the disease and FN = number of individuals who have the disease but receive a negative indicator. Note that the number of people with the disease = TP + FN.

specificity = (TN/(TN + FP)) * 100

where: TN = number who do *not* have the disease and receive a negative indicator for the disease and FP = number who do *not* have the disease but receive a positive indicator. Note that the number of people without the disease = TN + FP.

predictive value = (TP/(TP + FP)) * 100

Predictive value is the proportion of patients correctly diagnosed who displayed positive test results. The predictive value must always be greater than the proportion of the disease in the population. The predictive value of a diagnostic test depends largely on the population under study. This is because the predictive value of any less-than-perfect test depends on the prevalence of the disease in the population tested. It is hard to find a disease in a population in which the disease is rare. Likewise, when the disease is rare, the odds are small that the disease is actually present in a particular individual, so the probability of a false positive response is higher. If a disease is common, there will be many true positive (TP) results, and the odds will be greater, from luck alone, of having a high sensitivity and predictive value. In contrast, when the disease is rare and, therefore, most people are true negatives, specificity will be higher, just from luck alone.

17.1   Practical Exercise

A research study by Puyau et al. (2004) found the following:

1   The accelerometer prediction equations accounted for 76 to 79 percent of the variability in physical activity.
2   Sensitivity was 97 percent for the vigorous threshold.
3   Specificity was 73 percent.

What conclusions would you draw about the accelerometer device based on this information? (The investigator's answer is provided at the end of the chapter.)

Reading Quantitative Research

Table 17.1 lists the key parts of quantitative research papers. When you are reading research you need to be asking questions and looking for answers. Here is a summary of parts and some questions to ask.

While reading the methods section, keep in mind that the ideal approach is seldom feasible and that there may be multiple ways to answer the research question besides the method you envisioned. Key questions are: Are these methods valid, reliable, and objective? What information do the authors provide about validity, reliability, and objectivity? Do the methods appear to have content validity? Were the measurements made with care?

The methods section should conclude with a few paragraphs on the study's statistical design. Again, before reading this section, decide on the data analysis approach that you would consider ideal. Consider the issue of statistical power: Does the study have enough subjects to provide sufficient statistical power to find a difference if it

Table 17.1 Elements of quantitative journal articles and key questions to consider when evaluating them

---

Abstract
- What did this study find?

Introduction
- Why did this study need to be done?

Methods Section

Validity, Reliability, and Objectivity:
- Are these methods valid, reliable, and objective?
- What information do the authors provide about validity, reliability, and objectivity?
- Do the methods appear to have content validity?
- Were the measurements made with precision and care?

Statistical Design:
- Does the study have enough subjects to provide sufficient statistical power to find a difference if it exists?
- Does the study have so many subjects that extremely small differences will be reported as statistically significant?
- Did the researchers use the right subjects and test the right characteristics or outcomes?

Results:
- Are the data complete?
- Do the data make sense?
- Do the data look reliable?
- Do the data appear to be normally distributed?
- Does the sample selection appear to be biased?
- What would I conclude based on these data?
- How do the investigators' conclusions compare with mine?

Discussion:
- What do these findings mean and how are they applied?

---

exists? Does the study have so many subjects that extremely small differences will be reported as statistically significant?

The investigators may have devised another analysis plan as good as or better than yours, but even so, thinking about the study's statistical design in advance will help us evaluate the researchers' approach. For example, did they use the right subjects and test the right characteristics or outcomes?

Now you are finally ready to read the results section. At this point, it is best to try to forget any conclusions drawn in the abstract and focus on the data. Are they complete? Do they make sense? Do they appear to be reliable? For example, if measures were repeated and the treatment effect was small, then the data for each subject should be similar among trials. The data should appear to be normally distributed, and the sample selection should not show signs of bias.

After reading the results, think about them before you look at the discussion section. What would *you* conclude, based on these data? How do the investigators' conclusions compare with yours?

Finally, evaluate the paper as a whole. Whatever the findings are, if the design is good, the measurements accurate, and the statistical procedures correct, it is safe to accept the findings as true. One issue you may discover as you read several papers in the same research area is that different investigators often come to different conclusions about the same research question. For example, as was mentioned earlier, some investigators believe that urine color or urine specific gravity is a suitable measure of hydration status, while others don't believe either measure is valid for healthy ambulatory people. When you encounter such discrepancies among papers, try to determine why the discrepancies exist. Consider the qualities of each of the studies and decide which ones to trust the most. No research investigation is perfect, but, obviously, there are differences in quality among studies.

Application Questions

1   Why do professionals who are not involved in research need to understand the measurement issues in research?
2   What are some of the measurement challenges in research?
3   What are some of the statistical errors common to quantitative research?
4   Give an example from your specialty area for each of the following:

   a   Regression to the mean
   b   Floor effect
   c   Ceiling effect
   d   Low statistical power
   e   Statistical significance that does not have practical significance
   f   Practical significance that barely misses statistical significance

5   Explain and give an example of the following with regard to a test designed to diagnose mononucleosis:

   a   True positive
   b   True negative

    c   False positive

    d   False negative

6   For the below data, compute the sensitivity and specificity, and answer the questions that follow.

TP = 78

TN = 80

FP = 20

FN = 22

sensitivity = (TP / (TP + FN)) * 100

specificity = (TN / (TN + FP)) * 100

    a   How many people did *not* have this condition?

    b   How many people *had* this condition?

17.2   Practical Exercise

Is warm-up before exercising really necessary? Conduct a brief review of the literature. Is there a real research basis for warming up?

Answer to Practical Exercise 17.1

In this case, the researchers concluded that both accelerometer-based activity monitors provided valid measures of children's active energy expenditure (AEE) and PAR (physical activity ratio), and can be used to discriminate sedentary, light, moderate, and vigorous levels of physical activity. However, they require further development to accurately predict the AEE and PAR of individuals.

References

Balilionis, G., Nepocatych, S., Ellis, C., Richardson, M.T., Neggers, Y.H., and Bishop, P.A., Effects of Different Types of Warm-up on Swimming Performance in Collegiate Swimmers. *Journal of Strength and Conditioning Research* 26(12): 3297–3303, 2012. doi: 10.1519/JSC.0b013e318248ad40.

B.H. Robbins Scholars Series, Non-parametric tests, June 24, 2010, available at: http://biostat.mc.vanderbilt.edu/wiki/pub/Main/AnesShortCourse/NonParametrics.pdf, accessed June 3, 2018.

Bishop, P. and Herron, R. Use and Misuse of the Likert Item Responses and Other Ordinal Measures. *International Journal of Exercise Science* 8(3): 297–302, 2015.

Puyau, M. R., Adolph, A. L., Vohra, F. A., Zakeri, I., and Butte, N. F. Prediction of activity energy expenditure using accelerometers in children. *Medicine and Science in Sports and Exercise* 36(9): 1625–1631, 2004.

18 Qualitative Research and Reading Research

Abstract

Qualitative research was developed to investigate areas which are difficult to study quantitatively. Measurements in qualitative research attempt to maximize objectivity by disclosing the investigator's biases and predispositions.

Keywords: qualitative research

Introduction to Qualitative Research

Not everything that is important can be quantified. Quantifying teaching ability, for example, allows us to see some of the characteristics of teaching, but it does not account for the ways all the many variables in teaching come together. Frustration with the inadequacies of quantitative measurements provided some of the impetus for the development of qualitative research techniques. **Qualitative research** seeks to understand human behavior and the factors that motivate this human behavior. Generally, qualitative research employs small but intensely studied samples rather than the large and random samples used in most quantitative research.

Qualitative research uses an ecological approach to investigate phenomena in specified environments. In most cases, it is field research as opposed to laboratory research. **Quantitative research**, on the other hand, uses experimental measures to test hypotheses with the goal of extrapolating results from a sample to a larger population. Quantitative research may be conducted in the field, but in most cases is not because of measurement considerations. Both methods must be understood in terms of their own foundational assumptions.

Different research approaches produce different types of knowledge. Quantitative research seeks to determine causes for behaviors, make predictions, and generalize findings. Qualitative research seeks to illuminate, understand, and extrapolate to limited similar situations. Quantitative studies typically are based on random samples of a population, although *convenience samples* are probably more common. (A convenience sample is the sample that is most readily available. If it is an unbiased representation of the population, it is acceptable. If it is biased, then inferences to the population will not be as accurate as they should be.) Qualitative sampling is quite different, sometimes targeted to a specific and well-identified group, and certainly not random. It depends on selection of a sample that will provide an ample supply of the characteristics of interest. Hence, qualitative research depends on the availability of samples with an abundance of the characteristics of interest rather than the availability of measurement tools, as in quantitative research.

Challenges in Qualitative Research

Qualitative research has its own unique set of measurement challenges, particularly in regard to evaluation. Evaluating qualitative research is a bit "qualitative" itself. Readers should evaluate qualitative studies on the basis of logic, consistency, and relevance. That is, they should consider whether the results are believable, dependable, and confirmable, and whether the results can be applied to other situations.

Evaluating Validity in Qualitative Research

Validity in qualitative research is not judged on the basis of error, but on the honesty and completeness of the data collection. Qualitative methods require that investigators explain what they did, how much, and how often. A method called triangulation attempts to verify observations by viewing them from different angles. For example, a phenomenon may be investigated in large-group, small-group, and individual discussions. These will be carefully documented, and if the same observation is made from the large, small, and individual perspectives, a good degree of validity is assumed.

Evaluating Reliability in Qualitative Research

Test–retest reliability, critical in quantitative research, is not as highly valued in qualitative research because of the dynamic nature of qualitative research. That is, qualitative investigators see the context of their assessments constantly changing, so a finding of reproducibility in their research would merely be an unexpected coincidence. Since the ecology changes, qualitative researchers expect that the outcomes will vary over time. If you are studying high school athletes today in one school, you would expect a different outcome even a short time later due to the changing dynamics of society. Qualitative studies often take several months to complete, and the nature of the results are such that test–retest reliability doesn't make sense in this context. In qualitative research, therefore, reliability is evaluated only in terms of *internal-consistency reliability*. That is, it is viewed in terms of *confirmability*, or the likelihood that particular results will be repeated in similar situations, within the same study. The researcher tries to assess all the available information to make sure all observations are consistent with each other. If we have identified a key theme, for example, we want to be able to report that there were no contradictions to this theme in the data collected.

Evaluating Objectivity in Qualitative Research

In qualitative research, we evaluate objectivity by examining the biases of the investigators and the data collection methods used. In order to be fair in considering qualitative research thinking, we must abandon quantitative concepts of objectivity, since qualitative investigators agree that no research or investigative measurement is ever free of bias. The qualitative approach to objectivity is to acknowledge subjectivity and ask readers to consider the possible effects of the investigator's subjectivity. Conscientious qualitative investigators will provide considerable background information about themselves so that readers can estimate their potential biases. Table 18.1 is an example of a disclosure statement. By describing his or her own basic philosophy, the investigator enables readers to make their own evaluation of the likelihood of subjectivity. For example, suppose an investigator is strongly supportive of sport as a means of building positive character qualities but does qualitative research that provides findings contrary to this hypothesis. We may conclude that the investigator's subjectivity probably did not positively influence the results, although we may suspect that the findings may have been even starker if they had been reported by an investigator whose personal views did not conflict with them.

It can be argued that subjectivity really guides everything in both quantitative and qualitative research, including the choice of research topic, the hypotheses, methodologies, and data interpretation. On the other hand, recognizing this subjectivity may allow us to anticipate it, recognize it, and minimize it, and thereby become more objective.

Objectivity in qualitative research can sometimes be enhanced. Sometimes, multiple investigators will analyze the same data, and concordance criteria can be set in advance. Some computer programs (e.g., Nudist) use a semiquantitative approach to analyze qualitative data. This approach is intended to reduce subjectivity somewhat.

In addition, we can use the method of triangulation, mentioned earlier, to improve the objectivity of qualitative assessment. If there is agreement among three different perspectives, then we take this as evidence for reliability. Triangulation in a physical education study may mean that the researchers seek to examine a cultural setting using different approaches. They may interview the students in a class and find that a certain theme emerges (e.g., the theme of "high value was placed on participation" might emerge from a study of the sport education model). Next, they may conduct a formal interview with the class teacher and find that the same theme emerges. Finally, they may ask to examine the teacher's unit plans, lesson plans, and lesson evaluations and,

Table 18.1 A qualitative research disclosure statement

Researcher's Perspective

Driven largely by the researcher's creativity and thoughtfulness, interpretive research is a very personal endeavor. Researchers accept that different interpretations of context and data are not only possible but probable. Different individuals impose a bias that is unavoidable and should be acknowledged and even embraced. These researchers are compelled to deliberately disclose key personal information that may have influenced data collection and analysis.

Readers of this article should be aware that I am from England, and that I originally studied and first taught in my native country. I completed my master's and doctorate degrees in the United States in the Rocky Mountain area and have lived and worked in the southeastern United States for the last 14 years. Many local residents and most of my students would probably consider my views to be extremely "liberal"; however, my own personal view would place most of them "just left of center." My graduate training influenced my earliest efforts at teacher education to be strictly behavioristic. Recently, my approach has become more eclectic and diverse. For example, I have shifted from a focus on instructional behaviors to an emphasis on more effective implementation of different curriculum models. I have tried to develop a conservative reading of critically oriented training approaches to physical education. This conservatism is mainly because I have become concerned that teaching is becoming less professional, and I think that emphasizing technical teaching skills, while ignoring the social, political, and historical contexts of teaching, is wrong. Rather than seeking some "dark leftist political agenda," then, or imposing my own beliefs and values, I incorporate a critical orientation in my courses in order to achieve the difficult objective of producing teachers who are able to think and reflect on their work at a deep level.

Source: Modified from Curtner-Smith and Todorovich (2002).

again, identify the same theme. Because the theme emerges from three different data sources, the researchers and readers can be much more confident that the interpretation of the data is accurate and trustworthy, indicating its objectivity.

The field of qualitative research has grown significantly over the last 20 or so years. All researchers, whether they pursue qualitative or quantitative research, must constantly evaluate their techniques to ensure that they are using the best research approaches.

Reading Research Papers

Regardless of your profession in the sport, exercise, or health fields, you will need to know how to read research, in order to be informed on developments in your profession. Whether you are seeking to learn about a topic by reading the literature or conducting research of your own, your first step should be to review what is already known and to familiarize yourself with the measurement techniques and equipment used in similar previous research.

Finding Relevant Research Papers

Methods for finding research papers relevant to your area of interest have changed in the last few years. We used to start in the library; now, we usually begin with an Internet search. Several search engines and approaches are useful for this; for example, Google Scholar is free and universally available. One efficient technique is to use an online search to find a few recent papers on the topic. From the reference lists of those papers, you can identify pertinent additional references. Be careful not to rely totally on what others have done, but use their work to get started.

Reading Quantitative Journal Articles

After you have located articles of interest, read them from a critical perspective (see Table 18.2). You might assume, as I used to, that published papers are very close to perfect. Over the years my opinion has changed. I have been surprised at the errors that my students and I have identified, even in top journals. Everyone makes mistakes, and these are not always caught in the peer-review process.

The first item to read is the abstract, which provides a short description of the paper's research question, methods, findings, and conclusions. Do not rely only on the abstract for your understanding of the paper, because the limitation on the length of the abstract often means that vital information has to be omitted. For example, the participants are usually not fully described in the abstract. Details of the methods and the statistical analyses are also omitted.

Next, read the introduction, which tells why the study was done and should also include a clear purpose statement. Based on that purpose statement, ask what *you* think would be the best way to answer the research question that it suggests. Your own ideas about the ideal research design and measurements will help you evaluate the investigators' methods section.

Concluding Thoughts

To be an informed professional, you must stay abreast of the latest research in your specialty, whether it is an area of teaching, coaching, fitness, health, nutrition, or clinical sciences. To understand research requires understanding of measurement and evaluation.

Table 18.2 Issues considered in the peer review process

- How relevant is the topic?
- Is the research topic original?
- Is the approach to the research question appropriate?
- Are the measurement techniques appropriate?
- Are the study methods presented in sufficient detail to allow the study to be replicated?
- Is the analysis reasonable and free from major error?
- Do the conclusions arise directly from the data?
- Are any conclusions presented that are not supported by the data?
- Do reasonable alternative explanations exist for these results?
- Did the authors overlook any major issue?
- Does the manuscript meet its intended purpose?
- Are the subject and treatment appropriate for the journal's audience?
- Does the manuscript contribute significantly to the relevant body of knowledge?
- Does the manuscript conform reasonably to the journal's requirements?

Measurement is a key component of good research. Because no study is perfect, we must carefully evaluate each for its validity, reliability, and objectivity. Are the participants representative of an appropriate population? Are there enough participants to provide reasonable statistical power for finding true differences? Does the study have good ecological and external validity? Does the distribution of the data appear to be reasonable for that population? Were the statistical analyses selected and performed correctly? Is the interpretation of the results accurate?

With understanding of measurement and research, you are equipped to be a wise consumer of research.

Acknowledgment: The sections of this chapter on qualitative research were adapted from work by my colleague Matt Curtner-Smith (2002), with his permission.

Application Questions

1 What are some of the potential interpretive errors in both qualitative and quantitative research?
2 In qualitative research, why is it important that the investigators disclose their own backgrounds and viewpoints?

References

Curtner-Smith, M. D. Methodological issues in research. In A. Laker (Ed.), *The Sociology of Sport and Physical Education* (pp. 36–57). London: Routledge, 2002.

Curtner-Smith, M. D. and Todorovich, J. R. The Physical Education Climate Assessment Instrument. *Perceptual and Motor Skills 95*: 652–660, 2002.

19 Measuring Physical Fitness

Abstract

Measuring physical fitness involves defining the term, and then, typically, measuring cardiovascular endurance, muscular endurance, and sometimes strength. Body composition and range of motion may also be included and are discussed in Chapter 20. Measuring fitness in the elderly and in children requires special considerations.

Keywords: cardiovascular fitness, muscular endurance, strength, test battery

One of the unique aspects of measurement and evaluation in our fields is the need to measure physical fitness, exercise, physical activity, and health. This chapter introduces the fundamentals of measuring the various aspects of physical fitness.

Measurement of physical fitness is important in many professions. In physical therapy, frequently the patient's progress and percentage recovery must be measured. For coaches, fitness is foundational to most athletics. For athletic trainers, preventing loss of physical fitness while an athlete is recovering from a lower-limb injury is an important challenge.

What Is Physical Fitness?

In measuring physical fitness, we must start where we always start in measuring tasks: with definitions. Physical fitness has several possible definitions. One is that physical fitness is *a state of health that allows a person to do all daily tasks with a reserve of energy to participate easily in physically demanding activity*. This definition could be specified as health-related fitness. Other definitions could define physical fitness in relation to a particular sport. For example, a coach may say his football players are "in shape," meaning they are physically fit for football performance at a competitive level. This is quite different from an athletic trainer's declaration that a formerly injured player is "fit" to return to practice.

Another definition of physical fitness is *a measure of a person's ability to perform physical activities that require an elevated (above rest) rate of aerobic energy expenditure, endurance, strength, and flexibility (range of motion)*. In this case, fitness is determined by a combination of training and genetic potential. As you can see from these definitions, the way we measure fitness will depend on how we define it. You will recall from earlier discussions that all validity can be related to construct validity. That is, all evaluations of validity may be interpreted as evaluations of the underlying constructs that make up that knowledge or ability. Because the definition specifies the constructs, the way we validly measure must also flow from the definition we choose.

In most definitions, physical fitness comprises multiple components. Body composition, cardiovascular fitness, muscular strength, muscular endurance, and range of motion (flexibility) are common categories. Since the definitions of these are quite different from each other, at least four separate subtests are required to measure physical fitness. The combination of multiple subtests into a single measure of a more complex characteristic is called a **test battery**.

Measuring Cardiorespiratory Fitness

Heart disease has been a leading cause of death in the United States for many years. Therefore, **cardiorespiratory fitness** or the ability of the heart, and lungs to supply blood and oxygen and the muscles to use it is a key component of many fitness tests. The criterion method for measuring cardiorespiratory fitness is the graded continuous maximal oxygen uptake ($\dot{V}O_2$max) test. This test requires expensive equipment and well-trained technicians. Over the last few years, valid portable oxygen uptake measurement systems have been developed. Although these machines have made valid measures of field activities much easier, they remain quite expensive and, therefore, are not practical for use in most fitness testing situations.

Since maximal oxygen uptake ($\dot{V}O_2$max) is the criterion measure of cardiorespiratory fitness, and since the testing equipment is expensive and hard to operate, simpler field tests have been developed. Typically, maximal oxygen uptake is estimated from an exercise bout lasting eight minutes or more. In some cases, heart rate can be monitored following an exercise bout to see how quickly it responds in recovery. The faster heart rate recovers, the better the cardiorespiratory fitness of the person.

Before giving physical tests, administer and evaluate the Physical Activity Readiness Questionnaire (PAR-Q) (available at: www.acgov.org/wellness/documents/parQand Safety.pdf), and the ACSM Participation Screening (ACSM 2018, pp. 33–41) to ensure everyone is fit enough to take the test.

12-Minute Run/Walk Test

In this test, the subjects simply walk or run as far as possible in 12 minutes. The advantage of this test over other run/walk tests is that all test subjects start and stop at the same time. It can be conducted on any safe, flat running surface that can be marked in 100- or 200-meter increments. It may be advantageous for a large group to divide the group in half and assign partners, one from each group. One group runs and the members of the other group monitor the distance traveled by their partners in the running group. $\dot{V}O_2$max may be computed from the following equation (Cooper, 1968):

$$\dot{V}O_2\text{max} = ((\text{distance covered in meters} / 1609.3) - 0.3138) / 0.0278$$

Harvard Step Test

In the Harvard Step Test, a bench and a stopwatch are the only resources required. Directions and norms for the Harvard Step Test can be found at www.ptdirect.com/ training-delivery/client-assessment/harvard-step-test-a-predictive-test-of-vo2max (retrieved December 30, 2017).

Measuring Heart Rate Accurately

Accurately measuring heart rate is a little harder than many people realize. To measure it, we look at a timer and start the count with zero. We count for 10 seconds and then multiply the count by 6 (10 * 6 = 60 seconds). Alternatively, we can count for 15 seconds and multiply by 4 (4 * 15 = 60 seconds).

This illustrates an important measurement issue. The error will be greater if we measure for 10 seconds and multiply by 6 than if we measure for 15 seconds and multiply by 4. This is because we can't measure partial beats. That is, if we measure 10 beats in 6 seconds, we don't know if that is exactly 10 beats or 10 beats plus a fraction of another beat, such as 10.2, 10.5, 10.7, or 10.9 beats. When we multiply 10.0 beats by 6 to find the per-minute rate, we get 60, but if we multiply 10.7 by 6 we get 64.2. A measurement of 10.9 would give 65.4 beats per minute. These are obviously quite different heart rates. Also, a small error multiplied by 6 is bigger than a small error multiplied by 4. Since heart rate actually fluctuates a bit from beat to beat, measuring it continuously for several minutes and averaging over 4 to 6 minutes would give the most accurate result of all.

Heart rate monitor watches may be used to measure heart rates during field tests of fitness. These watches are generally more accurate than counting your pulse and multiplying, but it is important to ensure that the watch is averaging the detected heartbeats over at least one minute. If not, the watch can have the same "partial beat" errors as a manual count.

Validity is moderate. This test should be used only for self-monitoring or for rough general classifications of large groups.

The American College of Sports Medicine (ACSM, 2005) provided an equation that converts the score on any step test to a $\dot{V}O_2$max estimate:

$$\dot{V}O_2\text{max} = (0.2 * \text{step rate}) + (2.394 * \text{step height} * \text{step rate}) + 3.5$$

This equation gives $\dot{V}O_2$max in mL • kg^{-1} • min^{-1}, when step height is in meters and step rate is in steps/min. It is usable for step rates between 12 and 30 steps/min and step heights between 0.04 and 0.4 meters.

For people who have low cardiovascular fitness you should be able to devise a step test that starts at a low rate and gradually increases to reach the maximum. One possibility is to have the test subjects step up on progressively higher benches, at progressively faster step rates. When they are unable to continue, note the last step height and step rate, use this figure in the equation, and you will have an estimate of the $\dot{V}O_2$max. Setting up this equation on a spreadsheet makes this calculation easy.

The Rockport Fitness Walking Test

The Rockport Fitness Walking Test is a test of the time needed to walk (jogging is not permitted) 1,600 meters (just over one mile). The test subject is timed while walking an accurately measured 1,600 meters, and the subject's heart rate at the end of the walk is recorded. The test is fairly quick and very simple. However, the disadvantage is that the Rockport Fitness Walking Test is too easy for people in excellent physical shape. Thus, it would be most appropriate for those with a low level of fitness, such as individuals who are overweight or those who are older. Information is available at: http://walking.about.com/library/cal/ucrockport.htm and www.exrx.net provides calculators for estimating $\dot{V}O_2$max from various field tests, as well as norm tables and other useful features and forms.

What did the calculator on the website tell you about your own and your partner's fitness? What is your evaluation of the Rockport test?

Reading Between the Lines

Norm tables don't always give us the exact data we need. For example, consider Table 19.1 which shows a section from the $\dot{V}O_2$ norm tables. Suppose you are a 25-year-old male, and you performed a $\dot{V}O_2$max test in a laboratory. Your measured

(continued)

(continued)

$\dot{V}O_2$max was 50 mL • kg^{-1} • min^{-1}, and you want to know your approximate percentile rank. You will notice that a percentile rank is not given for your specific age and $\dot{V}O_2$max measurement. To find your rank, the first step is to note the difference between the 80th and the 90th percentiles. Your rank is somewhere between these. To find out where, subtract the 80th percentile number from the 90th percentile number: $51.4 - 48.2 = 3.2$ mL • kg^{-1} • min^{-1}. This tells you that for your age group, 10 percentile points corresponds to 3.2 mL • kg^{-1} • min^{-1}. Therefore, 1 percentile point corresponds to one-tenth of this figure, or 0.32 mL • kg^{-1} • min^{-1}. Your score of 50 is 1.8 mL • kg^{-1} • min^{-1} above the 80th percentile ($50 - 48.2$). How many percentile points is this? Since there are 0.32 mL • kg^{-1} • min^{-1} in each percentile point, divide 1.8 mL • kg^{-1} • min^{-1} by 0.32 mL • kg^{-1} • min^{-1}. The result, 5.6, means that you are 5.6 percentile points above 80. The answer, 85.6, rounds to the 86th percentile. Does this answer make sense? Yes, when you look again Table 19.1, it does look like you would be almost 6 percentile points above 80.

This process of "reading between the lines," or estimating a value between two known values, is called **interpolation**. Interpolation enables us to estimate a value that is not provided in a table. It is important to realize that it is only an estimation, so some error is likely. In interpolation, we usually assume that the difference between two values in a table is a constant proportion of the difference (that is, in mathematical terms we'd say that there was a linear relationship between the two values). This assumption may be wrong. In most cases we don't have to interpolate between points that are very far apart, so any error is likely to be small, but it is still important that we not have too much confidence in the details of an interpolation. For example, in the illustration I just gave for interpolating between 80 and 90, I would not argue with someone who said the percentile should be 85 rather than 86. And, to be honest, I would not be surprised to learn that the raw data used to complete the table actually showed that 50 mL • kg^{-1} • min^{-1} represented the 84th or 87th percentile rank. Very seldom do we need a very high degree of precision on norms, so interpolation can be helpful, even if it is not highly accurate.

We can also interpolate for age in this norm table. If the subject's age happens to be 25, 35, 45, or 55, right in the middle of the ranges, the table is probably quite accurate. But if the subject is 30, we could interpolate. Look back at the table. The 20–29 year group at the 90th percentile has a $\dot{V}O_2$max of 51.4 mL • kg^{-1} • min^{-1}, and the 30–39 year group has a $\dot{V}O_2$max of 50.4 mL • kg^{-1} • min^{-1}. The difference between these is 1.0 mL/kg. The age difference between the two groups is 10 years. If we divide 1.0 mL/kg by 10 years, we get 0.1 mL • kg^{-1} • min^{-1}/year. To adjust from 35 down to 30, then we find that 5 years * 0.1 mL • kg^{-1} • min^{-1}/year is 0.5 mL/kg. We then add this result to the table entry for 35 years: $0.5 + 50.4 = 50.9$ mL • kg^{-1} • min^{-1}. We added instead of subtracted, because we are moving in a "younger" direction, so the $\dot{V}O_2$max goes up. Again, we must double check: What answer would we expect? We know the $\dot{V}O_2$max should lie between 50.4 and 51.4, so the answer of 50.9 mL • kg^{-1} • min^{-1} looks correct. At any rate, a difference of about 1 mL • kg^{-1} • min^{-1} is negligible and is "absorbed" by the error of the test and its predictions/estimations.

Table 19.1 Norm table for $\dot{V}O_2$max (ml/Kg body weight, ACSM 2005)

	Percentile Rank	20–29	30–39	Age 40–49	50–59	60+
Men	90	51.4	50.4	48.2	45.3	42.5
Women		44.2	41.0	39.5	35.2	35.2
Men	80	48.2	46.8	44.1	41	38.1
Women		41.0	38.6	36.3	32.3	31.2
Men	70	46.8	44.6	41.8	38.5	35.3
Women		38.1	36.7	33.8	30.9	29.4
Men	50	42.5	41.0	38.1	35.2	31.8
Women		35.2	33.8	30.9	28.2	25.8
Men	30	39.5	37.4	35.1	32.3	28.7
Women		32.3	30.5	28.3	25.5	23.8
Men	10	34.5	32.5	30.9	28	23.1
Women		28.4	26.5	25.1	22.3	20.8

For more information on the Rockport Fitness Walking Test, visit the website www. rockport.com. The website at www.exrx.net provides calculators for estimating $\dot{V}O_2$max from various field tests, as well as norm tables and other useful features and forms.

Percentile ranks for $\dot{V}O_2$max can be calculated at www.kumc.edu/fitness-ranking. html (retrieved May 29, 2018). Tables to convert scores can be found on page 93 of the *ACSM's Guidelines for Exercise Testing and Prescription*, 10th ed. Wolters Kluwer, 2018.

19.1 Practical Exercise

Use that calculator to find:

a   The percentile rank for a woman who is age 40 with a $\dot{V}O_2$max of 40 ml/kg/min.
b   The percentile rank for a woman who is age 20 with a $\dot{V}O_2$max of 50 ml/kg/min.
c   The percentile rank for a woman who is age 20 with a $\dot{V}O_2$max of 20 ml/kg/min.

(The answers are at the end of the chapter.)

Measuring Muscular Endurance

Many occupations and activities require muscular endurance. In fact, in everyday life, muscular endurance is generally more useful than muscular strength. Remember the difference between strength and endurance: **muscular strength** is the maximal force one can exert, whereas **muscular endurance** is the ability to exert a force repeatedly. For example, workers on an assembly line may have to lift objects repeatedly, but these objects will be far lighter than the workers' maximal lifting capacity, and thus the task will challenge their muscular endurance, not their muscular strength.

Swimmers, runners, cyclists, basketball players, and soccer players, all need good muscular endurance because of the repetitive movements they must do. Physical therapists and athletic trainers often work to restore muscular endurance after an injury, since that is the fitness component needed for many daily tasks and jobs.

Muscular endurance measurements are tests that require the subject to move some amount of weight through some range of motion repeatedly. Think back to the hand grip endurance test you devised in an earlier chapter. You had to choose between absolute and relative, and between static (exerting force and holding it steady) and dynamic (repeated exertions) tests. The same choices must be made for muscular endurance tests. An endurance test can be absolute: all test takers move the same amount of weight. The National Football League uses an absolute muscular endurance test in evaluating potential players. In that test, the player bench presses 225 lb (102 kg) as many times as possible. Endurance tests can also be relative, requiring the subjects to move repeatedly an amount of weight that is relative to some other measure. For example, subjects might be required to bench press some fraction (50 percent, for example) of their body weight.

Push-Ups

A common relative muscle endurance test is repeated push-ups, which use the shoulder and triceps muscles. An advantage of push-ups is that almost everyone can do at least one push-up. Push-ups can be modified by raising or lowering the feet. If the subject's feet are elevated, push-ups are harder, and if the hand contact point is elevated, push-ups are easier. Disadvantages of push-ups are that if subjects fail (1) to go low enough on the down motion, (2) to keep their bodies straight, or (3) to lock out their elbows on the extension, the score will be erroneously high. Both of these extremes of motion can be hard to judge, especially when the push-ups are done very rapidly.

Pull-Ups/Chin-Ups

Pull-ups or chin-ups are popular measures of biceps and latissimus dorsi (the muscles connecting the upper-arm to the trunk) endurance, but both have several disadvantages. First, a strong pull-up bar set at an appropriate height is required. An even a bigger disadvantage is that many people cannot do even one pull-up. This is a serious measurement problem, because a score of zero implies no endurance, and this is rarely the case. Moreover, all people with scores of zero do not have the same endurance. In measurement, when we cannot differentiate among people's abilities, this is called a **lack of discrimination**.

Various attempts have been made to eliminate zero scores for pull-ups. Equipment has been built that supports a portion of the subject's weight. The bent-arm hang has been used for females. The arm-hang substitutes a static endurance test for a dynamic endurance test, which are two very different abilities. This difference has often been ignored in the past, a practice that could be considered bad measurement technique.

By changing the subject's body angle, we can adjust the pull of gravity against the body to make some of these tests harder or easier. A pull-up is very hard, but a partial pull-up, with the bar positioned low enough that the heels are resting on the ground and the body is angled, is easier.

Crunches

Crunches are a common method for measuring endurance in stomach/hip flexors. The numerous variations of crunches are derived from the older straight-legged sit-ups, which have been discouraged because they may be risky for low back injury. Even bent-legged sit-ups have been criticized as posing some risk for back injury.

Crunches are now the most popular method of measuring stomach endurance. There are several variations. One has the subject lie on her back with her knees bent at approximately 45 degrees and her feet flat on the floor. Her arms are placed by her sides, palms down. With her lower back in contact with the floor, she contracts her abdominal muscles to lift her head, neck, and shoulders up off the floor. She should keep her head and neck straight, and not tuck her chin. She holds the up position for one second and then slowly lowers herself back to the starting position. She should not rest between repetitions.

Often, a marker where the hands are placed is put on the floor or sit-up mat near the hips to ensure that an objective and reliable measurement can be made. The position of the hands and the extent of the crunch can strongly affect scores, so these elements should be carefully specified and enforced.

Other Tests

Other muscle endurance tests are available to measure various muscle groups. These include "wall-sits," where the subject maintains a sitting posture with the back against a wall and no support for the body weight except friction from contact with the wall. When equipment is available, bar dips may be used to test arm extension endurance (triceps endurance). In this test, the subject supports his or her weight while keeping the arms extended and the torso vertical. The body is lowered straight down until the upper arm forms a 90-degree angle with the lower arm, and then the arms are straightened again. Core endurance can be tested using plank hold-time. Chair stands are a good test of lower body endurance for use with elderly people. Some measurements for use with the elderly will be discussed later in this chapter.

Measuring Muscular Strength

Muscular strength is defined as maximal force output and is usually related to a specified muscle group such as quadriceps muscle strength or biceps strength.

Lifting Weights

Years ago, the only way to measure maximal muscle force was to take the subject into a weight facility and add weight to a barbell until we found the maximum that the subject could lift. This isn't as simple as it sounds; if we don't find the maximal lifting weight very quickly, then it is likely that fatigue will prevent accurate measurement of maximal strength until the person has fully recovered, which could take more than two days (McLester et al., 2003).

Maximal strength measured by lifting a weight is often referred to as one-repetition maximum or 1RM. It is dynamic strength, because the person moves through the specified range of motion one time only. Because strength varies with the angle of the joint, what most dynamic strength measurements really quantify is the weakest point in a lift (sometimes called the "sticking point"). The validity of 1RM strength measurements can be improved by specifying a consistent warm-up. 1RM can be predicted from other measures (e.g., www.exrx.net), which provide estimates that may help us measure 1RM with fewer trials.

Isometric Devices

Isometric strength can be measured with a cable **tensiometer** or a **load cell**, which measures the force applied to it. With a load cell, we can connect people in various ways via low-stretch cables to measure static strength. We fasten the load cell to a stationary object, such as the floor. To measure, for example, biceps curl static strength, we attach a stiff bar to the cable at the position we want to measure, then have the person pull upward against the immovable cable. The load cell registers the force for the curl at that particular angle. Strength varies with joint angle, so many static strength measurements could be made with this biceps curl exercise at different arm angles.

Isokinetic Devices

Isokinetic (same speed) strength measurements are made on devices with a coupling arm that is allowed to move only at a preselected speed, expressed in degrees per second. For example, to measure quadriceps strength, the test subject is strapped into a strong and stable chair. The adjustable coupling arm is strapped to the ankle and a speed of movement is selected. For eliciting maximal force 60 degrees per second is a common speed. As the person extends the leg upward, she must attempt to move faster than 60 degrees per second in order to register force. If she really pushes hard, the machine will not permit her to exceed 60 degrees per second, but instead records the force exerted. What has been found is that as the speed goes above 60 degrees per second, the force exerted against the machine decreases. Therefore, with isokinetic force, the strength must be recorded specific to the speed at which it was collected. The speed of the motion can be selected to match the application. For weightlifters, where slow speed is fine, a slower movement rate is best. For tennis players, where racquet speed is important, a faster speed can be used to measure strength.

Fitness Tests for the Elderly

Fitness tests for older people present some challenges. First, safety has to be paramount because many older people have undiagnosed disease, so exertion can present a serious health risk. Second, many older people have poor strength and endurance, so body weight must be used carefully and in such a way as to ensure informative scores (minimizing the number of scores of zero). Slips and falls may cause serious injury, so balance issues, as well as the potential for slips and falls, must be considered.

Lower-body strength in the elderly seems to be a very important characteristic in overall health. In fact, some have suggested it is the most important variable in predicting physical independence for the elderly (i.e., staying out of a nursing home). Physical independence is highly valued in this population. Following are some practical and valid lower-body strength tests for older adults.

The 30-Second Chair Stand

This test measures lower-body endurance. Directions for administering this test can be found at: www.cdc.gov/steadi/pdf/STEADI-Assessment-30Sec-508.pdf (retrieved May 29, 2018).

19.2 Practical Exercise

Using young, healthy subjects, practice giving the 30-second chair stand test. How challenging did they find the test? How well did they score? Why?

Two-Minute Step-in-Place

The two-minute step-in-place provides another measure of lower-body endurance. Directions for administering this test can be downloaded at: geriatrictoolkit.missouri.edu/cv/2min-step-rikli-jones.doc.

19.3 Practical Exercise

Using young, healthy subjects, practice giving the two-minute step-in-place test. How challenging did they find the test? How well did they score? Why?

Timed-Up-and-Go (TUG)

The timed-up-and-go measures more functional capacities than the chair stand. It tests the very practical function of arising from a chair, walking, and turning around. It is intended to test the constructs of leg muscular power (work per unit time), walking speed, and balance in walking and turning around 180° quickly. Repeated several times, it also includes the construct of leg endurance.

Directions for administering this test can be downloaded at: www.cdc.gov/steadi/pdf/TUG_Test-print.pdf (retrieved May 29, 2018).

Fitness Tests for Children

Evaluating the fitness of schoolchildren is an important task. Early experiences influence an individual's exercise habits throughout life, while inactivity and obesity result in negative health consequences. Happily, we have observed increased interest in youth fitness, particularly health-related fitness.

Numerous fitness test batteries have been developed especially for schoolchildren. The Presidential Youth Fitness program offers some good information on fitness testing in youth at: www.cdc.gov/healthyschools/physicalactivity/pdf/2014_09_12_14-249482-nihiser-collectingfitnessdata-final-508web_tag508_2.pdf. Also available is Plowman and Meredith's (2013) *Fitnessgram/Activitygram Reference Guide* (4th Edition), which can be found at: www.cooperinstitute.org/vault/2440/web/files/662. pdf, and at www.fitnessgram.net/home.

More measurement information is available at: www.shapeamerica.org//advocacy/ positionstatements/pe/upload/Appropriate-and-Inappropriate-Uses-of-Fitness-Testing-FINAL-3-6-17.pdf.

A list of international fitness tests for youth can be found at: www.ncbi.nlm.nih. gov/books/NBK241311/table/tab_2-6/?report=objectonly.

Fitness Tests for Differently Abled Individuals

Health, fitness, nutrition, and physical education professionals increasingly have opportunities to serve special populations, including those differently abled physically and mentally. The Brockport Health-Related Physical Fitness test was developed particularly for use with differently abled students 10–17 years of age. Details on all aspects of this test are available at: www.pyfp.org/doc/brockport/brockport-ch5.pdf.

Other procedures not specifically designed for these individuals, such as skinfolds and most range-of-motion tests, can be administered to almost any group. In other cases, these individuals may require modifications of some tests and require some special considerations for scoring and grading. For example, distance may be shortened for runs or walks. Some strength and endurance tests may be completed as usual, but others may need to be modified. The curl-up test may be made easier by allowing the subjects to put their hands on their thighs instead of across their chest. Some of the tests designed for the elderly may be used with differently abled people, when appropriate. For example, the two-minute step-in-place and the 30-second chair stand may be adapted to fit various needs. Each situation requires sensitivity, creativity, and common sense. The basic measurement and evaluation principles you have been learning should serve you well.

The FITNESSGRAM information available at www.fitnessgram.net/home includes information on assessment for differently abled students. For example, for assessing aerobic capacity in differently abled students, a swimming test or stationary cycle can be used. The FITNESSGRAM manual provides specific information on fitness administration modifications for differently abled students.

19.4   Practical Exercise

Review and application:

A group of 100 male students performed a 12-minute run test, and the results were converted to estimated $\dot{V}O_2$max scores. The mean $\dot{V}O_2$ score was 30, and the SD was 10. Compute the z-score for each of the following $\dot{V}O_2$ scores:

a $\dot{V}O_2$ estimated at 25 mL * kg–1 * min–1
b $\dot{V}O_2$ estimated at 35 mL * kg–1 * min–1
c $\dot{V}O_2$ estimated at 40 mL * kg–1 * min–1

Now you see how these scores could be combined with other measurements to form composite fitness scores.

Concluding Thoughts

Testing fitness is challenging and usually involves administering a test battery with multiple parts. Safety is always a concern, but especially when testing older adults. Tests must be carefully described and procedures exactly followed. Test administration for fitness testing is much more challenging than it is for cognitive testing.

Similarly, in athletic training and physical therapy, measuring and monitoring muscle strength and endurance and aerobic capacity are very important. As we mentioned earlier, measurements of strength and physical function very often play a role in diagnoses. Establishing initial levels is vital to monitoring progress and evaluating treatment plans. Only with knowledge of previous measurements of extension–flexion muscle strength ratios can rehabilitation goals be set. These same issues are important in cardiac rehabilitation. Valid measures of fitness are thus vitally important for these clinical professions.

It is important to note that although the administration of tests of fitness and tests of motor skills or sports skills are similar, the measurements themselves are quite different and should not be confused. Likewise, safety is important, and safety and screening is covered in the next chapter.

Application Questions

1 Give some different definitions of fitness as used by the following:

    a A tennis coach
    b An athletic trainer
    c A health educator
    d A nutritionist

2 Why is physical safety an important consideration in all fitness testing? Why is it especially important when testing elderly subjects?
3 Why are test batteries usually used for measuring fitness, rather than single tests?
4 Why should weight measurements, height measurements, and counts of repetitions be done by test administrators rather than test subjects?
5 Name a test that measures each of the following:

    a Muscular endurance
    b Aerobic fitness

6 What is the criterion measure for aerobic fitness?

Additional Practical Exercises

19.5 Practical Exercise

Find a good field test of each of the following characteristics. Be prepared to demonstrate one of these as assigned by your instructor.

(continued)

(continued)

a Body composition
b Muscular endurance
c Flexibility (range of motion)

What are the safety considerations for each of these tests? What information can you find about its validity and reliability?

19.6 Practical Exercise

Design a practical fitness test for a group of 100 high school students for the high school you attended. Name the specific sites where the students will be tested. How long will it take to administer the test? What is the plan for moving people between test sites? What is the plan for inclement weather?

19.7 Practical Exercise

Design a score sheet for a fitness test with the following measurements:

a One-mile run/walk
b Sit-ups
c Sit-and-reach
d Three-site skinfold measurement

19.8 Practical Exercise

Suppose you are a physical or occupational therapist. You have a 35-year-old male client who is just recovering from two years of Guillain-Barré syndrome. He has been paralyzed from the neck down for almost two years. You meet five times each week for 30 minutes per session. Describe how you would use measurement to improve your therapy programs. List the tests you would use, and explain why you picked each one. When would you retest? Explain why you made the decisions you did. You can consult with professionals, but not with other members of the class.

Answers to Practical Exercise 19.1

d. 99.6, 94.4 and 1.2.

References

American College of Sports Medicine (ASCM). *ACSM's Guidelines for Exercise Testing and Prescription*, 7th ed. Philadelphia: Lippincott Williams & Wilkins, 2005.

American College of Sports Medicine (ASCM). *ACSM's Guidelines for Exercise Testing and Prescription*, 10th ed. Philadelphia: Wolters Kluwer, 2018.

Cooper, K. H. A means of assessing maximal oxygen uptake. *Journal of the American Medical Association* 203: 201–204, 1968.

McLester, J. R. Jr., Bishop, P., Smith, J., Wyers, L., Dale, B., Kozusko, J., Richardson, M., Nevett, M. and Lomax, R. A series of studies—A practical protocol for testing muscular endurance recovery. *Journal of Strength and Conditioning Research* 17(2), 259–273, 2003.

Plowman, S. A. and Meredith, M. D. (Eds.). *Fitnessgram/Activitygram Reference Guide*, 4th ed. Dallas, TX: The Cooper Institute, 2013, available at: www.cooperinstitute.org/vault/2440/web/files/662.pdf, and at www.fitnessgram.net/home.

20 Measuring Body Composition and Range of Motion, and Administering Tests

Abstract

Body composition is sometimes included as a component of fitness testing, and is very valuable as a stand-alone test, as is range of motion. Effective administration of fitness and performance tests requires knowledge and planning.

Keywords: body composition, underwater weighing, hydrostatic densitometry, air-displacement plethysmography, body mass index, range of motion, data management

Measuring Body Composition

The concept of body composition has gained importance and attention in the United States because of the rise in the incidence of obesity. Many modern definitions of physical fitness include body composition as one of the components. Body composition measures offer several advantages over simple measurements of body weight. Body weight is made up of clothes, shoes, hair, muscle, bone, water, food, and drink and can change relatively rapidly over a 24-hour period. In addition, a person with very little muscle may be over-fat but not be considered overweight. Conversely, a person might be overweight because he or she is unusually muscular.

Estimates of Body Composition

Underwater Weighing

The criterion measure for body composition is underwater weighing with simultane-ous measure of lung residual volume (the amount of air remaining in the lungs after a person has blown out all he or she can). Several of the current methods of measur-ing body composition are derived from underwater weighing. Accurate underwater weighing requires sophisticated equipment and technical expertise. Consequently, underwater weighing is characteristically a research technique and generally not prac-tical as a field measure of body composition.

Measuring Skinfolds

The most practical method for measuring the body composition of a large number of subjects quickly is through measurement of skinfold thicknesses. Although the error in skinfolds is four to five percentage points (about twice that of underwater weighing), it is accurate enough for most fitness applications. Skinfold measurements are simple to do. ACSM Guidelines give the locations and procedures for measuring skinfolds (ACSM, 2018, p. 75).

The key issue with skinfolds is the use of proper measurement technique. Good technique starts with careful identification of the precise skinfold sites and angles. The skinfold sites that will be measured are specified by the mathematical equation used to convert the sum of the skinfold thicknesses (in millimeters) into a fat percentage.

Skinfold calipers

The fundamental piece of equipment in measuring skinfolds is the caliper. The caliper accurately gauges the folded-over (double-fold) thickness of the skin, together with the fat layer just under the skin. Since tissue is compressible, exertion of the proper pressure on the skinfold is crucial to obtaining an accurate reading. This is one of the key differences among the various types of caliper. More expensive calipers provide more precision.

How accurate the caliper must be depends on the purpose. For screening elemen-tary students or for a health fair, it doesn't matter if the caliper gives a bit more error. In these cases we are mostly trying to raise awareness and give people an approximate idea of their body fatness level. In research, however, we may require the higher preci-sion and validity of a top-notch caliper. Instructions and sites for taking skinfolds, as well as many equations for calculating body fatness, including the popular Jackson and Pollock equation for males and Jackson, Pollock, and Ward equation for females (see Table 20.1) are available on the Internet.

Table 20.1 Jackson and Pollock (1985) skinfold equations

Three-site equation for females based on a sample aged 18–55:
body density = 1.099421
  – (0.0009929 x sum of triceps, suprailiac, thigh)
  + (0.0000023 x square of the sum of triceps, suprailiac, thigh)
  – (0.0001392 x age)

Three-site equation for males based on a sample aged 18–61:
body density = 1.10938
  – (0.0008267 x sum of chest, abdominal, thigh)
  + (0.0000016 x square of the sum of chest, abdominal, thigh)
  – (0.0002574 x age)

Body density (D) from the appropriate equation is then converted to body fat percentage (%BF) using the Siri equation:
%BF = (495/D) – 450

20.1 Practical Exercise

On an Excel worksheet named "Female," create a column, starting at cell C4, of skinfold sums beginning with 21 and increasing by threes up to 69 (that is, cell C4 contains 21, C5 contains 24, C6 contains 27, and so forth). Across the top, in row 3, starting at cell D3, put ages starting at 20 and going up by three-year

Table 20.2 Sample table with the results of the three-site skinfold equation for females aged 20–35

I20		f_x	=495/(1.099421-(0.0009929*$C20)+(0.0000023*$C20*$C20)-(0.0001392*I$3))-450									
A B	C	D	E	F	G	H	I	J	K	L	M
1											
2					Age							
3	Skinfold sums	20	23	26	29	32	35				
4	21	9.7	9.9	10.1	10.2	10.4	10.6				
5	24	10.8	11.0	11.2	11.4	11.6	11.7				
6	27	12.0	12.1	12.3	12.5	12.7	12.9				
7	30	13.1	13.3	13.4	13.6	13.8	14.0				
8	33	14.2	14.4	14.6	14.7	14.9	15.1				
9	36	15.3	15.5	15.6	15.8	16.0	16.2				
10	39	16.4	16.5	16.7	16.9	17.1	17.3				
11	42	17.4	17.6	17.8	18.0	18.2	18.3				
12	45	18.5	18.7	18.8	19.0	19.2	19.4				
13	48	19.5	19.7	19.9	20.1	20.3	20.4				
14	51	20.5	20.7	20.9	21.1	21.3	21.5				
15	54	21.6	21.7	21.9	22.1	22.3	22.5				
16	57	22.5	22.7	22.9	23.1	23.3	23.5				
17	60	23.5	23.7	23.9	24.1	24.3	24.5				
18	63	24.5	24.7	24.9	25.1	25.3	25.4				
19	66	25.4	25.6	25.8	26.0	26.2	26.4				
20	69	26.4	26.6	26.8	27.0	27.2	27.3				
21											

increments to 50. Enter the three-site equation for females and drag it down and across the rows. Ensure that the equation has the right entries. If necessary, edit each cell to enter the actual age rather than using the cell location. The first part of your table through age 35 should look as shown in Table 20.2.

Now copy the data and headings from this worksheet and paste it on another worksheet, named "Males." Substitute the male equation for the female equation. You can print off and use the finished tables.

A practical approach to using skinfold measurements. We can measure skinfolds with high accuracy, but converting these to body fatness estimates introduces most of the error. This is because skinfolds are a measurement, but fatness is an estimate based on the skinfold measurements.

A solution to this problem is simply to measure and record the skinfold thicknesses *without* ever converting to body fat percent. With this technique, we choose the sites of the most interest (at least three sites, but possibly more). We add up the sites we measured, record the sites, and write down the date and the measurement for each site. On subsequent occasions, we measure the same sites, list the date, and show the sum. If the sum is increasing over time, then the person is gaining fat. If the sum is decreasing over time, then the person is losing fat. If the sum remains constant, then the person's fat is not changing, at least over the measured period. However, internal fat stores generally do increase with age.

This approach is especially useful when a person is changing exercise habits or losing weight. If the person has increased the amount of exercise, body weight may be increasing due to muscle weight gain even while the person is losing fat. Conversely, a person who is losing weight may be losing muscle along with fat. The skinfold technique is very quick and easy and provides very useful information.

Additional Body Composition Measures

Several other composition measures are available. **Bioelectrical impedance analysis** (often called **BIA**), is based on the notion that the total electrical resistance of the body reflects the fat content. Fat is low in water and, therefore, a poor electrical conductor (it has high electrical impedance, or complex resistance to electric current flow). Muscle is relatively high in water and electrolytes and conducts well (it has low electrical impedance). So, in theory, low conductivity (high impedance to current flow) reflects high body fatness. Despite the popularity of commercial versions of bioelectrical impedance body fat analyzers, the technique is not as valid as some other measures.

Another variation on underwater weighing was introduced in a commercial product called the "BodPod." The BodPod uses air displacement rather than water displacement. The advantage of air is that it is more comfortable for the test subjects; the disadvantages are that the equipment is very expensive and air is very sensitive to temperature changes. McCrory et al. (1998) reported that the BodPod had a validity of $r = .93$, using underwater weighing as the criterion reference.

Dual X-ray absorptiometry is useful because it can divide the body into segments and can measure bone density as well as body fatness. It works by using two X-ray frequencies, which allows clear identification of fat, bone, and muscle. Computers are used to analyze the X-ray pictures and convert the results to body fatness estimates. It has the disadvantage of exposing the test taker to X-ray radiation, which must be limited for health reasons.

The mere fact that a measurement system is sold in the marketplace does not mean it provides a valid measurement. Validity is often more important than convenience.

Indirect Estimates of Body Composition

As opposed to the more direct measures of body composition discussed above, indirect estimates, which are often used in health applications, are based on data that is readily available in large sample studies. Large-sample research studies have collected height and weight data for years. Based on these data, we can make rough estimates of body composition for large groups. Though indirect measures of body composition have their uses, the validity of these measures is much lower than that of the more direct measures.

Body Mass Index (BMI)

The body mass index is one of the most common indirect measures. Body mass index is calculated as follows:

BMI = body weight in kg / (height in m)^2

BMI = (weight (lb) / [height (in))^2 × 703

The calculation of BMI is quickly and easily done on a spreadsheet.

20.2   Practical Exercise

Use your skills in Excel to create a BMI table just as you did for skinfolds. Make a column of heights beginning with 54 inches and going up in one-inch increments to 72 inches. (Start these in cell B4 and go down from there.) Enter the weights in row 3 (starting in cell C3) and go across the row, increasing in 5-pound increments to 200. Your table might start as shown in Table 20.3.

Table 20.3 presents the BMI classifications.

Table 20.3 Sample table with results of body mass index calculations

---

BMI Classifications.
- Underweight: 18.5 kg/m^2 or less
- Normal weight: 18.5–24.9 kg/m2
- Overweight: 25–29.9 kg/m^2
- Obesity: 30 kg/m^2 or greater

The website www.cdc.gov/nccdphp/dnpao/growthcharts/training/bmiage/page5_2.html provides a BMI calculator, but with your Excel skills you can create your own.

Waist-to-Hip Ratio and Waist Circumference

An even simpler estimate of body composition that also predicts heart disease is the waist-to-hip ratio. To calculate the waist-to-hip ratio, simply divide the waist measurement by the hip measurement. Ideally for minimum body composition-related risk of heart disease, women should have a waist-to-hip ratio of 0.8 or less and men should have a waist-to-hip ratio of 0.95 or less. Even simpler yet, some recent research has suggested that waist circumference alone is a good predictor of diabetes and heart disease. Waist circumferences in males exceeding 40 inches (102 cm) and in females exceeding 35 inches (88 cm) have been associated with a greater risk of death.[1]

Measuring Range of Motion

Measurements of **range of motion** or flexibility are usually included in fitness test batteries. Measures such as touching the toes or reaching over the shoulder to grasp one's own hand can be useful in some applications. These tests may be modified to allow measurement of progress by measuring the gap distance between the fingertips or the amount of overlap of the fingers.

The Sit-and-Reach Test

The sit-and-reach test is a very popular measure of low-back/hip flexibility.

Instructions can be found on the www for administering this test at: www.exrx.net/Calculators/SitReach.html.

Norms can be found at: https://apps.carleton.edu/campus/rec/lifestyles/assets/Normative_and_Descriptive_Data_for_Fitness_Tests.pdf.

Several similar tests measure trunk, neck, shoulder, and wrist range of motion. All of these involve having the subject lie prone (face down) on a mat. The test administrator kneels near the subject's head, facing the person. For trunk and neck range of motion, a prior measurement is conducted with the subject sitting in a hard, flat chair. The trunk length is measured from the tip of the nose, with the head erect, to the seat surface. This trunk length should be recorded. The subject then lies prone, with hands on the lower back just above the hips. The subject then lifts the trunk slowly upward as high as possible, and the height of the nose tip above the mat is measured. The best of three trials is recorded. The score is the difference between the highest prone score and the trunk length. The lower the score, the greater the range of motion.

The shoulder and wrist range of motion can be measured similarly, except that the initial arm length measurement is from the tip of the middle finger to the bone protuberance at the top of the shoulder (acromial process). The subject keeps her chin on the floor and grasps a yardstick (the flat surface of the yardstick should be parallel with the floor) and raises it as high as possible. The score is her arm length minus the highest vertical point reached in three trials. The lower the score, the greater the range of motion.

Administering Fitness and Performance Tests

Administering cognitive tests is fairly easy. We devise the test and then announce it to the subjects and give them the time limit. We schedule a room and tell the subjects to bring a pencil. We give out the test and monitor it, then we grade it. Administration of a fitness test, however, is similar to administrating a sport skills test and is much more complex than administering a cognitive test. Devising the test is complicated by space and equipment requirements, time requirements, and, frequently, requirements for trained personnel. We have to be concerned for subjects' physical safety and ensure that they are healthy before performing the test. We must advise subjects to come prepared for exercise and to wear appropriate clothing. We also need a means for recording multiple scores. To score the test, we need norm tables or other means for analyzing and evaluating scores and perhaps some method for combining individual scores into an overall fitness assessment. None of these tasks are easy.

Safety

Since fitness tests can be demanding, safety must be a key concern. We must select tests that are both safe and appropriate for the group being tested. Before testing any group, it is important to consider their health status. A child may have a heart condition that would make it dangerous to perform some components of a fitness test. Even more problematic is that both children and adults may have health problems and not be aware of them. Rather than being intimidated, we simply need to be careful when asking individuals to exert themselves physically. Test takers who are obese are at risk not only of cardiovascular injuries but also of joint injuries because they have to carry so much weight. The American College of Sports Medicine gives comprehensive safety guidelines for testing physical performance in the ACSM's *Guidelines for Exercise Testing and Prescription* (2018).

Since safety of the participants is a primary concern in testing, we must make sure that the physical exertion required by the test procedures will not pose undue risk. We can do this by incorporating a pretest screening into the test administration procedures. Screening test takers is similar to screening participants about to begin an exercise prescription program. ACSM Guidelines (2018) offers comprehensive information on screening.

Time

Since most fitness tests are actually test batteries with multiple test items to examine each component of fitness, giving the entire test battery can be time consuming, particularly if a large group of people is being tested. When choosing or developing a fitness test, the time requirement should be a key consideration.

Equipment

An obvious issue in testing more than a very few subjects is the equipment required. More compromises in fitness testing result from time and equipment limitations than anything else. Most fitness tests typically need at least a few items of equipment. Skinfold calipers, stopwatches, and sit-and-reach boxes are often required. Sit-up mats and running tracks can be helpful.

In many cases, multiple sets of each type of equipment are needed so that subjects can move through the test battery without having to wait too long. This usually requires that multiple test stations be planned and set up in advance. In addition, the movement of test takers from one station to the next has to be planned and signs, arrows, or similar guides created. A scorecard for recording the scores must be developed, along with a way to make sure the scores aren't entered or changed by unauthorized people. Many of these concerns are similar for psychomotor and sport skills testing.

Trained Personnel

To test large numbers of subjects safely and validly, many personnel are often needed to provide adequate assistance. Unfortunately, it is rarely possible to provide adequate personnel. To maximize objectivity, everyone who supervises testing needs adequate training. With older test participants, some of the subjects can be trained to assist with the testing. With younger test participants, this is much more challenging, but in educational settings training can sometimes be incorporated into course objectives, and training can be combined with test familiarization for all subjects. Regardless of circumstances, safety is paramount. Sufficient supervision must be provided to ensure the safety of all. If test takers are to rotate among stations, the order of testing must be planned and followed. For example, running a long distance may erroneously lower the scores on a subsequent sit-and-reach test or other lower-body range-of-motion tests.

Facilities and Environment

Fitness tests often require lots of space and specialized facilities. If a running or shuttle test is to be given, then a running course has to be laid out and measured. If multiple stations are being run, they cannot be allowed to interfere with each other. If an outdoor space is needed, then weather will be a consideration. Hot weather is a concern because of the potential for a heat injury and because the heat will cause subjects to run more slowly, particularly in longer tests. Inclement weather will usually require rescheduling, so contingent alternative test schedules should be prepared in advance.

Data Management

Fitness test batteries generate large amounts of data that present a data management challenge. Whenever multiple scores have to be recorded, it is advisable to plan in advance how to do so. One good solution is to devise scorecards. As the test taker proceeds from test station to test station, the administrator records the subject's score on the card. If the administrator uses ink of an unusual color, the participants will be less tempted to alter grades. Another alternative is to develop a list of all the subjects and distribute the list to each administrator, who records the scores and submits them at the end of the session. If the list is prepared in Excel, it will be easy to produce as many copies as necessary and it will also be easy to compute grades.

Note

1 www.nhlbi.nih.gov/health-pro/guidelines/current/obesity-guidelines/e_textbook/txgd/4142. htm.

References

American College of Sports Medicine (ACSM). *ACSM's Guidelines for Exercise Testing and Prescription*, 10th ed. Philadelphia: Wolters Kluwer, 2018.

Jackson, A. S. and Pollock, M. L. Generalized equations for predicting body density of men. *British Journal of Nutrition* 40: 497–504, 1978.

Jackson, A. S., Pollock, M. L., and Ward, A. Generalized equations for predicting body density of women. *Medicine and Science in Sports and Exercise* 12: 175–182, 1980.

Jackson, A. S. and Pollock, M. L. Steps toward the development of generalized equations for predicting body composition of adults. *Canadian Journal of Applied Sport Sciences* 7(3): 189–196, 1982.

Jackson, A. S. and Pollock, M. L. Practical assessment of body composition. *The Physician and Sportsmedicine* 13: 76–90, 1985.

McCrory, M. A., Molé, P. A., Gomez, T. D., Dewey, K. G., and Bernauer, E. M. Body composition by air-displacement plethysmography by using predicted and measured thoracic gas volumes. *Journal of Applied Physiology* 84: 1475–1479, 1998. Available at: www.nhlbi.nih.gov/health-pro/guidelines/current/obesity-guidelines/e_textbook/txgd/4142.htm (retrieved December 30, 2017).

21 Measuring Exercise and Physical Activity

Abstract

To manage exercise and activity, we need to measure them. Exercise is measured by quantifying frequency, intensity, and duration, and describing the mode. Of these, intensity is important, but the hardest to measure. Commercial devices can estimate activity by steps and accelerations, but beware as not all these devices have been validated.

Keywords: frequency, intensity, duration, mode, accelerometry, pedometry

If you become an athletic trainer, a personal trainer, or a physical education professional, you will need to be able to describe physical activity and help clients understand how to assess their physical activities and diets. This chapter will discuss the fundamentals of measuring and evaluating physical activity and nutrition, and safety and medical screening prior to beginning an exercise program.

Measuring Exercise

In many situations, professionals must prescribe exercise for their athletes, students, clients, or patients. To prescribe exercise, we must·be able to describe it. Describing exercise requires clear measurements and complete descriptors.

To describe and prescribe exercise, we must specify these characteristics:

- *Frequency*: How often to exercise.
- *Duration*: How long to exercise.
- *Mode*: What type of exercise.
- *Intensity*: How hard to exercise.

Measuring Frequency, Duration, and Mode

Frequency, duration, and mode are easy to measure. Frequency is simply measured in terms of how many days per week an individual does a particular exercise. Duration is described as the number of minutes of exercise per session or per day. Mode isn't quantified at all; it's simply an exercise type.

Measuring Intensity

Intensity is the most challenging descriptor to measure and is also one of the most important to measure. Intensity may be the most important factor in physical training.

Measuring Heart Rate

Using heart rate to gauge intensity is convenient, but presents some problems. Heart rate can be sensitive to stimulants (such as caffeine), to hot environments, and to normal stressors (such as anxiety). Thus, heart rate may be artificially higher for a given intensity of exercise due to these outside factors. Nevertheless, heart rate *does* represent the total cardiovascular strain experienced by the exerciser—the sum of the exercise strain and the strain from other factors, such as a hot environment. The fact that heart rate includes other factors may seem to be a disadvantage, but it is also an advantage in that it does capture the total strain the person is experiencing. For example, if you were working with recovering heart attack patients, you would want to know the total strain on the heart, which heart rate would help you measure.

Upper-body exercise produces higher heart rates for a given metabolic rate than lower-body exercise. Other measures, such as direct measures of metabolic rate discussed a little later, are more accurate indicators of exercise intensity, but these are much more expensive and difficult to measure and are, therefore, often impractical. In any case, exact quantification of intensity often isn't crucial.

Heart rate watches. Measurement with a heart rate monitor watch has become very popular. Most heart rate watch transmitter systems have two sensors positioned on the chest just under the pectoralis major, usually on an adjustable elastic belt. The sensors detect and transmit the heart's electrical activity to the watch for each beat. A microprocessor in the watch calculates the beats per minute and displays the heart rate. More sophisticated watches feature high and low heart rate limits and alarms, electronic storage of heart rates, and additional functions.

EKGs. In some situations, particularly medical ones, we may measure heart rate from a printed electrocardiogram (EKG or ECG). The speed of the printout (how quickly the paper moves through the printer) must be known, and the number of heartbeats is counted for a given time period. For example, if the paper speed is 2 cm per second, then 20 cm represents 10 seconds. If we count exactly 12 beats in a 20-cm stretch of paper (remember, *the beat that starts the measurement is counted as zero*), the heart rate is 11 * 6 = 66 beats per minute (we multiply by 6 if we measure for 10 seconds, because there are 60 seconds in 1 minute). If we count 12 beats but the 20 cm point lands halfway between the 12th and 13th, we call it 69 beats per minute (6 * 11.5 = 69). Newer devices may use finger plethysmography or other means to compute not only heart rate but also heart rate variability.

Borg Rating of Perceived Exertion Scale

One of the best known ways to quantify an individual's subjective experience of exercise intensity is the **rating of perceived exertion (RPE) scale** developed by Gunnar Borg (Borg 1970, 1982). This ordinal measure is popular because it allows exercisers simply to indicate a number, perhaps by pointing to a sign—they don't have to speak. The Borg scale has received widespread acceptance and has been studied extensively.

Measuring Metabolic Rate

On some occasions, we need to know more precisely how hard a person is working. In such cases, we will want to measure metabolic rate because metabolic rate reflects exercise intensity.

Direct measurement of metabolic rate (calorimetry). Direct measurement of metabolic rate requires enclosing the individual within a large, well-insulated chamber (a human calorimeter, or heat measurer). The person's body gives off heat as it performs its processes, and the more intensely the person works, the more heat is given off. The chamber has water circulating through the walls and ceiling, which absorbs the heat. Every 1 °C of temperature rise for each liter of water represents 1 kilocalorie (Kcal). A kilocalorie (1,000 calories) is the basic measure of metabolism. These kilocalories (sometimes written as Calorie with a big "C") are the same as the calories (which are actually kilocalories) in food. Each calorie absorbed will require approximately 1 calorie of energy expenditure to "burn off." If that calorie isn't "burned" or consumed metabolically, it will be stored in the form of fat.

The Borg rating of perceived exertion (RPE is available in different forms on the Internet by simply searching "Borg Scale" then "images").

Human-sized calorimetry chambers are accurate, but, as you might imagine, they are very expensive and impractical for many metabolic measurements. For example, if we want to measure the energy (metabolic) costs of swimming, we couldn't do it in a chamber. In addition, the process is actually a bit more complex than was described above. Adjustments to the heat measurements have to be made for other heat sources, such as incandescent lights, friction, and so forth. These impracticalities of direct calorimetry gave rise to indirect calorimetry by spirometry.

Indirect spirometry calorimetry. In **spirometry calorimetry,** we measure a person's oxygen consumption rather than measuring the heat produced. Oxygen consumption is simply the difference between the volume of oxygen (not air) breathed in and the volume breathed out. We can measure the volume in several different ways. Air is about 21 percent oxygen, with most of the rest being nitrogen, some water vapor, a small amount of carbon dioxide, and tiny amounts of other gases. So, if we measure the volume of air a person inhales, we can calculate the volume of oxygen inhaled. For example, if a person breathes in 100 liters of air, at 21 percent oxygen, the person inhaled 21 L of oxygen (21 percent of 100 L = 21 L). Now all we need to know is how much oxygen the person breathes out.

To know how much oxygen a person breathes out, we can measure the volume of air exhaled and the percentage of oxygen exhaled. We need to know both the volume and the oxygen content, because people use more oxygen when they work harder. A lower percentage of oxygen (that is, less than 21 percent) is almost always exhaled. You might suppose a person would use all the oxygen inhaled, but we don't, because the body does not absorb all of it.

Indirect spirometry is called indirect because the heat production is not directly measured, but computed from oxygen utilization. With indirect spirometry calorimetry, we can measure the energy consumption of people while they are engaged in almost any physical activity. Recent advances in technology have resulted in portable battery-powered indirect metabolic measurement devices which can be worn by the exerciser. These work similarly to the laboratory indirect spirometry calorimeters, except that everything is done on a smaller, lighter scale. The validity of carefully calibrated indirect spirometry calorimetry laboratory equipment is very high. It is important to recognize that the validity of most measurement equipment depends on good calibration and careful use by trained operators.

Measuring Physical Activity

Health and physical fitness professionals also have an interest that is broader than exercise; they are interested in physical activity in general. Physical activity is a much broader classification than exercise, encompassing all physical activity and movement, including the incidental activities of daily living and work, such as walking or bicycling to do errands, doing chores, yardwork, and so forth.

Experts generally agree that one's total physical activity is a key factor in health (Fahey, Insel, and Roth, 2001; Housh, Housh, and deVries, 2006; Wilmore and Costill, 2004). Because US culture has become quite sedentary, intentional exercise is often the key component of physical activity. For some individuals, other activities can also be important. For example, mowing a large lawn with a push mower can provide exercise. Because physical activity encompasses everything physical that a person does each day, measuring physical activity can be very challenging.

Pedometers

One of the most popular means of assessing physical activity is the use of pedometers. A **pedometer** is essentially a small pendulum that the user attaches to clothing or a belt close to the waist. The pedometer registers any up-and-down motion, so that actions like walking, running, and jumping register, but cranking an arm cycle ergometer or lifting weights (except for a few lifts) won't show up at all. Because pedometers are inexpensive and unobtrusive and don't require a lot of attention or cooperation from the user, they are becoming popular for the assessment of physical activity. Pedometers work well for researchers studying groups that get most of their activity from walking, but pedometers don't work well for individuals who don't walk very much. Pedometers give a step-count as their only output. For most samples of people, pedometers provide an approximation of physical activity, but in evaluating results from the use of pedometers, we must remember that some modes of physical activity are not counted.

Accelerometers

Another tool for assessing physical activity is the one- or three-axis accelerometer. **Accelerometers** are similar to pedometers, except that they work in up to three planes of action (that's why the most sophisticated are called three-axis). Whereas a pedometer will not register for a person rowing a boat because no up-and-down motion is involved, an accelerometer can register motion in the horizontal plane.

Accelerometers typically provide output in terms of an activity count over the measurement time period. For example, you might see an output of $150 * 10^3$ counts/day ($150 * 1,000 = 150,000$) or $500 * 10^3$ counts/day ($500,000$). These counts do not indicate why or how strenuously the person was moving, but only signify that the person did move. Accelerometers can record much more activity than pedometers, but the cost of an accelerometer is also considerably higher. Despite their advantages, accelerometers do not record all motion, just *most* types of motion, and certainly more than a pedometer. Moreover, neither pedometers nor accelerometers show the amount of physical work done: someone who had climbed a mountain would not necessarily show much more energy expenditure than someone who had walked the same number of steps downhill.

Over the last few years accelerometers have been commercialized, and many people wear them. Clearly the validity of these devices depends on what is being displayed, but accelerometer-based activity monitors provide generally valid measures of the activity energy expenditure and could be used to discriminate sedentary, light, moderate, and vigorous levels of physical activity. Just keep in mind validity depends on the accuracy required.

Physical Activity Surveys

Another way to measure individuals' activity is simply to ask them what they did. Researchers have developed various survey techniques that ask users to recall their physical activity in the preceding day or days. This method has serious disadvantages. It is difficult for people to recall their activities accurately and completely. Asking people to keep a log of their activity requires cooperation, and it is almost inevitable that some activities will be omitted unintentionally. Surveys and activity recalls are relatively inexpensive, but the questionable validity means that the results cannot be fully trusted.

A supplemental issue of the American College of Sports Medicine's journal *Medicine & Science in Sports & Exercise* (volume 29, number 6, 1997) included 20 physical activity questionnaires intended for use with the general public and four designed for older adults. Examples of physical activity surveys include:

- Seven-day Physical Activity Recall.
- CARDIA Physical Activity History.
- Framingham Physical Activity Index.

In general, these questionnaires try to determine:

- The frequency of activity (number of times per day or per week).
- The type of activity.
- The duration of activity (how many minutes per day or session).
- The intensity of the activity (the rate of energy expenditure).

Survey results may be expressed in terms of energy expenditure or in terms of minutes of daily or weekly activity at a particular intensity.

The seven-day survey attempts to quantify a person's weekday and weekend activities so that the total energy expenditure can be estimated. Knowing a person's weekly energy expenditure is helpful in calculating the maximal number of calories the person can consume and remain in caloric balance for body fatness control. It also clearly identifies when people are not getting enough exercise in their weekly routine. A seven-day survey can be found at: http://sallis.ucsd.edu/measure_7daypar.html.

21.1   Practical Exercise

Find a report on the reliability and validity of a specific physical activity questionnaire. Bring the questionnaire to class to discuss its merits.

Application Questions

1   What is physical activity (as opposed to exercise) and why is measuring it important?
2   What are some means of measuring physical activity? What are some advantages and disadvantages of each?
3   What are some medical measurements that are critical to health?
4   What are the necessary elements to fully describe an exercise prescription?
5   Of the elements necessary to describe an exercise prescription, which is the hardest to measure and why?
6   Describe or demonstrate how to accurately measure exercise heart rate.
7   Why is there less error in measuring heart rate for a full minute, as compared to measuring for 6 seconds and multiplying by 10?

Additional Practical Exercise

21.2   Practical Exercise

Suppose you are a personal trainer. You have a 45-year-old male client who is overweight and has not exercised in many years. You meet three times per week for 50 minutes each session. Describe how you would use measurement and evaluation to establish and improve his training program. List the tests you would use and explain why you picked each one. When would you retest? Explain why you made the decisions you did.

References

American College of Sports Medicine (ACSM). *Medicine & Science in Sports & Exercise* 29(6), 1997.

Borg, G. A. Perceived exertion as an indicator of somatic stress. *Scandinavian Journal of Rehabilitation Medicine* 2: 92–98, 1970.

Borg, G. A. Psychological bases of perceived exertion. *Medicine & Science in Sports & Exercise* 14(5): 377–381, 1982.

Fahey, T. D., Insel, P. M., and Roth, W. T. *Fit and Well*. California: Mayfield Publishing Company, 2001.

Housh, T. J., Housh, D. J., and DeVries, H. A. *Applied Exercise and Sport Physiology*. Scottsdale, AZ: Holcomb Hathaway, 2006.

Wilmore, J. and Costill, D. *Physiology of Sport and Exercise*. Champaign, IL: Human Kinetics, 2004.

22 Measuring Health

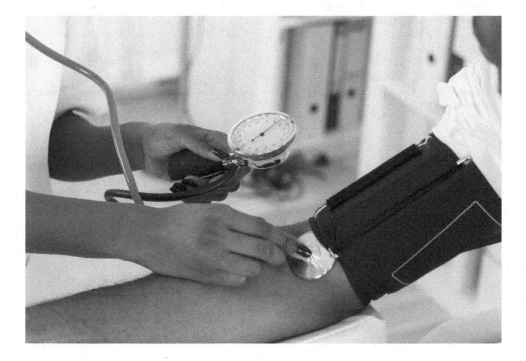

Abstract

Validly measuring the many components of health can be challenging, but can be essential in physical therapy, wellness, and medicine. Measuring our nutritional status, health status, and even our exercise preferences will allow safe and effective means for maintaining and improving health.

Keywords: exercise prescription, health status, exercise preferences

Measurement is essential in the evaluation of human health and well-being. By measuring key health indicators, such as the constituents of the circulating blood (e.g., different types of cholesterol), the blood's oxygen content, or blood clotting, the healthcare professional can identify potentially serious health conditions and possibly save a patient's life. Measurements of prostate-specific antigen (PSA), of the pressure inside the eye, and of bone density are crucial in diagnosing illnesses before the diseases become too advanced.

An overall health assessment often includes measures of physical activity, fitness, and function. Blood pressure, cholesterol levels, and body temperature are other important measures for a health assessment.

Measurement of nutrition is also essential to a health assessment, and this task can be as challenging as measuring physical activity, for many of the same reasons. Americans' eating habits make it difficult for them to recall or track what they have consumed. Nutritional surveys present the same problems as do physical activity surveys, but, for many of the same reasons we use physical activity surveys anyway, we use nutritional surveys, too. Software is available for converting food diaries to nutritional summaries. Some sources of nutritional analysis software are:

- Nutrition Analysis Software, Axxya Systems, Sudbury, MA (Nutritionist Pro).
- ESHA Software, Salem, OR (Genesis R&D SQL).
- www.fitday.com (Fitday).
- www.calorieking.com (CalorieKing).

An excellent article by Shim et al. (2014) describing the measurements of dietary history can be found at www.ncbi.nlm.nih.gov/pmc/articles/PMC4154347/.

The information gathered in surveys allows one to estimate the quality of the respondents' diet. For example, it identifies those at risk for not consuming five servings of fruits and vegetables per day combined. Obviously, the more accurate the responses, the more valid the dietary assessment.

Measuring food portion size is also important. Most people do not know what constitutes one serving in each food group. American portions are larger than anywhere else in the world, often larger than one "serving." Dietary guidelines in the food pyramid are established in terms of servings of each food group.

The Exercise Prescription

Physical educators, physical therapists, athletic trainers, coaches, and other fitness and health professionals often have occasion to prescribe exercise to students, patients, athletes, or clients. Good measurements provide a sound starting point for good exercise prescription. Before we can begin prescribing exercise, we need measurements of individuals' health status, physical abilities, and interests. We need measurements that tell us how healthy they are to ensure their safety, how fit they are so that we can start them off at the right level, and what their interests are, so that they will stick with the exercise program for the long term.

Medical Status/Health History

The first step in prescribing exercise, as in measuring fitness, is to determine the person's medical status and health history. Obviously, an exercise prescription for an obese person with a recent heart attack will be different from the prescription for a 16-year-old recovering from a soccer injury. The American College of Sports Medicine has developed a screening procedure for exercise testing and prescription,

ACSM's Guidelines for Exercise Testing and Prescription, which provides comprehensive information on protecting participants.

One of the most practical and popular means for screening fitness test takers is the Physical Activity Readiness Questionnaire, known commonly as the PAR-Q. It is available from the Public Health Agency of Canada (www.phac-aspc.gc.ca/sth-evs/english/parq.htm). Again, the definitive guide to screening people for fitness tests is the ACSM guide (ACSM 2018).

Any health status inquiry should be completed in writing and kept on file as long as the person is exercising under your supervision. The survey should be updated regularly to reflect any changes in health that might affect exercise safety.

Fitness Level/Exercise History

Along with the individual's health status, his or her fitness level is crucial to a good prescription. Clearly, the starting point of exercise for a highly fit sixth grader will be different than for a 50-year-old who has not exercised since high school. Measuring recent exercise history is also necessary for prescribing exercise. Prescribing too much exercise too quickly can cause students, patients, athletes, or clients to become discouraged, sore, or even injured. Too little exercise won't give results as quickly as it could.

Preferences and Interests

One aspect of exercise prescription that we sometimes neglect is the person's preferences and interests. Some people enjoy swimming, others detest it. Some people hate running. Others don't have convenient access to swimming pools or equipment. By assessing a person's experience with, and attitudes toward, exercise, we can prescribe types of exercise that the student, client, or patient is likely to adopt and continue.

Exercise Goals

It is important to help the client assess his or her own goals. Measurements of initial fitness levels reveal the person's strongest and weakest areas of fitness and may suggest initial goals. Sometimes the individual's expectations are unrealistic. If you have measured the person's initial fitness level, you can both start him or her at the proper point and encourage the person to establish more reasonable expectations. Also, by recording the initial fitness level, you can show the person his or her progress and provide encouragement when needed.

Concluding Thoughts

We cannot improve fitness and health optimally unless we can measure them. To describe and prescribe exercise, we must measure or specify frequency and intensity, among other things. Because intensity measurements are very important, you have learned ways to measure exercise intensity.

Assessing daily physical activity is much more challenging than measuring fitness. At best, we can only estimate—through use of surveys, accelerometers, and pedometers—the daily energy expenditure of mobile humans engaging in varying activities of varying intensities. Like all measurements, the various ways of measuring daily activity have advantages, disadvantages, and different size errors.

To ensure safety during exercise, we need to know the health history and potential problems of the individuals with whom we are working. To manage people's starting point and exercise progression, we need to measure their fitness capabilities. To help people enjoy and stick to their programs, we want to know what they like and dislike. Measurement also allows us to motivate people by helping them set realistic goals and see that they are indeed progressing.

Application Questions

1   Why is it important to assess a person's health status before prescribing exercise for him or her?
2   Why is it important to determine a person's exercise preferences before prescribing an exercise program for him or her?

References

American College of Sports Medicine (ACSM). *ACSM's Guidelines for Exercise Testing and Prescription*, 10th ed. Philadelphia: Wolters Kluwer, 2018.

Shim, J-S., Oh, K., and Kim, H. C. Dietary assessment methods in epidemiologic studies. *Epidemiology and Health*. 36:e2014009. doi:10.4178/epih/e2014009 2014.

23 Measuring Psychomotor Performance and Sports Skills

Abstract

Validly measuring motor performance is challenging. Using Harrow's taxonomy, allows us to order measurements in difficulty. Measurements for each level of the taxonomy can be devised.

Keywords: reflexes, basic intentional movements, sensing, differentiating, and responding to the environment, basic physical skills, skilled movement, communicative movement

Testing psychomotor skills and sports skills can be more difficult than it might first appear. Both mental and neurological ("psycho") and movement (motor) skills are involved, and the two coordinated components must be tested simultaneously. Fortunately, this type of testing can also be fun.

Before we begin, it will be useful to talk about a taxonomy of motor performance. *Taxonomies* are ordered levels of related items. A **taxonomy of motor performance** is an ordering of information about human movement ability. Thinking of measurement in terms of a taxonomy gives us an organized basis for setting performance expectations and helps us devise strategies for teaching, coaching, or advising.

Using Taxonomies in Human Performance Measurement

Taxonomies are simply ways of organizing and ordering information according to complexity (that is, in a hierarchy). In a physical performance taxonomy, each successive movement or ability builds on the ones beneath it (see Table 23.1). An individual who has not mastered basic physical skills cannot succeed in more complex skilled movements. Taxonomies are useful in measurement because they can guide our thinking and help us design developmentally appropriate assessments. They provide a foundation and structure for understanding a set of abilities, such as psychomotor abilities. In both teaching and measuring physical performance, the hierarchy of skills determines the order in which skills are taught and the test items that should be included in a test battery. It makes little sense to test too high—at skill levels to which students have not been exposed. In contrast, it *is* often useful to test at the lower levels of a taxonomy, to help identify weaknesses in fundamental abilities.

Table 23.1 shows a simple taxonomy for physical performance, also called motor performance (adapted from Harrow's Taxonomy of the Psychomotor Domain, 1972).

Reflexes

The lowest level of physical function is reflex movement. Reflexes occur without conscious thought, in response to a stimulus. The withdrawal reflex, for example, controls multiple movements. When a person touches a hot stove, an entirely automatic reflex is activated, which involves no learning. The reflex causes the sudden withdrawal of the hand in response to pain (the stimulus). Reflexes are good, because generally they protect us from injury. A doctor may check a patient's reflexes to ensure the motor nerves that control the muscles are functioning correctly. An athletic trainer may shine a light into the eyes of an injured player to see if the pupil responds to light (a reflex).

Table 23.1 Taxonomy of the psychomotor domain (adapted from Harrow, 1972)

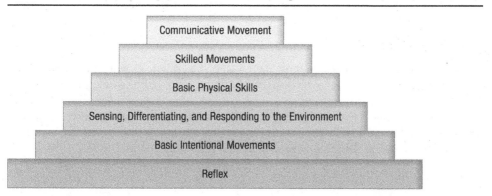

Reflexes are tested because they reflect the responsiveness of the nervous system, which controls the most fundamental movements a person can make.

Basic Intentional Movements

Just slightly above the basic reflexes in the taxonomy are the basic intentional movements. Newborn babies quickly learn to reach for things and to move from side to side. Eventually babies master walking a few steps. If we consider all the sensory information that must be integrated, the balance required, and the muscular coordination that is necessary, we recognize that the simple act of walking is very complex. A taxonomist could break a baby's movements into: (a) random movements of limbs (most basic), (b) movements of locomotion, and (c) movements that require fine motor skills, such as when the baby grasps an object and puts it in her mouth.

Sensing, Differentiating, and Responding to the Environment

At the next level in the taxonomy are abilities to sense (perceive), differentiate, and respond. These abilities include basic hand–eye coordination. It should be clear that basic neuromuscular function and basic physical movements are required before one can perform complex skills. Included in the sensing, differentiating, and responding level of function is the ability to identify things by feel, to detect differences in sounds, to pick things out visually, and to sense the position of the body in space.

Throughout life, we develop higher and higher skills in the ability to sense, differentiate, and respond. Even experienced adults vary greatly in these abilities. A springboard diver or a gymnast has a much better sense of body position in space than I do.

Basic Physical Skills

The next level of performance ability includes basic physical skills. This level includes fitness items that are fundamental to psychomotor and sports performance. Thus, it includes flexibility and cardiovascular endurance, as well as agility and balance. Basic physical skills are not specific sport skills but are the basic abilities foundational to sport competition: cardiovascular and muscular endurance, anaerobic power, muscle strength, range of motion, and agility. Every person can develop all of these abilities to differing degree.

Skilled Movement

Next on the taxonomy is skilled movement—specific athletic movements such as complex gymnastics moves, soccer passes and shots, accurate ball throws, etc.

Clearly, there is a range of skilled movement. Most people can perform motor skills to some degree, but excellence in these skills often requires hours of instruction and practice. When an athlete can adapt movements to varying circumstances and combine complex movements, the athlete has achieved a high degree of mastery.

Communicative Movement

According to many experts on movement, nonverbal communication through purposeful body movement is the highest level of psychomotor performance. This type of movement includes skillfully playing musical instruments, skilled dance, ballroom dancing, ice dancing, and balance beam and floor exercises in gymnastics. To evaluate the degree of skill at the pinnacle of the taxonomy requires judges who possess skills themselves, in order to appreciate the performance.

Only the most highly skilled athletes exemplify this communicative level. Their level of expertise has been clearly recognized by many, though probably only fully appreciated by experts in their own sports.

Measuring Performance Based on the Psychomotor Taxonomy

The taxonomy given in Table 23.1 can help us structure our concepts of psychomotor and sports skills. It is helpful to recognize that all sports skills are basic psychomotor skills adapted to specific sport purposes. A student, athlete, or client must be able to perform basic intentional movements in order to perform any sports skill, such as the squat in weightlifting or hitting a golf ball. Therefore, understanding a bit about the psychomotor skills, including reflexes, can help us in our instruction. Understanding the hierarchical nature of motor skills also helps us establish appropriate plans for instruction and for measuring and evaluating performance.

Measuring Reflexes

Reflexes are such fundamental sensory-nervous system and motor responses that they are not normally tested, with a few exceptions. For example, the reflex response of the pupil of the eye indicates brain function, useful in diagnosing a concussion.

Measurements of reflexes are sometimes criterion-referenced. Athletic training and physical therapy professionals typically evaluate their patients' reflexes on a five-point scale (0–4). By measuring the functioning of the reflexes, trainers or therapists can determine the level on the spine and degree of lesion in spinal cord injuries.

Measuring Basic Intentional Movements

In testing performance, we usually start with basic intentional movements. We may measure such skills as walking, running, and jumping. With children or the elderly, we may simply have them walk a straight line on a smooth, hard, flat surface while we look for gait irregularities, such as excessive toe-in or toe-out.

These evaluations are often formative rather than summative. Most basic intentional movements are learned in childhood, and, therefore, are most appropriately assessed in young children. In most cases, we perform formative measurement with the purpose of finding deficiencies in students. At the same time, it can be important to identify those abilities in which young children excel, so that the children can be encouraged to pursue activities for which they show ability.

Tests at this level may be criterion-referenced or norm-referenced (for example, balance tests). Tests that measure basic intentional movement skills include the balance test and hand steadiness test.

Balance Test

A person's balance can be tested by having him or her stand on one foot as long as possible, with eyes open or closed. The test with eyes open is easier, because with the eyes closed, people lose their ability to monitor their surroundings and adjust their posture accordingly. For most people, having sufficient (as opposed to highly developed) balance is the important issue; therefore, the test could be criterion-referenced and might simply require standing on one foot for a certain time, say, 20 seconds.

The stork stand is an example of a norm-referenced balance test with face validity and a reported reliability of 0.87 and objectivity of 0.99. To perform this test, the subject stands on the ball of the foot of choice and places the other foot on the inside of the supporting knee. The hands are placed on the hips. It is best to perform this test without shoes, because shoes vary in their ankle support and the width of the sole. On command, the subject raises the heel off the floor, and the timing device is started. The time that the subject is able to maintain balance on the ball of the foot without moving it or allowing the heel to touch the floor is recorded. The score is the longest time of three trials (Johnson and Nelson, 1986).

23.1   Practical Exercise

In this exercise you will measure a person's response time using a yardstick. Hold the yardstick near the end marked "36" and let it hang down. Have another person put his or her hand next to the bottom, without touching it. Tell the person that you will drop the yardstick sometime within the next 5 seconds and that they should catch it as fast as they can after you drop it. Record the level (inches or centimeters) at which they catch the yardstick, and convert the distance into reaction time with the equation below. Test the same person three to five times. Vary the time of dropping the yardstick within the 5-second "drop zone" so the person cannot guess when you will drop it.

The website http://faculty.washington.edu/chudler/chreflex.html converts the distance on the yardstick to reaction time. For example, if you caught the yardstick at the 8-inch mark, then your reaction time is 0.20 seconds (200 ms). There are 1,000 milliseconds (ms) in 1 second.

If you want to be more precise, use the following formula:

$$\text{reaction time} = \sqrt{\frac{2 * \text{distance in cm}}{980\text{cm}} / \sec^2}$$

Measuring Sensory Ability and Response to Environmental Challenges

At the next level in the taxonomy, we measure such sensory and response skills as touch sensitivity, vision, hearing, identifying objects by feel, detecting differences in sound, picking objects out visually, and sensing the position of the body in space. Following is a test of touch sensitivity that measures sensory and response ability.

Two-Point Touch Test

Two-point touch—the ability to distinguish two points of touch that are close together—can be measured with very simple equipment. You will need a set of dividers (you could use a compass with a very sharp pencil—both points must be similar in sharpness) and a good-quality ruler marked in millimeters.

The subject closes her eyes or is blindfolded. Place the points of the dividers as close together as possible and touch the subject's skin at a designated site (the pad of the index finger, for example), firmly enough to indent the skin slightly (be careful not to damage the skin). Tell the subject that this is one point. Next, separate the pointers by 5 mm (using the ruler to measure), and touch the site again so that both points touch simultaneously—this is very important. Ask the subject if she feels two points. If the answer is yes, then reduce the distance to 3 mm and try again. If the answer is no, then widen the distance between the two points until the subject can detect two different points of contact. Keep repeating until you find the smallest distance that the test subject can detect as two distinct points of touch. This is the score.

23.2   Practical Exercise

Use the two-point test described above to measure two-point detection on several class members. Calculate the mean and the standard deviation of the group. Measure at three different places: the pad of the index finger, the back of the hand, and the hairy side of the forearm, just below the elbow (measure the forearm perpendicular to the bone).

- How much variability was there among the participants?
- How much variability was there among measurement sites?

Evaluate the test–retest reliability and the objectivity of your measurements. What would you say about the content validity of your test? What does the definition of two-point touch have to do with content validity?

Measuring Basic Physical Skills

When measuring basic physical skills, we are measuring the components of physical fitness, as well as some additional abilities such as agility and balance. Previously we covered the basics of fitness testing. Many of the same tests described in that chapter may be used in the context of sport fitness, but for specific sports, some tests will be more readily applicable than others. For example, for baseball or football, a very long endurance run might not be as appropriate as a sprint test. Tests of upper-body muscular endurance will be more appropriate for wrestlers than for soccer players.

Two common tests of the basic physical skill level of functioning are the Margaria-Kalamen test and the Wingate Anaerobic Power test.

The Wingate Anaerobic Power Test

The Wingate Anaerobic Power test is conducted on a mechanically braked bicycle ergometer, ideally the type with "basket" loading, such that the resistance can be applied all at once. After a warm-up, the athlete begins pedaling as fast as possible without resistance. Within 3 seconds, a predetermined resistance is applied to the flywheel and the athlete continues to pedal as fast as possible for 30 seconds. An electronic counter records the number of flywheel revolutions in 30 seconds. The flywheel resistance used depends on the test subjects.

Suggested resistance used and procedures for the Wingate Anaerobic Power test can be found at: https://en.wikipedia.org/wiki/Wingate_test.

Measuring Skilled Movements

Measurements become more difficult since tests now must measure a person's skill both in isolation and in the context of competition.

Consider how we might construct basic skills tests for a sport such as racquetball. For example, we could do a serve test. For a scoring system, we might use a small scoring circle in each back wall corner corresponding to a good serve to the opponent's backhand. We could establish scores for different serve placements. This looks easy enough, but there is a problem.

If a player hits a drive serve that bounces straight back from the front wall to the high-score circle, the opponent may get a very good return by hitting the ball on the rebound from the front wall. For the serve to be a good one, it must come into the back corner from a very high angle, so high that the opponent cannot get to the ball until it has bounced off the floor. We must find a way to take that into account.

Even if we set up a series of tests that evaluate almost all elements of the game, we will still be lacking at least one ingredient. That ingredient is an opponent. Racquetball is played against another player, not against a series of targets. How do we deal with this?

We could have two people play against each other and then measure each component of the game during play. What's the problem here? It is very possible that the opponent will influence the measurement. Doesn't everybody look more skilled against a weaker opponent? This turns out to be the problem with many sport skills tests. The face validity of the target-based test is questionable, because it doesn't look much like a real racquetball game.

A partial solution to the problem of involving other players is to use machines. You are probably familiar with mechanical shooters like pitching machines, tennis serving machines, and skeet and trap throwers. Machines offer the advantage of greater consistency than most humans can attain. Machines also present the *disadvantage* of greater consistency than most humans can attain. That is, we don't play sports against highly consistent machines, but against humans who often adopt variety as one of the strategies for beating us. Nevertheless, when machines are available and practical, they can often be put to good use.

The only other practical approach is to evaluate all players against the same (non-fatigued) opponent. For example, a teacher might try to play against each student to provide a "consistent" opponent. This requires that the students not only hit a target, but also do so in a manner that is difficult to return, which is the objective. We must also consider "process" and "product" measurements. The distinction is parallel to formative and summative evaluation. In process measurement, we are collecting data on how well someone has performed the fundamentals that will ultimately lead to good performance. In product measurement, we are collecting data on the outcome—that is, what was "produced." Ultimately, we are hoping for a good product, but often the best way to achieve this is by focusing first on the process.

Measuring Communicative Movement

Communicative movement is movement at its highest level. Evaluation at this level requires a very sophisticated approach. Individuals who are evaluating dancers, gymnasts, or skaters require an expert level of knowledge of the sport.

Evaluations of communicative movement tend to be summative, but they certainly may be formative in coaching contexts. They are most often norm-referenced. Over the years of sport competition, the norms are constantly raised so that better performance is required for the same scores. In gymnastics, for example, when some gymnasts begin to score the maximum of ten, the standards are raised to keep the scores meaningful (if many athletes score the maximum, the ability to discriminate among competitors is lost). Gymnasts must now perform better and at a higher level of difficulty than their counterparts from 40 years ago, to achieve the same score.

Issues in Measuring Human Performance

Measurements of human performance, like all measurements, must be valid—they should measure what we intend to measure, with an acceptable degree of error. Human performance measurements also encounter some specific challenges, including variables that may interfere with the measurement, the learning effect, and cheating. This section covers all these topics, plus a few more aspects of human performance testing—the use of test batteries, over-testing, misleading testing, ways to resolve deficiencies in a test, discrimination in tests, and nonteaching applications.

Variables That May Interfere with Measurement: Body Fatness

An individual's body fatness sometimes affects their sports skill performance. That is, two athletes may have the same level of skill, but the one with higher fatness will achieve lower scores simply because of the fatness. Skills that require lifting, moving, accelerating, and changing directions of the body are more difficult for people who have more body fat. In fitness tests, body fatness may have a large enough impact to result in misinterpretation.

In fact, a person who is large, even if he or she is not fat, is penalized in weight-supported tests. This is because as a person gets larger, body mass goes up faster than muscle cross-sectional area. The mass of a person is proportional to volume, which is expressed in cubic meters (m^3). The muscle that moves this mass increases its cross-sectional area as a squared meter (m^2). Obviously cubing a number (raising it to the third power) makes it go up faster than merely squaring it (raised to the second power).

Experience

Experience should enable test takers to perform better and score better. Those who have taken a particular test several times may learn how to achieve a higher score. This is referred to as a **learning effect**. The learning effect can give an unfair advantage. However, the learning curve usually plateaus fairly quickly, so one way to negate it is to allow all test takers to become familiar with the test before they take the test for score. The more complex the test item, the more important the learning effect and the more time necessary to allow test takers to become familiar with the task.

It may not always be practical to allow test takers to become familiar with the test. In these cases, it is important to recognize that the learning effect will reduce the validity of the test.

Cheating

Cheating adversely affects the validity of motor skills testing. "Cheating" includes both deliberately skirting the rules and unintentionally failing to follow details of the test precisely (strictly, this is simply carelessness, not cheating). For example, if a long-jump test specifies that the subject not swing the arms, but when the test administrator looks away the person swings his arms, the measurement will have increased error. The best approach to this problem is to design or modify test items to minimize cheating. By studying the test or test battery, we can detect the areas most subject to both kinds of cheating.

Using Test Batteries

Skill tests frequently involve test batteries. Test batteries for skills are like test batteries for fitness. A skills test battery for racquetball, for example, would include a variety of types of serves, forehand and backhand strokes, a variety of types of shooting, a variety of types of returns, and perhaps some evaluations of tactics. A single test would not give a complete picture of the individual's skills. Devising a test battery for motor skills requires a balance between practicality and good measurement technique. Generally, the best measurements are very difficult and time consuming. In most cases we have to compromise and settle for less valid, objective, and reliable measurements for the sake of practicality.

Resolving Deficiencies

The purpose of a skills test, in part, is to reveal deficiencies in the test takers, but it is possible for the testing process to reveal the skills test to be deficient. In fact, the evaluation of the test itself should be an ongoing part of the testing process. Following are some good questions to ask during and after test administration:

1   What worked, and what didn't work? Was the test practical? What could make it more so? Does it have content and construct validity?
2   What could be done to enhance the test's validity, reliability, and objectivity? Would changes to the rules make it more valid and objective? What do we need to clarify in order to enhance the test's validity, reliability, and objectivity?
3   How could the test be modified to make it more practical?

4   What can be changed to speed the test?
5   What can be done to simplify test administration?
6   What can be cut from the test without reducing its validity and reliability? Lengthening a test generally increases its reliability, but redundancy makes the test longer. Is the test length appropriate, in terms of validity and practicality?
7   Are there any objectivity issues? What might be misunderstood or misapplied?

Keep in mind that if you change the test to correct problems, you will probably not be able to use the original norms. On the other hand, if the modified test is much more useful, then changing the test is probably a good idea. View every administration of the test as an opportunity to critique and improve it.

Discrimination in Skills Tests

A useful motor skills test must be able to discriminate among skill levels. As stated earlier, when we cannot differentiate among people's abilities in measurement, it is called lack of discrimination. Highly skilled players should do well on the test, and novices should do worse. Tests that fail to discriminate among skill levels are virtually worthless—there is no sense in giving a test that does not yield useful information about individuals' performances.

Administration of Psychomotor Skills Tests

Administering psychomotor tests can be very challenging, in terms of preparation, organization, supervision, and scoring. Typically, one of the greatest challenges is to provide the time required for these tests. Sports skill testing often involves test batteries, in which each subject must take multiple tests. These can take considerable time. One solution to the time requirements of skills tests is to set up multiple test stations.

Planning for Psychomotor Skills Tests

Valid, safe, and efficient motor skills testing requires considerable preparation. Safety is always paramount, so we must anticipate dangers and screen test takers to make sure that no one is placed at unacceptable risk. We must also ensure that sufficient equipment is available. If targets must be marked, they should be done so accurately, clearly, and well in advance of testing. Scoring sheets, if needed, must be developed, tested, modified, and reproduced. Individuals who will assist in the testing should be trained well in exactly how to administer their portion of the test battery.

Despite thorough preparations, things may still go wrong. As long as we learn from mistakes, we can take comfort that at least we are progressing. Recording a few notes each time you give a test will prove valuable the next time you give it.

Concluding Thoughts

The administration of psychomotor skills tests is one of the most challenging aspects of measurement and evaluation. Validity is difficult to assure, scoring is often complicated, and many factors can interfere with accurate measurement. In the next chapter I'll discuss some practical alternative approaches to skills testing.

Application Questions

1   What do taxonomies have to do with measurement?
2   Outline some of the key aspects of Harrow's taxonomy for psychomotor performance.
3   What are some factors that could reduce the validity of performance tests? How can these threats to validity be eliminated or reduced?
4   What are some common mistakes made in using motor skills tests?
5   Describe the steps in developing a motor skills test.
6   What are some of the key issues in planning the administration of a motor skills test?

References

Barry, L., Johnson, B. L., and Nelson, J. K. *Practical Measurements for Evaluation in Physical Education*. Minneapolis, MN: Burgess Publishing, 1986.

Harrow, A. J. *A Taxonomy of the Psychomotor Domain: A Guide for Developing Behavioral Objectives*. New York: David McKay, 1972.

24 Measuring Skills with Rubrics

Abstract

Many measurements of sports and psychomotor skills are best done with rubrics. Rubrics can be holistic or primary trait rubrics, depending on the circumstances. Good rubrics are helpful in increasing the objectivity and reliability of measures of complex skills. Skillfully selecting and training judges who will use these rubrics will enhance the validity of the measurements by improving objectivity.

Keywords: holistic rubric, primary trait rubric

Rubrics

A **rubric** is a ranked set of descriptors that specifies the components of a skill. Rubrics may be used to measure skills at various levels of the psychomotor taxonomy, from skilled movement to communicative movement.

The highest level of the rubric describes the desired level of performance. For many motor skills, this upper end should be high enough that it will not be commonly attained. For normative evaluations, if the desired level of performance is too commonly attained, the rubric will not discriminate between very good and extremely good performers. On the other hand, if it is a criterion measure, we may hope that most test takers will attain this level. At the low end of the rubric, the descriptor should adequately describe the lowest level of performance imaginable. The rubric scale should encompass every performance we might ever view. If it does not, the rubric will not provide a good assessment.

A rubric should include all of the key criteria. If a performance has several components, the instructor or evaluator may write a single scoring rubric that covers all the parts (a **holistic rubric**) or, alternatively, they might compose several rubrics that cover each part (a **primary trait rubric**). Both types have advantages and disadvantages. A holistic rubric is simpler to handle and faster to use than a primary trait rubric. For dealing with large groups of performers, it is probably the more practical approach. For example, a holistic rubric for basketball play might be a single large rubric that provides one global score for the skills demonstrated during an observation. In contrast, primary trait rubrics would separate basketball offense from basketball defense. Within offense, there may be several primary trait rubrics for shooting, since there are several different types of shots. There may be a primary trait rubric for free throws. There may also be a ball-handling rubric, or separate rubrics for passing, dribbling, and positioning on the court. Breaking down the rubric into primary trait parts takes a lot more time and effort, but, if carefully accomplished, should yield a rubric with greater reliability and objectivity than a holistic rubric. We would expect these characteristics to be at least slightly superior for a primary trait rubric, because the skill is broken down into smaller parts and this gives more emphasis to process as opposed to product evaluation. Multiple careful measurements typically yield higher reliability than a single measurement.

An Example of the Development and Application of a Rubric

To illustrate the development and employment of a rubric in a real situation, let's consider the example of cheerleader selection. Cheerleader selection is an interesting example, partly because cheerleader disputes can be very emotional and are, therefore, to be avoided when possible. What can we do to ensure a valid, reliable, and objective assessment system for cheerleading abilities? What basic principles of good measurement can we use? We will begin with the basic principles of measurement.

Defining what will be measured. As with any assessment, we should start with a definition of what we want to measure. It is not enough to say "cheerleading"—we need to be more detailed. To define high-quality cheerleading, we might sit down with a few knowledgeable colleagues. Once we define the skill, we might do further research in order to create a list of skills a cheerleader should possess. We might come up with a list such as the one shown in Table 24.1.

Once we are satisfied with the list of skills, we can move to the next step: establishing levels and writing the rubric.

Establishing levels and writing the rubric. The best place to start developing a rubric is at the top level. Opinions vary as to how to structure the top level of the rubric. One approach is to write the ideal or optimal criteria, so that very few of the performers

Table 24.1 List of skills defining the quality of cheerleading

---

1   Athletic skills, including agility, balance, and tumbling skills.
2   "Dance-like" skills, including rhythm, grace, and poise.
3   Skill in communicating enthusiasm and conveying charisma.
4   Voice and projection.
5   Stage presence.
6   Originality/creativity.
7   Ability to perform classic cheer types:

    a   Individual cheers
    b   Group cheers
    c   Tumbling/gymnastics types.

8   Academic qualifications (it is extracurricular).

---

will reach this level. This approach helps us differentiate among very good performers and is useful when the level of performance is extremely high. It sets a very high standard that may encourage some individuals to work hard, but it also might discourage others. Perhaps a more reasonable approach is to write the rubric's top level in such a way that top performers will be challenged but will clearly be able to attain this score. This approach is probably better when the skill level is highly variable among the performers.

Most rubrics have four to six levels. As you move down the rubric, each level is easier to achieve than the one above it, since the standards become progressively less demanding. Perhaps the most crucial level is that of *minimal competence*. The instructor, evaluator, or teacher must decide what the minimal level of performance will be and set up the scoring system so that this minimal level is included. As far as possible, the levels of the rubric should be evenly distributed and gradually change from the highest to the lowest level.

Rubrics for cheerleading are available on the Internet, such as:

www.albertacheerleading.ca/score-sheets-rubrics/

www.sectionxi.org/v2/sports/2016-17%20Cheerleading%20Rubric%20&%20 Scoring%20Guidelines.pdf

www.rcampus.com/rubricshowc.cfm?code=X3CCX8&sp=yes&

http://championcheercentral.com/cheer-competition-score-sheets/

Weighting rubrics. Obviously, some skills and qualities of cheerleaders are more important than others. Hence, in addition to rubrics for each quality to be assessed, we need a weighting system to reflect the importance of each quality. One way to do this is to use a 100-point scale and set up the rubrics to reflect the weightings. If we settle on five selection criteria, they will have to add up to 100 points, but each will have a different number of points because not all categories are equal. For example, suppose we chose the following five qualities for selecting cheerleaders:

1   Athletic skills, including agility, balance, and tumbling skills.
2   "Dance-like" skills, including rhythm, grace, and poise.
3   Skill in communicating enthusiasm and conveying charisma and stage presence.
4   Voice and projection.

5   Ability to perform classic cheer types:

    a   Individual cheers
    b   Group cheers
    c   Tumbling/gymnastics types.

Let's assume category 5 is most important and should be weighted most heavily. For this category, then, we might set the top rubric rank at 40. Now let's assume category 3 is least important. We assign it a top score of 5, meaning it is only one-eighth as important as category 5. We continue this weighting with each category until we have distributed all 100 points. During this process, we may decide that 40 is too much for category 5 and drop it to 30 points. We then will need to adjust the other scores so the total is 100. Of course, there is nothing magic about 100 points; if we wind up with 120 or 130 points, that is fine. The advantage to 100-point scales is that we are used to dealing with 100 points in course grades, and it is easy to convert to percentages—a score of 33 is easily conceived as 33 percent or one-third of the total. When a student scores 90, or 50, she has a good idea of how well she did.

Scoring. Now we need to decide on a scoring system. With a holistic rubric, the rubric score may comprise the entire performance score. With a series of primary trait rubrics, we will need to decide how to combine the rubrics' scores. To do this, we can either build a weighting system into the rubric itself or use multipliers.

Building a weighted scoring system into the rubric would mean setting up a different scoring system for each skill or quality, so that the more important skills or qualities contribute more points to the overall total and the less important qualities or skills contribute less. For example, one skill or quality might be scored on a scale of 0 to 40 and another on a scale of 0 to 20. The first would be weighted twice as much as the second.

The alternative is to give each skill or quality the same scale, say from 0 to 10, and simply assign a multiplier to each rubric depending on how important it is relative to the others. For example, if we think that "Athletic skills" should be twice as important as "Enthusiasm," then we could assign "Athletic Skills" a multiplier of 10 and "Enthusiasm" a multiplier of 5. We would apply the multipliers to each rubric and add them up for the final score. To convert the final score to a percentage, we simply divide the final score by the highest possible final score and multiply by 100. Here's an example of using multipliers:

1   Athletic skills, including agility, balance, and tumbling skills (multiplier: 10).
2   "Dance-like" skills, including rhythm, grace, and poise (multiplier: 5).
3   Communicating enthusiasm and conveying charisma (multiplier: 5).
4   Voice and projection (multiplier: 9).
5   Creativity/originality (multiplier: 4).
6   Ability to perform classic cheer types (multiplier: 10):

    a   Individual cheers
    b   Group cheers
    c   Tumbling/gymnastics types.

7   Academic qualifications (multiplier: 8).

Each category will be scored on a 0 (lowest) to 5 (highest) basis.

If a cheerleading candidate scored 4 on each of the seven primary trait rubrics, then the score would be:

$$(4 * 10) + (4 * 5) + (4 * 5) + (4 * 9) + (4 * 4) + (4 * 10) + (4 * 8) = 204$$

After all of this work, now we must ask the most important question: does the scoring plan seem to give a valid outcome? Don't forget—the goal is to produce a valid, reliable, and objective assessment.

24.1   Practical Exercise

You have already acquired the skills to assess the measurement qualities of validity, reliability, and objectivity. How would you construct an evaluation for the cheerleading rubric? Use the skills you learned in Chapter 4 for evaluating validity and in Chapter 5 for evaluating reliability and objectivity to devise an evaluation of the scoring system.

Creating the judging form. With the rubrics and scoring system established, we are ready to draw up the judging form. This form should help the judges or evaluators provide valid, objective, and reliable scoring. It should yield a written record showing how all judges used the rubrics to determine the scores. And, the score sheets may be used to evaluate the objectivity of the judges, by showing the level of agreement among them.

Selecting judges. To administer the cheerleading rubric, we will need to select a panel of judges. For valid, reliable, and objective measures, we need to select judges carefully. What qualifications would we look for in cheerleader judges? We might seek some of the following qualifications:

- Judges must be out of high school for at least three years or have been recommended by their high school cheer coach at another (non-rival) school. This is to ensure judges are experienced and unlikely to be friendly with anyone who is trying out.
- Judges must be currently unaffiliated with anyone participating in the tryouts they are judging. This is to maximize objectivity (by minimizing bias).

Cheerleader scoring sheets are available on the websites listed earlier.

- Judges must have experience as cheerleading coaches, squad members, or camp instructors and must have completed the judges' workshop. This requirement would help to ensure that the judge has training in cheerleading and cheerleader judging and to maximize validity, reliability, and objectivity.
- There must be an odd number of judges, preferably five. Odd numbers of judges cut down the likelihood of tie votes. Since rubrics yield scores rather than just yes/no votes, the likelihood of a tie should be small, anyway. Using five judges rather than three should increase reliability, just as multiple measurements usually improve measurement reliability.

- If possible, all judges should be from a school district outside that of the school being judged. This helps maximize objectivity.
- All minority and ethnic groups represented in the school should be represented in the judging panel, if at all possible. This helps maximize objectivity.

Note that many of these guidelines are aimed at maximizing objectivity. Why do you think that this is important? The answer is that judging qualities such as poise, stage presence, creativity/originality, and enthusiasm is inherently subjective. This raises the suspicion that the judging may be arbitrary, with judges simply choosing the contestants they "like" without regard to the contestants' qualifications. Perceptions are important, so in measurement situations where subjectivity is suspected, good measurement requires extra effort. In these situations, we must do all we can to instill confidence in the evaluation program and offer measurements that are as valid and objective as possible.

Application Questions

1   Describe the key factors in selecting judges for subjective situations such as selecting a school's dance line.
2   Describe the basic steps in developing a rubric.

Additional Practical Exercises

24.2   Practical Exercise

Find a skills test and administer it to some of your classmates (remember: safety first!). How good a test is it? How could it be improved?

24.3   Practical Exercise

Devise a sports skills test of your own. Write out a set of detailed instructions. Devise a scoring system. Give the test to some of your classmates. Have them evaluate the test for validity and point out any potential objectivity or reliability problems.

Alternative: Devise an athletic training skills test of your own. Write out a set of detailed instructions. Devise a scoring system. Give the test to some of your classmates. Have them evaluate the test for validity and point out any potential objectivity or reliability problems.

Alternative: Devise a health skills test (e.g., measuring heart rate or blood pressure, or performing the Heimlich maneuver or CPR) of your own. Write out a set of detailed instructions. Devise a scoring system. Give the test to some of your classmates. Have them evaluate the test for validity and point out any potential objectivity or reliability problems.

24.4 Practical Exercise

You have been asked to be head judge of a high school cheerleading contest. Draw up a judge's form that provides for the most valid, objective, and reliable judging of such an event. Be sure that the instructions you provide are clear.

25 Measuring in Sports and Coaching

Abstract

For fair competition, valid, reliable, and objective measurement is essential. Changes in sport sometimes present new measurement challenges, and technology in sport can improve measurement. Coaching and athletic training all require good measurement. Athlete recruiting at the college and professional levels is based on measurements, which are sometimes restricted. Research is needed to improve measurements in all aspects of sport and therapy.

Keywords: formative and summative evaluation, qualitative and quantitative measurement

Sport presents us some of the biggest challenges in measurement and evaluation. For example, sport umpires and officials have to make precise measurements and evaluations quickly and in front of thousands of critics. It is not surprising that sport officials make mistakes. In fact, it is amazing that their measurements are nearly correct (valid) as often as they are.

Measurement Challenges in Competitive Sport

Competitive sport presents some measurement challenges that are not common in other situations. These include training for officiating, discarding scores, the complexity of rules, and changes to the structure of competition.

Rules

Measurement challenges occur when the rules for a sport change. Basketball rule changes, for instance, have brought a new dimension to measurement in that sport. In NCAA basketball, for example, the three-point rule for the 2008–2009 season specified that three-point field goals be from beyond 20 feet 9 inches for men and 19 feet 9 inches for women. This rule has both made the game more exciting and increased the demands on officials. Exactly where the athlete was at the start of the shot determines whether the basket counts two or three points, which can impact the outcome.

This rule change represents a challenge for coaches as well as for officials. The three-pointer is worth more, but the success rate is lower. What's the trade-off? This measurement and evaluation decision is complicated by who shoots well on the team and what type of defense the other team is playing.

Changes to the Structure of Competitions

Sometimes the structure of a competition changes because of pressure by the public, advertisers, or the media, and this change affects the measurements in the sport. For example, one-day cricket matches were developed in response to such pressures. Traditional cricket matches, which went on for days, did not necessarily appeal to modern audiences. Similarly, soccer has adopted the tie-breaker shootout, in part because today's audiences want a clear winner in competitions.

25.1   Practical Exercise

In small groups, identify some measurement issues in sports not already mentioned in the text. What solutions would you recommend to address these issues?

Measuring in Coaching

The measurement challenges of coaching may be more complex than they first appear. In most coaching situations, the objective is to select the best team possible to compete against each opponent and to adjust the playing strategy and the players in order to maximize the team's advantages while minimizing the opponent's advantages. In some cases, however, coaches have the objectives of exposing a lot of people to sport participation and teaching them to enjoy the game regardless of the outcome.

Teachers of physical and motor skills, athletic trainers, and physical therapists also engage in a form of coaching. Teachers don't have to select teams, but they do have to assess and motivate their students. Trainers and therapists must evaluate the extent of injuries, pain levels, and functional capabilities in order to give injured athletes exercise and other therapeutic prescriptions. In many cases, patients must be taught to perform exercises or other therapy. Therapists often have to motivate players to complete uncomfortable rehabilitation regimens, and they must measure frequently to evaluate the efficacy of treatment and progress.

When coaches choose the players to compose the best team, they are using evaluation, the highest level of cognitive function. They must use good measurement technique to inform that evaluation. Strength, speed, endurance, agility, experience, and sport-specific skills can all be measured, and all influence an athlete's ability to succeed. Many good coaches take these measurements, but those who understand measurement and evaluation can do so more effectively than those who don't.

Coaching provides a good illustration of formative and summative evaluation. When coaches measure and evaluate players during practice and during games, this is formative evaluation. Coaches may film their football, soccer, or track teams during practice with the express purpose of correcting flaws, improving techniques and performance, and evaluating abilities. Ultimately, coaches have to make summative evaluations to pick the starters or, at the end of the year, to select award recipients.

For coaches, measuring involves both quantitative measures—of scoring, strength, fitness, general performance, and skill ability—and qualitative assessments—of coachability, leadership, and determination. Not only must these factors be assessed, they must also be evaluated and integrated to achieve success.

Measuring Recruits in Professional Sport

Professional sports organizations, such as those for baseball, basketball, soccer, and American football, are very interested in measuring potential players. For example, the National Football League (NFL) draft represents a major investment in their employees. Consequently, the NFL invests a lot of time and effort in examining every aspect of each of its potential "investments." Typically, following the NFL combine (an invited "tryout" used to determine which players to draft), scouts will visit those college football programs which have good prospective players who may be drafted. These evaluations are typically less extensive than those done at the combine. Each team's scouts individually record the performance scores for each player of potential interest to them. Most NFL teams employ eight to ten full-time scouts.

After these tests are completed, scouts are free to put prospects through any additional testing they want the prospect to perform. Scouts are interested in position skills and may have quarterbacks throw, receivers run patterns, and defenders backpedal to assess specific skills.

Measuring Recruits in College Sport

At the college level, measurement and testing of prospective athletes is more restricted than at the professional level. For example, NCAA rules for collegiate football recruiting are restrictive as to the number of coaches who may visit prospects at one time.

College coaches are not allowed to test prospects as the NFL coaches or scouts do. College coaches instead rely on analysis of films and reports by trusted high school coaches. If high school players attend a football summer camp at a university, they may be tested in that context.

College recruiters also have to consider factors not related to athletic performance, such as the prospect's academic performance, attitude, and cooperation (coachability). These qualities are most often evaluated by contact with principals, coaches, teachers, and counselors.

25.2   Practical Exercise

Suppose you are a college coach recruiting for any sport of your choice. What key qualities—physical, emotional, and cognitive—would you seek in players? List these. How would you evaluate each quality in prospects? Keep in mind that the NCAA restricts you from making direct measurements.

Measuring in Athletic Training

The evaluations that trainers make can impact an athlete's long-term health. For example, if the trainer misses the diagnosis of a concussion, the mistake could result in a brain injury. Injury assessment, rehabilitation prescription, and progress evaluation are all challenges for the athletic trainer. Since most injury assessments must be done with very little diagnostic information, trainers must learn to make measurements quickly and accurately and know which measurements are most helpful. Many times, these measurements are more qualitative than quantitative, but in either case they must be valid measurements to ensure the athlete's safety and health.

After making an accurate injury assessment, the trainer must design a therapeutic regimen that will return the athlete quickly to health. Technology offers new treatment modalities, which means trainers have lots of evaluations to make. Currently, some athletic training and physical therapy decisions tend to be made based on tradition rather than available research data. You may find opportunities to develop techniques for measuring rehabilitation progress and design comparative measurements that will help athletic trainers optimize their work. The challenges are great, but good quality measurements are foundational to progress.

Assessing Hydration Status

One of the greatest challenges to trainers is assessing athletes' hydration status. Since dehydration contributes to heat injury and possibly muscle cramps, knowing an athlete's state of hydration can be crucial in protecting athletes and promoting performance. Currently, the only practical method for estimating hydration status is to observe a rapid change in total body weight. This is a crude measure, since water in the stomach or bladder contributes to body weight, although water in these locations does not immediately contribute to the hydration of the muscle cells.

Application Questions

1 What are some rule changes in sports that resulted from measurement issues?
2 What are some rule changes in sports designed to improve athlete safety?
3 What are some key measurement issues in athletic training or physical therapy?
4 Give examples of how measurement errors in athletic training might put an athlete's life at risk.
5 List three examples of measurement challenges in sports not mentioned in the text.
6 What are the key components of measuring the environment on a hot day?
7 If a coach is using multiple practice fields, why should Wet Bulb Globe Temperature (WBGT) or other environmental measurements be made on each practice field?
8 Give some examples of how technology has affected coaching and officiating in various sports.
9 How would you go about equating the three events in a triathlon (swimming, cycling, and running)?
10 Why does officiating sports present special measurement challenges?

Additional Practical Exercises

25.3 Practical Exercise

Call or visit an athletic trainer. What measurements does she or he routinely make? How does the trainer measure and evaluate potential environmental heat stress? How does he or she measure and evaluate athletes' hydration status?

25.4 Practical Exercise

Call or visit an athletic coach of a sport of interest to you. What measurements does she or he routinely make? How do these measurements influence his or her coaching?

26 Alternative Approaches to Measurement and Subjective Measurement

Abstract

Validly measuring performance in complex skills such as teaching and some sports requires special approaches. Authentic assessment seeks to measure in ecologically valid ways. Rubrics also find application here. Systematic observation is useful in several measurement situations.

Keywords: authentic assessment, rubrics, systematic observation, interviews

Many physical educators use scores on traditional tests of physical fitness, sports skills, and knowledge as a basis for giving grades. These tests usually have acceptable validity, objectivity, and reliability, and for many of them, norms or other standards are available—hence, they appear to provide a solid basis for grading. However, it is important to recognize that not everything that is worthwhile can be quantified, and not everything that can be quantified is worthwhile. Many important aspects of life and work cannot be reduced to a number. Many of the things we need to measure and evaluate don't lend themselves to measurement in minutes, or meters, or kilograms. Plus, the typical traditional test environment often lacks ecological validity, that is, it doesn't resemble the real world. For example, tennis skills test items seldom replicate actual match play. For these reasons, several alternative assessment methods have proved useful in teaching, coaching, athletic training, and physical therapy.

Alternative assessment usually involves such instruments as rubrics, questionnaires, rating scales, and portfolios and involves such techniques as systematic observation and interviews. Except for the necessity of achieving certifications and similar requirements, such as licensing exams (e.g., for athletic trainers, physical therapists, and NCAA strength and conditioning coaches), most of the skills that are important in the working world relate to what we can do rather than how we can score on a test. Alternative assessment, therefore, attempts to be more creative in identifying the skills actually used in task performance and evaluating those skills in a variety of ways.

The focus of alternative assessment is on an individual's product or quality of performance. Alternative assessments tend to use formative evaluation (evaluation designed to improve performance) and criterion-referenced scoring (scoring tied to a specific level of performance and independent of what others may do), and they tend to assess higher levels of learning or performing (i.e., the higher skill levels) compared to traditional evaluation based on testing. In many cases, students may be involved in developing the assessment and the final evaluative product. Alternative assessments may be used to assess the affective domain (attitudes, emotions, and feelings) as well as the physical domain.

Authentic Assessment

One complaint regarding many measurements is that they lack ecological validity. That is, the measurement situation is so unlike the real situation that the measurement lacks strong content and ecological validity. A tennis skills test battery that requires only that the test taker hit artificial targets on the court doesn't "look" at all like tennis and does not necessarily reflect the skills actually necessary to play tennis well. For example, the test may require students to hit forehand volleys against a wall marked with targets, and the closer to the target center, the higher the score. The problem with such a test is that it has very little to do with actually playing the game of tennis (it lacks ecological validity)—which requires one to hit the ball hard, with spin, and to some place where the opponent isn't.

Authentic assessments are when the skill, performance, or task evaluations are conducted in realistic environments that people actually face in real life. That is, an authentic assessment is conducted with ecological validity.

The basis for authentic assessment is that for many sports skills, observations can be made while students or athletes are actually playing the game. These observations may then be handled in a manner to provide a valid, reliable, and objective assessment. Such assessments are more "authentic" because they are ecologically relevant, in that they are done within the context of game play. It is usually just as important to know *when* to use a particular sport skill as it is to know *how* to do that skill, and authentic assessments attempt to measure both.

An advantage of authentic assessment is that it gives the students more time in a realistic environment. The process may be somewhat laborious for the assessor, but, with practice, it becomes more efficient. One disadvantage, however, is that some students will inevitably feel that the assessment was not accurate. On the other hand, this is a common complaint for many types of assessment.

Authentic assessment may be used for both formative and summative evaluations. To review, formative assessment is ongoing assessment, primarily for the purpose of identifying problems, weaknesses, and opportunities for improvement, in order to provide feedback to students and teachers. In contrast, summative assessment is typically done at the end of a unit or semester, primarily to assess achievement and often to determine a final grade. Technique and progress, as well as outcomes, may be assessed through authentic techniques. That is, authentic assessment techniques can both target how a sport skill is done and assess the outcome of the skill. For example, you can assess how a student executes a volleyball spike, and you can also assess where the ball went with respect to the defenders.

Although the term "authentic assessment" is most commonly used in education, you should not think of authentic assessment as limited to the assessment of students' sport and fitness skills. It is also appropriate for evaluating employees in the workplace and clients in a health club. With regard to athletic training or physical therapy, authentic assessment is probably most applicable in training athletic trainers and therapists to perform new-patient evaluation and therapeutic skills. For example, athletic trainers or physical therapists might be asked to perform actual evaluations on "simulated" patients who have a scripted set of symptoms and responses. To assess the students authentically, we would evaluate them in the context of a real clinical setting, as if these were real patients.

Alternative Assessment Instruments

Rubrics

Previously we discussed the use of rubrics to measure the performance of athletes at various levels of the psychomotor taxonomy, including the communicative skill level, but they can also be used to measure student performance in educational settings. Rubrics used in educational settings are normally written by the instructor or teacher and shared with students as the evaluation scheme is explained, but to some extent students can participate in the development of the rubric and evaluation scheme. Even when students do not help with development of the rubric, they can be given the evaluation criteria very early. Knowing the criteria will help them improve their own performances, and the ability to judge their own work empowers them to decide how well they choose to perform.

Teachers can also use rubrics for student self- and peer assessment. In self-assessment, students are given the rubrics to use in evaluating themselves. Based on their own assessment, they can work on their weakest skills. Alternatively, peers can evaluate each other to guide their own and their peers' skill development. It's helpful to make the rubrics available to all students in advance of the actual assessment so that they can evaluate themselves and their peers in preparation, and so they know the expectations of the teacher. For the "official" assessment, students may be required to evaluate one another, while the teacher evaluates the evaluator. Evaluating others is the highest form of cognition, requiring a high level of knowledge, comprehension, application, analysis, and synthesis on the part of the student.

Common Errors in the Use of Rubrics

A few specific errors arise frequently in the use of rubrics. One is called the "**halo effect.**" The halo effect occurs when prior information biases an observer positively or negatively. For example, if a student usually demonstrates good skills and is also cooperative, friendly, and supportive, the rater will have a natural inclination to rate that student erroneously high. By the same token, if a student typically performs poorly and is uncooperative or otherwise unpleasant, the rater may unintentionally penalize that student with an erroneously low score—even though the student may have performed well during that particular assessment.

Error may also arise from the fact that raters tend to be reluctant to use a rubric's full rating scale. That is, most raters seldom use the extremely high and extremely low scores. This tends to compress the rating scale—for example, turning a five-item scale into, in practice, a three-item scale, with the top and bottom scores almost never used.

The best practical solution, in most measurement situations, is to be acutely aware of the potential for these errors and be on guard against them. In some cases, definite steps can be taken. For example, a "guest rater" who is not familiar with the performers helps eliminate the halo effect.

Alternative Assessment Techniques

In authentic assessment, the techniques of systematic observation and interviewing are frequently used. This section discusses these techniques and provides sample forms for data gathering.

Systematic Observation

The technique of systematic observation has been used extensively in research on teaching and is also applicable in everyday measurement situations. **Systematic observation** is the process of first identifying behaviors of primary interest and then recording the presence or absence or the time engaged in those particular activities. Considerable effort is devoted to developing scoring sheets for a particular set of behaviors, which guide the observations. For example, Table 26.1 is a coding sheet developed and used by my colleague Dr. Matthew Curtner-Smith.

This sheet was developed for a systematic observation aimed at determining the proportion of physical education classes devoted to ego- versus task-orientation. In this coding sheet, the definitions and descriptions of the two classifications are first given. Then the class is broken down into parts, with each of six elements listed. These six elements are classified as task oriented, ego oriented, or neutral (neither task nor ego oriented).

In this systematic observation, interobserver objectivity was evaluated by requiring the two coders to code independently ten videotaped physical education lessons. These codings were compared to a third reviewer's codings of the same lessons. Objectivity percentages of agreement between raters varied from 85 percent to 100 percent. To check for intra-observer (within the rater) reliability, two coders re-coded one lesson

Table 26.1 Coding sheet for the Physical Education Climate Assessment Instrument

Subject: Hockey	Class: 6th grade	Teacher: B
Start: 8:00	Stop: 8.30	Time: 30 min.

Here are definitions of the elements coded by the Physical Education Climate Assessment Instrument. A strong ego-involving motivational climate is produced during a physical education lesson or sports practice under the conditions described under "Ego-Involving" below, whereas a strong task-involving climate occurs under the conditions described under "Task-Involving."

Definitions of Coding Elements

Alterable Element	Ego-Involving	Task-Involving
Task	All pupils attempt the same task. Goals for the task are determined by the instructor.	Pupils choose to attempt different tasks. They are permitted to set their own goals.
Authority	The instructor makes all decisions about what pupils will learn, sets up all equipment, and carries out all pupil evaluations.	Pupils choose what they will attempt to learn, are given the opportunity to set up their own equipment, and are encouraged to evaluate their own performances.
Rewards	Recognition of pupils' accomplishments is made public, and rewards are given for superior performances.	Recognition of pupils' accomplishments is kept private, and rewards are given for improvement,
Grouping tasks	An entire class or squad works on one task, or pupils are grouped according to their ability.	Pupils work individually or in small cooperative groups. Grouping is flexible and heterogeneous.
Evaluation	Evaluation is norm-referenced or rank-ordered and public. Progress is judged on the basis of whole group objectives and level of performance.	Evaluation is self-referenced and private. Progress is judged on the basis of individual objectives, participation, effort, and improvement,
Time	The instructor gives strict time limits for all pupils to complete tasks and establishes timelines for improvement.	Time limits for task completion are flexible. Pupils help to schedule timelines for improvement.

(continued)

Table 26.1 (continued)

Task #1 Task Description: *Warm–up*

Alterable Element	Task	Ego	Neutral
Task	X		
Authority			X
Rewards		X	
Grouping		X	
Evaluation		X	
Time		X	

Task #2 Task Description: *Dribbling practice*

Alterable Element	Task	Ego	Neutral
Task		X	
Authority		X	
Rewards		X	
Grouping		X	
Evaluation		X	
Time	X		

Task #3 Task Description: *2 V 2 game*

Alterable Element	Task	Ego	Neutral
Task		X	
Authority	X		
Rewards	X		
Grouping		X	
Evaluation		X	
Time		X	

Task #4 Task Description: *Passing to partner*

Alterable Element	Task	Ego	Neutral
Task	X		
Authority	X		
Rewards		X	
Grouping		X	
Evaluation		X	
Time	X		

Task #5 Task Description: *Warm-down*

Alterable Element	Task	Ego	Neutral
Task	X		
Authority	X		
Rewards		X	
Grouping		X	
Evaluation		X	
Time		X	

15 days after the previous comparison. The two codings for each coder yielded reliability percentages of agreement between test and retest of 95 percent and 100 percent.

Table 26.2 shows an example of a summary sheet for the number of observations and the percentage of the total for each of the three categories of climate (task, neutral, or ego) for each of the six elements comprising the class (task, authority, rewards, etc.).

Table 26.3 is an assessment form, also developed by Dr. Curtner-Smith, that you can adapt for your own application, whether it be training other athletic trainers, new fitness center employees, or teachers.

Table 26.2 Summary data sheet for the Physical Education Climate Assessment Instrument

	Task		Neutral		Ego	
	Raw Score	*%*	*Raw Score*	*%*	*Raw Score*	*%*
Task	3	60	0	0	2	40
Authority	3	60	1	20	1	20
Rewards	1	20	0	0	4	80
Grouping	0	0	0	0	5	100
Evaluation	0	0	0	0	5	100
Time	2	40	0	0	3	60
Total Score	9	30	1	3	20	67

Table 26.3 Physical education intern teacher behavior assessment form

Date: Student teacher:

School: Student coder:

Time started: Time ended:

Observation length:

Definitions of behaviors:

1 _____

2 _____

3 _____

4 _____

Behavior 1	Behavior 2	Behavior 3	Behavior 4
TOTAL:	TOTAL:	TOTAL:	TOTAL:

Comments:

_____

_____

_____

_____

Interviews

You may not think of interviews as a useful measurement and evaluation technique, but interviews are a useful method of data collection, and involve many of the same principles of data collection as other types of assessment. Even when you are speaking informally with someone, you are gathering information. In interviews that you conduct for specific measurement purposes, you simply need to gather the information in a more careful and systematic manner than in casual conversation. When you are interviewing several people to learn what they think or how they feel about some issue, you will need to plan in advance what you will ask. Once you have completed the interviews, you should then review them carefully, looking for common themes or points of agreement and disagreement. Whereas we normally hope to find points of agreement, a discovery that several knowledgeable and experienced people disagree on many issues is also very helpful.

An interview is most useful when it is recorded in audio or video, to capture exactly what was said. At some point, these recordings must be converted to text for processing. This conversion is typically done by a good typist with a transcription machine. Transcription software is available, which may be useful if a lot of interviews must be transcribed. This software can be found on the Internet by searching for "speech to text."

Once the interviews are converted to text, they can be analyzed to identify major points and themes, either manually or with specialized software. These themes will help you discover the desired information.

Conducting a good interview takes knowledge and practice. Then, being able to identify the emerging themes from a collection of multiple interviews of the same people takes both skill and patience. Valid assessment based on interviews requires all the measurement skills you possess, plus training, experience, and practice. If you choose to use interviews for assessment, you will need to invest time in developing this skill.

Application Questions

1 What are some of the key characteristics of authentic assessment?
2 Describe the advantages of authentic assessment.
3 Differentiate between primary trait and holistic rubrics. What are the advantages and disadvantages of each?

Practical Exercises

26.1 Practical Exercise

Interview two people in any one of the following categories: physical education teacher, former collegiate athlete, experienced athletic trainer, health professional, fitness specialist, fitness business owner, high school coach, or college coach.

Ask five questions about these individuals' experiences. Record the key descriptors of their responses. Did they agree on each question? Why or why not? What did you learn about the category? What did you learn about the respondents?

26.2 Practical Exercise

Use the rubric you developed in Practical Exercise 13.1 or one taken from another source to evaluate a candidate for a job in your own field of interest. If necessary, modify the rubric so that it is appropriate for this task. How would you weight each item? How might use of this rubric improve the evaluation of candidates?

27 Measuring the Affective Domain

Abstract

Valid measurements of the affective domain are valuable to anyone leading or working with teams or groups. Rating scales of various types are typically used, but caution is needed in analyzing ranked data.

Keywords: rating scales, Likert scales, rating of perceived exertion, Myers-Briggs personality factors, comfort scales

Measures of affect are measures of qualities such as values, interests, and emotional responses. The affective area also includes such aspects of behavior or personality as sportsmanship, leadership, initiative, attitude, and others. Thus, anyone in leadership, whether the teacher of a class, the leader of a work group, or the coach of a team, should be concerned with affective measurement. Often, leaders desire to change their groups in a positive way—to elicit the best performance, the most effort, the most learning possible. Understanding a bit about the affective area of measurement can make you a better coach, teacher, athletic trainer, health professional, and leader. Simply recognizing that people are different from you can be an important insight in life. When we recognize that others see things differently, we are better able to coach, teach, treat, serve, and communicate.

The affective domain is difficult to measure for many reasons. Values, interest, and emotions are hard to measure, partly because they are often transient. In addition, individuals are so different from each other that the underlying constructs for some of these qualities may also vary.

Rating Scales

Rating scales, particularly Likert-type scales, are widely used for assessing subjective qualities in the affective domain, such as attitude, comfort, and preference. A **Likert scale** asks the respondent to rate items, usually on a horizontal five-point scale, with the negative or low aspect of the quality at the low end of the scale, and the positive or high aspect of the quality at the high end.

Table 27.1 is an example of a Likert-type scale.

An alternative to the Likert-type scale is a 100-mm line, set up just like a Likert scale, but instead of having to choose a discrete score (1, 2, 3, 4, 5), the person simply puts a mark on the line that represents her or his selection. To score the scale, the evaluator measures the line from the left end to the person's mark. This type of scale gives people more choice in scoring, because the line represents a continuous rather than a discrete scale. A **discrete scale** (sometimes called a semantic differential scale), which is ordinal, requires the respondent to choose a specific answer, as the Likert scale makes one choose 1, 2, 3, 4, or 5. In contrast, a **continuous scale** allows the respondent to choose any point. Table 27.2 shows how the same question as in Table 27.1 would look, expressed as a continuous scale. Likert scale measures should be treated as ordinal measurements as we pointed out in a research paper (Bishop and Herron, 2015).

Table 27.3 provides yet another example, a scale that my colleagues and I have used in research on clothing comfort during a 45-minute exercise bout.

If you use a Likert-type scale, a 100-mm line, or some variation of these, it is very important that you always design them so that *the left end is the less desirable end* and *the right end is the most desirable*. Otherwise, it can be very confusing for both the respondent and the evaluator when some items are rated from left to right and others from right to left. I've made this mistake, and learned that it can be frustrating to those completing the questions, and more so for those analyzing the data.

Table 27.1 A Likert-type numeric scale

Mark the answer that best describes your perception.
I find this Measurement and Evaluation class to be:

1	2	3	4	5
Irrelevant	*Somewhat relevant*	*Moderately relevant*	*Very relevant*	*Extremely relevant*

Table 27.2 A Likert-type 100-millimeter line scale

Mark the place on the line that best describes your perception.
I find this Measurement and Evaluation class to be:

Not relevant		Extremely relevant

Table 27.3 Clothing comfort scale

Questionnaire for ALL Work Bouts

Time POINT of measurement: _____initial _____25 min _____45 min (at end of exercise bout)

Please rate the work experience on the following characteristics. Mark the line anywhere, with the left end representing the lowest amount of that quality and the right end representing the highest amount of that quality.

Not comfortable	**OVERALL COMFORT**	*Very comfortable*

Not sticky	**STICKING TO SKIN**	*Very sticky*

Not wet	**WETNESS**	*Very wet*

Not cool	**COOLNESS**	*Very cool*

Not hot	**HOTNESS**	*Very hot*

General comments (please make any observations about the work bout and any suggestions for improvement):

_____

_____

_____

27.1   Practical Exercise

Create a relevant example of each of the following scales:

a   Likert-type scale
b   100-mm scale

Borg Rating of Perceived Exertion Scale

The Borg Rating of Perceived Exertion (RPE) Scale, or Borg Scale, has been extensively studied and proven very useful in regulating exercise intensity. It asks participants in exercise to subjectively rate their level of effort.

Myers-Briggs Personality Factors

The psychologists Katharine Cook Briggs and Isabel Briggs Myers developed an eight-part description of the human personality that is now a commonly used personality inventory (Myers et al., 1998). In this description, each individual has a "preference" in attitude (Introvert or Extravert), perceiving (Intuition or Sensing), judgment (Thinking or Feeling), and "lifestyle" (Judging or Perceiving). An individual may tend strongly to one side or the other on these elements or may be balanced between the two.

The four characteristic pairs (lifestyle, judgment, perception, and attitude) combine to result in 16 possible personality "types." I am characterized as an Extravert, Intuitive, Thinking, Judging person, with very strong Thinking characteristics. In contrast, my wife is almost the exact opposite: an Introvert, Sensing, Feeling, Perceiving person. One of our children is similar to me—an Extravert, Intuitive, Thinking, Perceiving person—except for being more Perceiving than Judging.

Myers and Briggs use these terms a bit differently from the way they are used in general conversation, so it is necessary to understand their usage in the Myers-Briggs system; for more information, refer to the following website: www.myersbriggs.org/my-mbti-personality-type/mbti-basics/extraversion-or-introversion.htm (retrieved on May 29, 2018). The Myers-Briggs personality descriptions may not definitively capture human personality, but their system can be a useful way of looking at students, colleagues, trainees, and clients. These personality factors can help us understand how individuals with different personality types are likely to receive our instruction and react to our particular style.

Other Affective Measurements

Affective measurements are available to measure a variety of characteristics that are important in sport and health. For example, sport competition anxiety can be assessed in children with the Sport Competition Anxiety Test questionnaire, available at www.brianmac.co.uk/scat.htm (retrieved June 3, 2018). A similar measurement for adults is available from the same source. R. K. Dishman and W. Ickes have developed a motivation inventory, available in the *Journal of Behavioral Medicine* (1981). The Competitive State Anxiety Inventory-2 (CSAI-2) is another popular measure (Lundqvist and Hassmén, 2005).

Concluding Thoughts

Valid, reliable, and objective measurement in the affective area often requires the use of alternative assessment methods. Considerable progress has been made in developing assessments that can be conducted while test takers are actually performing the skill. Rubrics are often an important part of this alternative approach to evaluation. Rubrics may be developed for all sorts of measurements, and existing rubrics, including those shared in this chapter, may be modified for other applications. Interviews, observations, and surveys are also useful in measurement of the affective domain. One of the key issues in affective assessment is to understand that different people see, experience, and learn in very different ways. Learning to adapt teaching, communication, and interaction to the variety of individuals who will receive it is a valuable skill.

References

Bishop, P. and Herron, R. Use and misuse of the Likert item responses and other ordinal measures. *International Journal of Exercise Science* 8(3): 297–302, 2015.

Dishman, R. K. and Ickes, W. Self-motivation and adherence to therapeutic exercise. *Journal of Behavioral Medicine* 4: 421–428, 1981.

Lundqvist, C. and Hassmén, P. Competitive State Anxiety Inventory-2 (CSAI-2): Evaluating the Swedish version by confirmatory factor analyses. *Journal of Sports Sciences* 23(7): 727–736, 2005.

Myers, I. B., McCaulley, M. H., Quenk, N. L., and Hammer, A. L. *MBTI Manual: A Guide to the Development and Use of the Myers Briggs Type Indicator*, 3rd ed. Mountain View, CA: Consulting Psychologists Press, 1998.

28 Measuring and Evaluating Knowledge

Abstract

As we saw in measuring in the psychomotor domain, taxonomies can help us organize our measurements and expectations. In measuring knowledge, Bloom's taxonomy gives us guidance in creating valid cognitive measurement. It also allows us to evaluate different types of questions.

Keywords: knowledge of fact, comprehension, application, analysis, synthesis, evaluation

Testing and grading are not just issues for professional teachers. All of us teach, at least once in a while. Even without the formal role of teacher, you may teach younger and less experienced professionals or athletes. You may discuss an injury with an athlete and train her on prevention and rehabilitation techniques. In conjunction with this teaching or training, you may play a part in developing formal tests, such as determining qualifications for certifications, licensure, and so forth. If you are in physical education or other teaching, you will test students formally and informally to find out what they have learned. Understanding the nuances of measuring knowledge through asking questions, testing, and assigning grades will be helpful no matter which field you work in.

Many teachers find grading challenging, but the task of assigning grades in physical education is particularly complex. Most other subjects have only a cognitive component, but physical education has fitness and skills components as well as a cognitive component. Physical education teachers cannot grade simply on performance, but must consider participation, improvement, and effort, and they must sometimes subdivide classes into ability groups. However, there is less ability grouping in physical education than any other subject area, which adds to the challenge of grading. When students are not grouped by ability, any measurement must span a wider range of abilities. Fairly assigning physical education grades is indeed a challenge.

Why Test and Grade?

There are many reasons to evaluate cognitive abilities as well as performance. In physical education, one of the key reasons to test knowledge is that our minds can hold information much longer than our muscles can hold their trained status. If a skill is learned cognitively as well as physically, then even if the skill is not used for a period, the person can still duplicate it at a later time because of the cognitive knowledge. In fitness, the principle of *reversibility* means that when we stop training, the physiological changes associated with training begin to disappear. However, if we know *how* to get fit, that knowledge will remain and help us regain fitness later. This is why I always recommend that people who teach a fitness or skill activity include a cognitive component. In testing the cognitive portion, we motivate students to learn that portion so if they find themselves unfit or do not use a sport skill for some time, they will know how to become fit or skillful again. If I know how to exercise properly, I can initiate a program, even after being inactive for a while.

Another reason to test students in all fields is that most will admit that testing and grading motivate them to study. Testing students' knowledge and performance abilities increases the amount of learning.

Testing and grading also give students valuable feedback on how much they are learning and in which areas they need to study or practice more, whether cognitive, skill or fitness testing. By the same token, testing gives the teacher, instructor, or coach information on the effectiveness of the instruction. If everyone in a class or in some group does very poorly on some area of instruction, then the problem is probably with the teacher, not with the students. We normally expect a range of student abilities, but if *everyone* does poorly, even the good students have not learned. Therefore, evaluating students can provide valuable feedback regarding the effectiveness of instruction.

Measurement of cognitive abilities occurs in many other situations in sport, beyond physical education. The NFL requires potential players to take a test of cognitive skills (called the Wonderlic test). CPR certification requires a written test. Professions such as athletic training, adult fitness, and physical therapy require a written test of knowledge.

Many other professions require various forms of testing, certification, and so on, and some criterion level of knowledge (that is, the minimal level of knowledge deemed necessary for competence) is also required to be a competent medical/health/fitness professional. Once on the job, professionals are likely to be involved in formal and informal testing of patients or clients. For example, a fitness professional might test clients, perhaps informally, to determine when they are ready to supervise their own training. You might question personal training clients on their knowledge of the signs of a heart attack, or ask them about hydration in hot weather, or symptoms of heat injuries. Testing of health educators, physical therapists, and athletic trainers' knowledge indicates when they are ready to go out on their own.

Planning for Testing and Grading

Although teaching takes place in every profession, this section will focus on formalized education. The principles are applicable, however, in many contexts outside the classroom.

Planning for testing and grading should start when the teacher outlines what he or she wants to accomplish in a given course. Often, teachers neglect this task of determining where the course will go and what destination it will reach. The course's definition can be conceived in a variety of ways. In general, the conception may be *content oriented*, *assignment oriented*, or *student oriented*.

Devising Cognitive Tests

Asking good questions—the essential skill for devising cognitive tests—is important for any professional. A test is simply a series of good questions intended to elicit the student's knowledge. We ask questions of teachers, colleagues, and friends in order to learn from their often considerable knowledge and experience. And in conversation, we ask questions in order to focus the conversation on a topic of interest to us, to slow down the speaker so that we can absorb more, and to elicit more information.

Devising good questions is an acquired skill. Like most skills, we learn to ask good questions through practice. Each time you have the opportunity to ask questions, make a point of asking at least one. Often, asking one question, or the answer to one question, leads to others. Listen to others asking questions, too. You can improve your questioning skills by imitating others.

Asking questions will increase your knowledge and extend your education. What's more, this practice will serve you well when you find yourself composing test questions for formally or informally assessing people you are teaching or training. It is a skill that must be developed, and to do so may take an investment of time. The result will be large dividends in the quality of your thinking and your students' learning.

Using Bloom's Taxonomy of Cognition to Measure Knowledge

You may recall Harrow's taxonomy of the psychomotor domain. There is also a well-known taxonomy for the cognitive domain, **Bloom's taxonomy**, named after the educator Benjamin Bloom. Bloom's taxonomy is presented in Table 28.1.

Table 28.1 Bloom's taxonomy of cognition

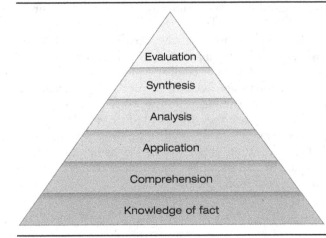

Knowledge of Fact

Knowledge of fact, the lowest level of cognitive functioning, consists of simply learning isolated facts. In physical education, these facts might include the rules for a sport, the length of a football field, the sizes of various balls, or the equipment used in various physical activities. In health, the facts may be symptoms of sexually transmitted diseases. In athletic training, they may be medical terminology. In exercise science and physical therapy, they may be the names, origins, and insertions of muscles.

Teaching facts is popular, and testing facts is even more popular. Facts are essential. Facts have value because they form the foundation for further learning, but overemphasis on learning isolated facts can actually hinder learning. Overemphasizing facts can encourage students to memorize the facts and then forget them as soon as the course is over, because they don't see the importance of the facts or they do not use the information on a regular basis.

Comprehension

The next level in Bloom's listing is comprehension. *Comprehension* is understanding the nature and meaning of facts. You might memorize a long list of terms (facts), such as the names and formulas for statistics, but comprehension requires that you know what these terms mean—what the statistics signify and how they may be used. Testing comprehension is almost as easy as testing facts. How a question is asked usually sets the level of cognition required to answer it. For example, "Explain the relationship between validity and reliability" requires deeper comprehension than, "Is reliability related to validity?"

Application

The next level above comprehension is application, which Bloom described as the first level at which real learning takes place. *Application* is simply applying one's understanding in an appropriate situation; for example, knowing the symptoms of various athletic injuries and applying this knowledge to diagnose an injury in an athletic training situation. Questions at this level may pose a realistic situation and ask students to solve a problem. Questions that require calculation are usually application questions. For example, asking you to compute means and SDs from supplied data would be an application question in this class. Application is popular to teach, but testing application is a little more demanding than testing knowledge of facts or comprehension. This is because it takes more effort to write scenarios and calculation problems.

Analysis

The level above application is analysis. *Analysis* means taking something apart to study its parts. If you have disassembled scuba gear, you have analyzed it in a mechanical sense. Coaches analyze the opponent's offense and defense by strategically examining it. Baseball and softball batters try to analyze both the pitcher and the defense. Teachers analyze material to develop a plan for teaching a unit or a course. Physical education teachers may be required to analyze complex movements in order to develop an instructional plan and a curriculum. Athletic trainers may be required to analyze situations to see how to prevent injuries, learn what is causing injuries, or determine the best combination of treatments to rehabilitate injuries. Therapists analyze an injury or disability before they devise a treatment plan.

To measure analytical abilities, a teacher will create situations and ask test takers to break them down into parts. For example, a senior-level athletic training student might be asked to identify the key knowledge, skills, and abilities required to function as an independent high school athletic trainer for a school with a full sports program.

Synthesis

Taking something apart is a fairly high level cognitive skill. Putting it back together is even more demanding. If you have ever disassembled something and not been able to get it back together, you know what I mean. In terms of cognition, we call the assembly process *synthesis*. Coaches must be able not only to analyze an opponent, but also to synthesize effective tactics and strategies to win a competition. Teachers must be able to synthesize information from a variety of sources to teach a lesson. Athletic trainers and physical therapists must be able to synthesize facts about an injury or a person's physical abilities with their knowledge of possible interventions to develop a treatment plan. Health professionals must be able to analyze health issues and synthesize effective interventions. For the most part, synthesis is not very popular to teach, and it is even less popular to test. This may be because it requires considerable creativity on the part of the teacher to write test items on this level, normally requiring an essay-type question.

Testing a student's ability to think on the synthesis level usually requires that the test taker create something. For example, the teacher might pose a common injury, such as a sprained ankle, and ask the student athletic trainer to devise a treatment program based on a list of available modalities. Or the test might pose a situation wherein athletes are performing hard workouts in hot environments, and ask the test taker to devise a program to minimize the risk of heat injury.

Evaluation

According to Bloom, *evaluation*, or making judgments about value, is the highest cognitive skill. Since this is a taxonomy, meaning that the skills build on one another, all the underlying skills are necessary for one to be able to evaluate accurately. That is, one must be able to learn facts, to comprehend facts, and to apply, analyze, and synthesize knowledge in order to evaluate well. Evaluation, in this context, is exactly as we defined it in Chapter 1. Evaluation is the process in which one combines all the measurement data, decides which data are most important, and then assigns a value to each possible choice.

Evaluation is needed when an athletic trainer examines an injured athlete to determine whether she can be safely moved. In fact, we call this process injury evaluation, because the trainer must know and comprehend facts, analyze the symptoms, synthesize a diagnosis, and finally evaluate the diagnosis and treatment possibilities to decide what needs to be done for the injured player. Evaluation is vital to coaches' selections of players and starters and their decisions about the offensive and defensive schemes to run, because failure to evaluate well will substantially reduce the chances of success in close competitions. Physical education teachers need evaluation skills in designing courses and assigning grades. For example, teachers must evaluate which material is most important and the order in which their students will be learning the material. Teachers must make these decisions themselves, rather than follow a prescribed curriculum. Just because material is in a textbook doesn't mean it's important, and just because the text is presented in a particular order doesn't mean that order is optimal for a particular group of students. Teachers must evaluate the level of their students before they initiate instruction, to know where to start. At the end of a course, assigning final grades constitutes the summative evaluation of the students' mastery of the class material.

Good evaluation skills are useful in every aspect of life, from making a purchase to giving an award to voting in an election. Evaluation may be the most important skill any of us ever perform. Bad evaluations can have very serious results. For example, if an athletic trainer incorrectly evaluates a possible spinal cord injury, an injured player could be paralyzed. If a teacher incorrectly evaluates students' effort or students' progress, this may damage the students' self-confidence and have long-term negative effects. If you have ever been seriously misevaluated or misjudged, you know how harmful this can be.

Most evaluative questions are fairly long and require the evaluation of a product, program, service, or idea. A test of evaluative skills usually requires individuals to use all of their cognitive skills to assign a value or worth to whatever is being evaluated. Requiring students to critique paragraphs, programs, or products tests their evaluative abilities. For example, I have collected newspaper and magazine advertisements for health and fitness products and asked the students to evaluate the stated claims for the product based on their knowledge of exercise, fitness, and safety.

Application of Bloom's Taxonomy

It is vital to consider Bloom's taxonomy in designing any cognitive instruction or evaluation. Generally, it is best to start at the fact level and then proceed through comprehension and application. Unfortunately, in practice, we almost never get beyond application, and we spend the majority of our time on the lowest two cognitive levels.

Nonetheless, students do need to learn to analyze, synthesize, and evaluate. What we want in teachers, athletic trainers, health professionals, and coaches is higher-order thinking. How can we expect to get it, if we don't teach it?

Application Questions

1 Describe the levels of Bloom's taxonomy.
2 How does Bloom's taxonomy relate to the measurement and evaluation of knowledge?
3 What are some common errors in grading?
4 How can professionals such as teachers and physical therapists use evaluation and measurement principles to do their job better?
5 Your school principal has decided that every teacher at Frog Eye High will grade only on improvement. Tell her what measurement and evaluation problems might arise from this approach.
6 Many of your fellow teachers give nothing but multiple-choice tests. One day they casually remark that you're dumb for giving essay tests.

    a Explain to them why you might use essay versus multiple-choice questions.
    b They complain that essay questions lack objectivity relative to multiple-choice questions. Explain why this may not be true.
    c Give your fellow teachers specific steps they can take to improve the objectivity of all tests, both cognitive and skill.
    d One of your fellow teachers doesn't understand how to write questions on the higher levels of the cognitive domain. Write out examples of questions on evaluation and measurement on the application level or higher. (Use any type of questions you wish.)

28.1 Practical Exercise

Suppose you were part of an examination committee that had developed a certification exam for coaches, athletic trainers, PE teachers, personal trainers, or some other group. When you gave this exam to a large group of competent candidates, almost all of them failed the exam.

a Why might this have occurred?
b What are some possible short-term (immediate) remedies for this group?
c What should be done before this exam is given again?

Reference

Bloom, B., Englehart, M., Furst, E., Hill, W., and Krathwohl, D. *Taxonomy of Educational Objectives: The Classification of Educational Goals. Handbook I: Cognitive Domain.* New York, Toronto: Longmans, Green, 1956.

29 Creating and Evaluating Cognitive Tests

Abstract

In creating valid measures of knowledge, we have a lot of decisions to make. There are several different types of questions we can ask, and our choice of which type and what portion of each type will determine the validity of our measurement. Discrimination and difficulty assessments will allow us to evaluate individual questions.

Keywords: multiple choice, short-answer, fill-in-the-blank, essay, item-analysis, discrimination of questions, difficulty of questions

Types of Test Questions

Doubtless you have seen a lot of tests during your years as a student. In taking all those exams, you have learned quite a bit about testing. For example, you have seen a variety of types of questions: multiple choice, short answer, fill-in-the-blank, matching, true–false and essay. Each of these types of questions has advantages and disadvantages. Let's review some of these.

Multiple Choice

The most commonly used test questions are multiple choice. The greatest advantage of multiple-choice questions is that they are extremely easy to grade. If we are testing a large number of students, this can be a very important consideration. As we will discuss in a later section, multiple-choice questions also give the appearance of being objective. They allow us to cover a lot of material very quickly, and they are quite popular with students.

On the other hand, multiple-choice questions seldom test higher-level thinking. With a lot of work, it is possible to devise these questions to test higher levels of thinking, but most multiple-choice questions test knowledge of fact. It is also fairly easy to cheat on these test items, because all a student has to do is see how another person marked the question. Despite the fact that answering multiple-choice questions doesn't require an in-depth understanding of the material, writing good multiple-choice questions is hard. Often the biggest challenge is to come up with three plausible false answers to go along with the correct answer. Experts tell us that four different choices are optimal and that offering "both a and b" or "a, b, but not c" choices is not good. We also need to avoid clues such as number agreement—asking a question that suggests a singular answer, but giving some plural answers from which to choose. We should avoid using words like *always* and *never*. We ought to avoid using silly or irrelevant false answers. For handy information on writing multiple-choice test items, I recommend these tips from several years back from the Center for Teaching and Learning at the University of North Carolina, Chapel Hill: www.smu.edu/-/media/Site/Provost/assessment/Resources/MultipleChoices/Improving-Multiple-Choice-QuestionsUNCCH.ashx?la=en.

Finally, multiple-choice questions are largely irrelevant in the real world, with perhaps only a few exceptions. I can't recall anyone ever coming up to me and posing a multiple-choice question about fitness, health, nutrition, coaching, or anything else.

Matching

Another type of test question that is easy to grade is matching. Matching questions have the additional advantage of being slightly easier to write than some of the other types. You can ask a lot of matching questions, because they can be answered quickly. For a few situations in our specialties, matching would be a very good examination technique. For example, in anatomy, matching may be a useful technique for pairing muscle and bone names with locations and functions. Keep matching questions in mind for those occasions. If you can write enough questions, you can cover a lot of material.

Matching has some of the drawbacks of multiple-choice questions, the most important being that it is very hard to reach even to the application level of Bloom's taxonomy. Writing higher-level matching questions is a real challenge, because the task of matching generally requires only knowledge of fact or comprehension. It is very difficult to write matching questions that test higher-order thinking.

As with multiple-choice questions, test takers merely have to recognize the answers in matching questions—they don't have to supply the answers. This is one of the reasons why they are easy.

Just as multiple-choice items very seldom arise in real life, I don't think I've ever been asked a matching question. You probably haven't either.

True–False

Another testing option is the true–false question. True–false questions are easier to write and easier to grade than even multiple-choice questions—we don't have to come up with multiple wrong answers. Students can answer a large number of questions quickly, if the questions aren't too long. In life, as in true–false tests, false statements are often presented as true, so learning to read carefully to distinguish true from false statements is worthwhile.

The major disadvantage of true–false questions is that only lower levels of cognitive function are easily reached. This is because, usually, it is only facts that are identified as true or false. If we want to test higher-order thinking, it is very difficult to boil down issues to just two clear options of true and false. The second major disadvantage is that random guesses on all the test questions will usually get a score close to 50 percent. A third disadvantage is that cheating on these tests isn't very hard, by simply copying another person's answers or reading a text message that is just Ts and Fs. Again, this is a type of question that is not often asked in the real world.

Here are some additional points to consider: First, in terms of good teaching, it may be confusing for some students to be exposed to a series of wrong and barely wrong statements in an area in which they are trying to learn what really is true. Second, when you think about whether these questions have real-world application, although you may argue that it is fairly common for someone to begin a question with "Is it true that . . . ," your answer will rarely be a simple yes or no. In fact, the answer will often begin with "It depends . . . ," followed by a longer, more in-depth, detailed discussion that may involve application, synthesis, analysis, or evaluation.

Fill-in-the-Blank

An advantage of the fill-in-the-blank type of question is that it at least requires students to supply information instead of simply recognizing answers. Fill-in-the-blank questions are not quite as easy to cheat on as multiple-choice or true–false questions.

A disadvantage of these questions is that they, like all of the question types discussed so far, tend to test lower levels of Bloom's cognitive taxonomy. In general, one cannot give higher-order thinking answers in a few words, though that is not impossible. Also, like the other question types described so far, they don't tend to come up in daily life.

Short Answer

Short-answer questions are more difficult to grade because there is potentially more subjectivity in the answers. On the other hand, they are easier to write than multiple-choice or matching questions because you don't have to supply wrong-answer choices.

With some thought, short-answer questions can be devised to reach higher levels of thinking. Short-answer questions that ask specific questions requiring analysis, synthesis, or evaluation achieve this. For example, you might provide something for the student to evaluate that only has a few facets, or you could break a larger question into smaller parts that have short answers. This is the first type of question we have considered that requires the student to supply substantial information—to write something, even if it is just a few words. For example, I could ask you, "What are one advantage and one disadvantage to a multiple-choice question?" You should be able to answer by writing a couple of sentences.

Essay

Essay questions are often easier to write than the other types, and with just a bit of practice, it gets easier. Essay tests are very hard to cheat on, even if students get the test in advance. After all, if students are willing to prepare a good essay answer before the test, at least they have mastered the material—if only for a short while. Essay questions have a reputation of being very difficult to grade. There are some steps to take to facilitate validly grading these which are covered in the next chapter.

Essay questions are the best type of question to reach the highest levels of Bloom's taxonomy. We can start the question with the words *analyze*, *create*, and *evaluate*, and the format allows students enough time and space to provide appropriate responses. For example, we might ask students to "Evaluate the following fitness program," and this would call on all levels of cognitive ability.

Essay questions are the type you will most commonly hear in real life. For example, athletes, clients, students, or patients may ask you to explain complex issues dealing with fitness, injuries, treatments, or physical problems, or they may pose problems that they face. Even more than short-answer questions, essay questions give students excellent opportunities to practice written communication. The importance of giving students practice in writing and expressing themselves should not be underappreciated. Everyone needs to be able to communicate clearly in writing—in order to fill out applications for jobs, programs, or other opportunities, and to communicate by writing letters and emails. Once students finish school, there aren't many opportunities to have someone help them with their writing. Essay questions give students a valuable chance to practice and receive feedback on their written communication skills. (See Practical Exercise 29.1 for sample essay questions.)

Types of Test Questions and Bloom's Taxonomy

29.1   Practical Exercise

Writing questions is harder than you think. That's why you've had to answer so many ridiculous test questions over the years. Using the guidelines provided in the text, write seven questions as specified below. Questions should be taken from the subject matter of this class.

(continued)

(continued)

1   Write a short-answer question on the *application* level.
2   Write a multiple-choice question on the *application* level.
3   Write *two* true–false test questions on the *application* level and *two* on the *comprehension* or *knowledge of fact* level.
4   Write a matching question on as high a cognitive level as possible.

Item Analysis for Evaluating Tests

As with all measurement techniques, after you administer a test, you should evaluate it to determine how to modify it to make it better. The first step occurs as you grade the test. To make this evaluation, ask yourself the following questions during the grading process:

- Are test takers misunderstanding a test question?
- Do several students have wrong answers based on a misunderstanding of the question rather than simply not knowing the answer?
- How can the questions be improved?
- Were there any questions that everyone got correct or mostly correct? Why?
- Were there any questions that everyone got wrong or mostly wrong? Why?
- Were there any questions to which the answers were especially weak? Why?

Once you complete an initial general review, then you can do an *item analysis*. In item analysis, we assess each item with regard to its discrimination and difficulty.

Calculating Discrimination

Discrimination means the ability of a test to distinguish between those who have the relevant knowledge and those who don't. We calculate discrimination by first dividing the class into thirds based on their scores on this particular exam. To do this, list the scores in order and then divide them into thirds. Now, to calculate the discrimination index for a particular question, subtract the number of those in the bottom third who got the question correct from the number of students in the top third who got it correct. Finally, divide this answer by the number of students in each group (the two groups should have the same number of students). Here's an example:

number of people taking the exam = 42

14 students scored in the top third, and 6 of these got question #1 correct.

14 students scored in the bottom third, and 2 of these got question #1 correct.

Subtract number in the bottom group from number in top group who got it correct: 6 − 2 = 4

Divide 4 by 14 (the number in each group): 4 / 14 = 0.29

If you think about it for a moment, you can see that the maximum discrimination index would be +1. This would happen if all the top group got the question right but none of the bottom group got it right. The minimum discrimination index would be −1, and this could happen if *none* of the students in the top group got it right but all of the students in the bottom group did. Ideally, discrimination indexes should be above 0.2. A score above 0.3 is very good item discrimination, see https://testingservices. utexas.edu/scanning/interpreting-test-results (retrieved May 29, 2018).

The discrimination index is based on the assumption that those who scored in the top group are the "best" students and ought to get the question right. (By eliminating the middle third, we give a little more distance between the top and bottom groups, so that the discrimination index is more meaningful.) This assumption is probably only partly correct, so don't take discrimination as "the law."

Test item discrimination is difficult to identify with essay questions, and it hardly makes sense with matching questions. It is most clear with multiple-choice questions and slightly less so with short-answer questions. Evaluation of discrimination for essay questions is difficult partly because most students receive at least some partial credit. The calculation is also more complicated for essay questions, since we score essay questions along a scale, rather than just marking them right or wrong. For example, on a 20-point question, test takers can score anything between 0 and 20 points. For essays, we evaluate discrimination as follows: As before, divide the group into top and bottom thirds. Then, calculate the *mean* score for the two groups. If there isn't much difference in the means between these groups, then the discrimination is low. If the bottom group scored better than the top group, there is "reverse" discrimination, and you should carefully consider the question's value.

Items that do not discriminate or that are too difficult or too easy can be modified. Although you should use discrimination to help in your overall evaluation of test questions, the discrimination index should only be an aid to your thinking, and not a replacement for it. When test questions lack discrimination, they should be reworked to improve their validity in measuring the specific constructs you are trying to measure.

Calculating Difficulty

Computing the difficulty index of a set of test scores is a bit simpler. To calculate difficulty, simply divide the number of students who got the question correct by the number who took the test.

difficulty = number of correct responses / total number taking test

Following is an example of a difficulty calculation:

number of people taking the exam = 42

number of correct answers = 11

difficulty index = 11 / 42 = 0.26

If no one gets a question correct, then the difficulty index is 0. If only one person in the above example got it right, then the difficulty index would be 0.024 (1 / 42 = 0.024). If only two got it right, the difficulty index would be 0.048. If everyone got it correct, then the difficulty index would be 42 / 42 = 1.0. Keep in mind that the higher the difficulty index, the *easier* the question. This might seem a bit backward, but that's how it works. Test items with difficulties greater than 0.80 or less than 0.20 are generally unacceptable, with a difficulty near 0.50 being ideal and difficulty indices between 0.3 and 0.7 being the goal. However, the difficulty index is affected by the "guess" factor. With a true–false question, a person has a 50 percent chance of guessing correctly, so the standard should be adjusted to halfway between 0.50 (guess alone) and 0.0 (maximal difficulty), or 0.25.

As with discrimination, test item difficulty is most easily determined for multiple-choice and short-answer questions and harder to determine for essay and matching questions. You can evaluate the difficulty of essay questions by performing the calculation with the mean score for each question. A question with a very high or very low mean score (very high or low difficulty index) would need review. A very low mean score (or difficulty index) suggests that most test takers didn't have the concept or that the grading key was wrong or demanded too much. A test question with a high difficulty index (high mean score) may indicate that test takers have mastered the concept or that the grading key didn't demand enough.

Interdependence of Discrimination and Difficulty

If you think about it, you can see that test item difficulty and discrimination should be related. If no one gets a certain question right, then the discrimination will be 0. If everyone gets the question right, then the discrimination is also 0 (16 – 16 / 16 = 0). If difficulty is extremely high or extremely low, therefore, the question does not discriminate between the students who know the material and those who do not. Ideal discrimination occurs when the difficulty is close to 0.5 (that is, when half of the class get the question right and half get it wrong). When this is the case, *all* of the students in the top third got the answer correct, and none of those in the bottom group got it right, giving maximal discrimination. (Note that the middle third of the test takers contribute to the difficulty index but not to the discrimination index, so the two qualities are not strictly linked.)

Don't get too carried away with the concepts of difficulty and discrimination. There can be good reasons to start students off with a fairly easy question that gives them confidence. On the other hand, if you want to get students' attention, you might choose to ask a few very hard questions. These are issues of motivation and pedagogy that only a good teacher can decide.

29.2   Practical Exercise

Given the following information, compute the discrimination and difficulty indices.
Number of people taking the exam = 33
Eleven students scored in the top third, and 6 of these got question #1 correct.
Eleven students scored in the bottom third, and 2 of these got question #1 correct.
Of the 11 students remaining, 3 got question #1 correct.

Application Questions

1 Calculate the difficulty for the following questions:

   a   Out of 30 students taking the test, 8 of them got the question correct.
   b   Out of 40 students taking the test, 24 of them got the question correct.

2 Calculate the discrimination index for the following data:

   a   Question 3 data:

   Number in top one-third (10 students) who got question correct = 6
   Number in bottom one-third (10 students) who got question correct = 2

   b   Question 4 data:

   Number in top one-third (10 students) who got question correct = 3
   Number in bottom one-third (10 students) who got question correct = 7
   What might be wrong with this question?

3 Explain how difficulty and discrimination are related.
4 Describe how difficulty and discrimination might be calculated for essays or short-answer questions.

30 Grading

Abstract

In many settings, including some sports, ultimately, we must assign grades. In Physical Education, unlike some other disciplines, there are multiple criteria which can be used for grading, instead of strictly grading on performance. Each of these options provides advantages, including motivation. Actually calculating grades provides additional options too.

Keywords: performance, improvement, effort participation, weighted averages, standard scores, grading "on the curve," T scores

Grading is a complex and challenging task. Grading in physical activities and sports is even more challenging. To grade a student's knowledge, one has to measure only the knowledge, but to grade activity and sports, one must measure knowledge, fitness, psychomotor skills, the ability to think and adjust quickly to changing circumstances, and, in some cases, teamwork. The degree to which each of these qualities is present and important varies from situation to situation, and testing poorly in any one of these areas may result in a poor overall score, even if the student is proficient in the others. For example, a very fast, skilled person could come in last in an obstacle course, if the person exhibits poor ability to adjust to the tasks of the course. In this case, only considering time for completion of the obstacle course would lead to the conclusion that the student is not very fast, when in reality the individual's decision skills were the determining factor.

Options in Physical Education Grading

Teachers of physical education have several options on which to base grades: on performance, participation, effort, or improvement.

Grading on Performance

In coaching, physical education, athletic training, and physical therapy, what is most commonly evaluated is the person's performance. There are numerous good reasons for this—the most important being that performance is what most often counts in the real world. In sports, performance is essential. In the fitness business, fitness centers that don't perform (make money) can't last. In health professions and medicine, including athletic training, competent performance can make the difference between life and death. Evaluation based on performance simply makes sense.

Why, then, would teachers not grade on performance all the time? The answer is in the reasons for grading. Some students in physical education will never perform extremely well on certain skills. There may be physiological, psychological, and cultural reasons for this. For most school subjects, students progress gradually through a series of skills until they reach high school, where students are often divided into different academic tracks. Hence, all students entering an algebra class or a consumer math class are at least somewhat close to the same level, at least somewhat prepared. On the other hand, in physical education classes students often arrive with huge variability in their aptitude for, and experience in, a given physical activity, or physical activity in general.

If our desire is to use grading to maximize student learning, then performance-based grading may be totally discouraging for many students. If a student has no hope to pass a class, why should she or he do anything? Conversely, if the grading is too easy, then students have little external motivation to try to learn more.

Grading on Participation

The line of thinking described above may lead us to consider rewarding students just for showing up and participating. Giving students a grade for merely "dressing out" has the advantage of motivating students to participate, so that their fitness and skills will at least progress somewhat.

This approach has several disadvantages. First, this approach is unlike that for any other academic subject. This inconsistency with other classes may be more important than it first appears. Second, this approach is largely inconsistent with the real world. Can you think of any jobs where you would be paid just to "dress out"? Third, motivation is only partially effective if people are motivated only to dress and pretend to participate. In fact, it can be hard for teachers to distinguish between students who are really participating and those who know how to "look" like they are participating. Faking participation in physical education is common enough to have a name: "competent bystanding."

Rewarding students just for participating raises a question about the appropriateness of the standards set for students. Research suggests that students will adapt to the standards that we set. If we set low standards, that's the level to which students will aspire.

Grading on Effort

Giving grades based on effort may encourage students to engage in the class. Effort is necessary for anyone to improve fitness and learn skills, so encouraging effort is good.

However, this approach also has disadvantages. First, this approach, like grading for participation, is unlike that for any other academic subject. Grading for effort is also largely inconsistent with the real world. Few jobs will pay an employee based on effort as opposed to accomplishment. Finally, as with grading for participation, motivation is only partially effective if people are motivated only to feign effort. As with participation, distinguishing between real effort and a pretense at effort may be impossible. All of us who have been involved with sports know what effort looks like, and grunting, holding one's sides, breathing deeply, and appearing ready to vomit may give the *appearance* of good effort.

Grading on Improvement

Anyone can improve his or her fitness and learn new skills. Improvement is rewarding in itself, and provides intrinsic motivation. Continuous improvement over a long period of time is likely to result in good to excellent performance. Encouraging improvement is good.

Once again, however, there are disadvantages to this approach: It is unlike that for most other academic subjects, and it is inconsistent with the real world. One of the biggest disadvantages to this approach is that it usually takes at least two measurements, an initial and a subsequent one, to get one assessment of improvement.

Another disadvantage of grading based on improvement is that it is much harder for highly skilled, compared to low-skilled, students to make improvements. You may recall that we discussed "regression to the mean" in Chapter 2. Anytime a person achieves an extreme score and then retakes the same test, the score is statistically likely to move toward the average score. For example, a person who makes 14 out of 15 basketball free throws at the start of the unit will be hard-pressed to show any improvement. On the other hand, a person who misses all of the free throws can improve the score simply by getting a little bit lucky on the second test.

Selecting Between Grading Options

Each of these grading systems—performance, participation, effort, and improvement—has drawbacks as well as advantages. How, then, should one choose among them? I would suggest that each of these is superior in certain situations. For example, if we need to relate performance to the "real world," grading on performance would be helpful. For very discouraging or difficult skills, grading on effort may keep students engaged in trying to master the skill. On the other hand, if the goal is to maximize learning, then some combination, depending on the situation, will probably give the best results. The key is to plan, think through the plan, and make sure the students understand the basis for their grades. As in developing any evaluation scheme, we research it, design it, test it, modify it, and continue the process, perhaps indefinitely (see Chapter 11).

In addition, each of the grading systems presents some validity concerns. On its face, it appears invalid that a superior performer should receive a lower score than a very poor performer, but this often happens when grades are based on effort, participation, or improvement. The trade-offs may depend on the context. Fitness and health professionals have to adjust their thinking, because most of the individuals who come to classes, gyms, and clinics are not athletes. Basing success on performance would put most gyms out of business, because patrons wouldn't tolerate negative treatment because of poor or average performance. Encouraging participation and effort is essential to successful adult fitness and physical therapy programs. In academic settings, basing a grade entirely on skills may be very discouraging to those who have lower skills. Their lower grades may result in their developing disdain for whatever fitness activity was being taught. The likelihood of their participating in the activity later in life will likely be small, which means they will never receive any health and fitness benefits from that particular activity. Depending on your goals, this may be an enormous disadvantage.

Methods for Calculating Grades

Weighting scores and using standard scores are two methods for calculating grades. Each method has advantages and disadvantages. Thorough knowledge of and comfort in using both methods will result in better evaluation.

Weighting Scores

Not all scores are equally important—some should count more than others. Chapter 24 showed how to assign different values to different parts of a rubric. Weighted scores appear on almost every class syllabus. Final exams, projects, and quizzes are typically worth different numbers of points or are given different percentages in calculating the final grades. Weighted averages are very common in grading, so it is important that you understand how to calculate them and how to adjust them when necessary. Let's look at a common weighted average that is important to many teachers, coaches, and athletic trainers.

Calculating a weighted grade average in a 100 percent grading system. Here's an example:

quizzes = 20 percent of grade

projects = 25 percent of grade

homework = 5 percent of grade

other exams = 20 percent of grade

final exam = 30 percent of grade

For each element except the final exam, we would use the mean—for example, the mean of the homework scores or the mean of the quiz scores. For the calculation to be accurate, all of the elements must be expressed on the same scale. The calculation is:

> grade = quizzes * 0.2 + projects * 0.25 + homework * 0.05 + other exams * 0.2 + final exam * 0.3

Calculating a weighted grade average in a non-100 percent grading system. When we are not using a 100 percent grading system, the calculation is somewhat different. For example, rubrics may have a total that is not expressed as a percentage. Suppose a class has only three scores: a practical exam in athletic training, a project, and a written exam similar to the certification exam. We want to count the practical as 50 percent of the final grade, the written exam as 50 percent, and the project as 20 percent. But now the total is 50 + 50 + 20 = 120 percent. In a situation like this, we simply multiply each score by its weighting, as we did earlier. Then, to convert the final to a 100 percent basis, we divide the answer by 120. Table 30.1 presents an example.

In all of these examples, the scores of each element were expressed individually on a 100-point scale. This is not always the case, however—a practical exam may have a maximum score of 135 instead of 100. In this situation, the simplest solution is to convert the practical exam to a 100-point basis. To do this, divide the practical exam score by 135 and multiply the result by 100 to express it as a percentage. Table 30.2 shows the previous example with the practical exam worth 135 points instead of 100.

30.1   Practical Exercise

Set up spreadsheets as shown in Table 30.2 and calculate the weighted grade averages for three additional students.

Table 30.1 Calculating a weighted grade average in a non-100 percent grading system

F6		f_x =E6/120			
A	B	C	D	E	F
1					
2	Practical exam	Project	Written exam	Grade	Grade
3	50%	20%	50%	120%	100%
4	87	80	88	103.5	86%
5	77	87	90	100.9	84%
6	95	85	72	100.5	84%
7				0	0%
8				0	0%
9				0	0%

Table 30.2 Here is the previous example with the practical exam worth 135 points instead of 100

	G7	▼	f_x =F7/120				
	A	B	C	D	E	F	G
1							
2		135-point	Practical exam				
3		Practical exam	(100-pt scale)	Project	Written exam	Grade	Grade
4		50%	50%	20%	50%	120%	100%
5		117	86.67	80	88	103.33	86%
6		104	77.04	87	90	100.92	84%
7		128	94.81	85	72	100.41	84%
8						0	0%
9						0	0%
10						0	0%

Expressing Scores as Standard Scores

As you have learned already, there are advantages to using standard scores, such as z-scores, to measure things. You have probably heard the expression "grading on the curve" many times, yet few people have any idea that this method uses z-scores. Let's look at some applications of standard scores in grading.

Recall that a z-score is calculated by comparing a score to a mean and dividing the difference by the SD, to determine by how many SDs the score is better or worse than the mean.

z-scores on the curve. Using z-scores gives us the advantage of being able to control the distribution. In other words, we can use z-scores to set a new mean and a new SD for almost any scores we wish. In fact, z-scores are the principle behind "grading on the curve." We can add any number to the z-score, and this number becomes the mean for the distribution (0 + what we add = the mean). Likewise, we can multiply the z-score by any number, and this number becomes the SD. For example, if you want the mean for a set of scores to be 75 and the SD to be 10, then you can take the raw scores, compute the mean and SD, and convert each raw score to a z-score. Once you have the z-scores, you can multiply them by 10 and add 75 to create the new distribution. Here's the equation:

new score = (Z * 10) + 75

In fact, if you ever asked a teacher to "curve" the grades in a class, that's really what you were asking the teacher to do. In Figure 14.1 (the z-curve), you can see that if the grades are close to normally distributed, and you then make the mean 75 and the SD 10, then about 68 percent of the scores will fall between 65 (75 – 10) and 85 (75 + 10), and about 95 percent will fall between 55 (75 – 20) and 95 (75 + 20).

This would be an acceptable grade distribution on a 100-point scale. Keep in mind that the actual scores the students earned don't really matter, because you can transform them to produce any mean score and any SD you choose, as long as the grades are close to a normal distribution.

For example, you may find that the mean score on an examination was 55 and the SD was 7. Just by looking at the raw scores, you see that about 68 percent of the scores are going to fall between 55 + 7 and 55 − 7, that is, between 62 and 48. You don't want that many students to fail (score below 60), so you can adjust these scores by converting the raw scores to z-scores and adding 75. By doing this, you assure that the mean score for the class is 75. If you multiply each z-score by 10, then about 68 percent of the scores will fall between 75 − 10 and 75 + 10, or between 65 and 85. This means that most students (about 85 percent) will make better than a 65.

To grade on a curve, you need a stable standard deviation and mean, so this method must be restricted to situations with more than about 40 or 50 data points (the more data, the greater the stability). All data points drawn from the same measurement and population can be combined to obtain the mean and SD.

In all honesty, this type of grading is almost never done, because very few people— besides you—know how to do it. Now that you have this skill, however, you have a useful tool for transforming grades in order to make sure that the grades actually represent degrees of learning.

"Grading on the curve" can be a double-edged sword. This method "forces" a distribution to conform to our wishes. In some cases, the result may be that some students score above 100. To avoid this situation, you may have to lower the mean and SD. Then, you may find that other students are now scoring very poorly. Perhaps at this point we should remind ourselves that we measure for a reason—in order to make good evaluations—and measurements are simply tools to help us do that.

It is important to think about what "curving" grades does and doesn't do. Grading on the curve is simply a process of transforming scores—converting scores from one scale of numbers to another. It doesn't mean anyone knows more or less than they did before you transformed the scores. Grading on the curve *does* force you into a norm-referenced approach, in which students are compared chiefly with each other rather than to some external standard of mastery (criterion-referenced grading). Norm-referenced grading offers the advantage of predictability but the disadvantage of forcing students into a competitive situation, where their grade depends as much on the other students in the class as it does on mastery. Recall from an earlier example that using norm-based scores could result in a student scoring 90 percent on an exam and being awarded a B. Conversely, a student could score 62 and be awarded a C. Whether to use norm-referenced or criterion-referenced grading depends on the situation. To make a good decision, you must evaluate the circumstances.

Theoretically, now that you know the method, you can use z-scores to transform scores in any way that benefits your measurement system and the test takers. If you have a mean and an SD, or can calculate them, you can convert any set of raw scores to a set of z-scores. Once you have z-scores, you can then scale them by multiplying the z-score by any number you choose. The larger the multiplier, the flatter the curve and the wider the scores will be spread. The number that you add to the multiplied z-score will move the mean in whichever direction you choose. If you like, you can even name the new score distribution after yourself.

T-scores. T-scores are just a special variation of the z-score that makes all z-scores positive. The T-score is simply the z-score multiplied by 10 and added to 50.

$$T = (Z * 10) + 50$$

T-scores are not necessarily easier to handle than z-scores. Their advantage is that all but the most extremely bad scores (greater than five SD below the mean) will have a positive sign (no negative scores). The T-score is occasionally used to report standardized test scores.

Common Errors in Grading

There are many ways to go wrong in grading. As stated earlier, one common error in grading is too much focus on facts. Because it is easy to test on facts, teachers sometimes place too much emphasis on facts in testing and grading. Facts are important, but when we teach and test primarily factual knowledge, we inadvertently teach test takers that facts are the only important issues in education.

Keep in mind, also, that in general grading is a lot less precise than we might think. Grading is almost always based on an arbitrary volume of material. The required mastery level for an "A" or an "F" is, likewise, usually at least a bit arbitrary. You may have had the experience of being in the "hard" (or maybe the "easy") section of the same course taught by two different teachers, and seeing that grade expectations can vary widely. Although grading can be better or worse, it is seldom an exact science.

It is impossible to list all the ways that testing and grading can go wrong (people are very creative), but you should be able to avoid most errors if you keep in mind—and apply—the basic measurement principles of validity, reliability, and objectivity.

Validity

The key issue in measurement is always validity. Anything that hurts validity hurts the measurement. For example, one may ask invalid questions. On a measurement exam, the teacher may ask a question about some current event that has nothing to do with measurement. Or, the teacher may grade on factors that have little to do with the student's knowledge of the subject. For example, if I were to grade students on "dressing out" in a physical education class, I may have a legitimate reason, but this will nevertheless lead to an invalid grade. This practice may be motivating and may prevent attendance problems, but it does not seem valid, in most cases, to base a grade on something that does not reflect knowledge (or skill or performance). Validity requires valid application as well as valid measurement.

Invalid grading can also result from invalid tests and invalid scoring.

Invalid tests. To be valid, each test question should relate to a learning objective. For each test question, we ought to be able to show which course objective the question addresses. Questions tied to objectives help reinforce the objectives' importance, encourage clarity of thinking, and determine whether students have grasped the concept. Whether we are quizzing an injured athlete on his therapy program or a soccer player on her defensive responsibilities, we have to make sure the testing is related to what we want the test taker to know and retain days, weeks, months, or years later.

Invalid scoring. Invalid scoring can result when the measurer creates a valid measurement but fails to ensure a valid scoring system. When testing students, it is helpful to tell them what each question is worth before they answer it, and then adhere to the relative value. This enhances the validity of scoring because it helps define each question's contribution to the total score. That is, when the cognitive test is constructed, each question has both individual validity (or invalidity), and the collection of the test items has an overall validity. The overall validity of the test can be reduced by giving one item too much weight. For example, if you gave a final exam on evaluation and measurement and gave most of the weight to the question or questions on significant digits, the test questions might be individually valid. However, the overall test may be invalid as a measure of knowledge of measurement and evaluation.

Objectivity

A more common grading error is basing too much of a grade on opinion. If we grade a class on participation, effort, and "attitude," it is likely that this grading system will be weak in objectivity. Similarly, if we determine course grades based mostly on "participation," "cooperation," and "instructor's evaluation," then this grading system probably also has too much potential for subjectivity.

Most people think of multiple-choice tests as very objective, and essay questions as just the opposite, very subjective. Is this view justified? First, let's review objectivity. In its most basic sense, objectivity means that it shouldn't matter who is doing the measurement and evaluation, the outcome should be consistent. Notice that it is the entire process, not just the grading, that comprises objectivity. That is, there may be subjectivity (the opposite of objectivity) in writing the test items.

Multiple-choice questions. Since multiple-choice test items are hard to write, there is likely to be subjectivity in writing 30 or 50 of these questions. The big opportunity for subjectivity in multiple-choice questions is in writing the "best" or "correct" answer. You have probably had experiences with multiple-choice questions where you disagreed with whoever wrote the test key. Sometimes subtle differences in interpreting questions will result in different opinions about the correct answer. For example, I might ask you on an exam, "Which type of cognitive question is the best?" You might interpret that question several different ways depending on what ideas enter your thought process. If you are concerned with an exam to be given in many locales with many issues to cover and little time for administering or grading the test, you might give one "correct" answer. If you are thinking in terms of reaching the highest levels of thinking according to Bloom's taxonomy, then you would likely choose a different answer.

Short-answer, fill-in-the-blank, matching, and true–false questions. Short-answer, fill-in-the-blank, matching, and true–false questions are considered more or less objective. This is because, hypothetically, each of these types of questions can be asked in such a way that it has only one "best" answer. As you saw with multiple-choice questions, however, subjectivity arises from the person who decides which of the options is the "best." So once again, applying the key is objective, but developing the key can be subjective. Two different knowledgeable people might come up with different answer keys, both of which contain reasonable answers.

Essay questions. A discouraging aspect of essay questions is grading them, because this task can be very subjective. Steps can be taken, however, to make this process more objective. When preparing the test, you can ask a few people, some who are at the same level as the students and some who are very knowledgeable, to read through the questions to try to eliminate potential misunderstandings. You would give them a copy of the questions and ask them to tell you or write down what constructs they think are being measured. If their responses differ from what you were thinking, you need to examine the questions to see where the misunderstanding arose.

The next task is to determine and indicate the point value for each test question so that test takers know how much each question is worth. The point value should not be changed until the test is modified for the next administration. All test answer sheets turned in by students should be anonymous so that the grader will not have preconceived biases. This is easily done by having test takers put their names on the back of the last answer sheet.

Before grading the tests, the grader should make up an answer key. The answer key should be a very thorough answer written by a knowledgeable person. When you use this type of key, do not demand that the test takers reproduce every aspect of the answer "key," and be prepared for the students to come up with some acceptable answers that may not have been included on the key. I usually only require about 80 percent of the key's answer for full credit for the question. This 80 percent requirement is my arbitrary choice, and you may pick a different requirement. In addition, you will need to devise a grading scheme that indicates how many points each question and each subpart of a question is worth.

Table 30.3 presents an example question, answer key, and grading scheme.

When grading essay answers, it's best to grade all of the answers to question number 1 before grading any answers to question number 2. This is important because of the halo effect. If you recall, the halo effect is the phenomenon in testing when prior information about a person or performance biases an observer's evaluation. For example, if someone does very well on a question that was just graded, we may expect, and interpret, their next answer to be a little better than it probably is. If we grade one student's exam all at once, and that student does very well on the first question, we will be biased to think that student will do well on the next question, and so forth. Likewise, if a student does poorly on one question, we may be biased against the student for the next question.

It's best to grade all students on a particular question at one time so that you are in the same frame of mind for evaluating everyone's answer. Both using an answer key and grading all the answers to one question at a time give better consistency and better objectivity. If it happens to be a long exam or you have many students, it is acceptable to start one day and finish the next. However, make certain to stop at a definitive point. Don't grade questions 1 through 6 and half the class on question 7 and then pick back up the next day on question 7. This introduces potential bias. You may have had a really bad day when you started and then a really good day the next day. If so, half the class will suffer your wrath on question 7.

Table 30.3 Example question, answer key, and grading scheme

Question:

Crucial qualities for a good measurement and evaluation are:

A Validity
B Reliability and
C Objectivity.

Use the analogy of a horseshoes contest (or another suitable analogy of your choosing) to explain to a teaching colleague what each of these terms means. Be complete and clear in your explanation. (Points for the question = 25)

Answer Key:

A Validity is a person's ability to hit the center of the target (with arrows, horseshoes, etc.) with minimal (acceptable) error. Validity means that the error is acceptable and we are measuring what we say/think/desire to measure. It also refers to correct interpretation and application of the measurement. (Maximal points = 10)
B Reliability means we hit the same spot consistently—that our error in direction and magnitude is nearly constant. If we are always hitting the bull's eye (or other target), we are both reliable (consistent) and valid, but we could be consistent, yet far from the target's center—that's good reliability without good validity. (Maximal points = 8)
   Less desirable alternative answer: Reliability means having a consistent scheme for scoring such that the horseshoes are always scored the same when they lie in the same position relative to the post and other shoes. (Maximal points for alternative answer = 6)
C Objectivity means that whoever is throwing gets about the same awarded score, i.e., that the scores are similar regardless of who does the measuring.
   Alternatively, it could be that the person throwing is given the same score, no matter who scores them. (Maximal points = 7 for either response)

Concluding Thoughts

Cognitive measurement is simpler than fitness or psychomotor measurement, but it is still extremely challenging. Like the psychomotor taxonomy, the cognitive taxonomy is useful in evaluating cognitive measurements. Cognitive tests typically have many test items (questions), and these questions should be evaluated with respect to their difficulty and ability to discriminate.

Each cognitive test question type and each grading method offers some advantages and some disadvantages. The choice of question types and grading method depends on the context. Often, different question types and grading methods are combined in a single course of instruction.

Valid cognitive measurement requires that we avoid common mistakes and that we use all the cognitive measurement tools available. Experimenting with different approaches will help professionals do a better job of cognitive measurement.

Additional Practical Exercises

30.2   Practical Exercise

Suppose you are an eighth-grade physical education teacher. You have 30 students per class, and you meet two times each week for 50 minutes. The school year is divided up into six, six-week grading periods. You are supposed to teach the major US spectator sports (football, basketball, baseball) plus physical fitness. Set up a grading scheme to award grades A–F in a way that motivates students to participate. Explain why you made the decisions you did.

1 Write out your plan.
2 Justify it.

30.3 Practical Exercise

Suppose you were evaluating employees at a hospital, fitness center, or similar facility. How could grading relate to employee evaluation? Interview someone who gives or receives employee evaluations and ask him or her to discuss this topic. Write a summary of this person's comments.

Application Questions

1 What are some types of test questions and what are the key advantages/disadvantages of each?
2 Frame an argument to show that multiple-choice questions are not altogether objective. Give examples.
3 What are some options for grading in physical education or physical activities? What are the advantages and disadvantages of each?

Glossary

Accelerometer A small device that detects the acceleration of a body or limb (e.g., leg) to provide data related to the amount of physical activity performed over time.

Analysis of variance (ANOVA) An analysis used to make more than two comparisons, or to compare more than two means at the same time.

Authentic assessment An assessment in which the skill, performance, or task evaluations are conducted in realistic environments that people actually face in real life. For example, the measurement of sport skills in the context of sport play, where they are actually used.

Bimodal distribution A distribution curve with two peaks, indicating that two different scores could be described as the highest frequency.

Bioelectrical impedance analysis (BIA) A body composition measure based on the notion that the total electrical conductivity of the body reflects the fat content.

Biomechanical analysis Analysis of the physics of human motions, which may be done through the use of software with the ability to produce an animated figure based on measurements of an actual performance.

Bland-Altman Analysis A simple approach to evaluating criterion validity through error analysis.

Bloom's taxonomy A taxonomy for the cognitive domain, named after the educator Benjamin Bloom, which shows the lowest to highest levels of cognition.

Cardiorespiratory fitness The ability of the heart, blood vessels, and lungs to supply blood and oxygen to all parts of the body during prolonged physical activity (also known as aerobic or cardiovascular fitness).

Ceiling effect The limitation on high scores when a certain high value is impossible or very difficult to exceed.

Coefficient of determination The number that equals the square of the correlation coefficient.

Communicative movement Nonverbal communication through purposeful body movement.

Construct validity The correspondence between constructs for a characteristic and the actual measurement that is being used to measure that characteristic. A measurement of an ability has construct validity when the factors measured correspond with the underlying qualities needed for success in the performance of that ability.

Constructs The underlying qualities that make up ("construct") the state, trait, quality, performance, or behavior to be assessed.

Content validity The degree to which a measure, upon careful inspection, logically appears to measure what it claims to measure.

Continuous measurement A measurement for which an infinite number of scores are possible, as the measurement may be anywhere on a scale.

Continuous scale A scale that allows the respondent to choose any point.

Correlation The measure of the strength of the relationship between two variables.

Correlation coefficient *See* r value.

Criterion-referenced measurement Measurement that compares a person's knowledge, ability, or performance against a standard or criterion that is considered appropriate for mastery in the area. Criterion-referenced measurements determine whether one has a specified ability level. "Criterion" here means the same as for "criterion validity," it is simply a different usage of the word.

Criterion validity The degree to which a measure compares well with a criterion, or master gauge, measure.

Cronbach's alpha A statistic that is the equivalent of averaging all possible split-half estimates of split-half reliability.

Descriptive statistics Statistics whose main function is to describe a set of data. The mean, median, and mode are all considered to be descriptive statistics.

Discrete measurement A measurement for which a finite number of scores are possible.

Discrete scale A scale that requires the respondent to choose a specific answer from listed choices; for example, a Likert-type scale requires respondents to rate some characteristic using supplied choices.

Discrimination (of a cognitive test item) The ability of a test to distinguish between those who possess knowledge and those who do not.

Ecological validity The extent to which conditions in the laboratory reflect real-life conditions of the environment where the results will be applied.

Equipment reliability The dependability of a machine; its ability to work on demand.

Evaluation The process in which you combine all available data to make an informed decision.

External validity The degree to which a study's results may be generalized to other situations and groups.

Floor effect The limitation on low scores when a certain low value is impossible or very difficult to go below.

Formative evaluation An evaluation made during a program or process to guide that program or process as it continues.

Frequency distribution A way of organizing scores to show how often a particular score appears.

Halo effect The phenomenon in testing when prior information about a person or performance biases an observer's evaluation.

Holistic rubric A single scoring rubric that covers all the parts of the item being measured.

Independent t-test A test that compares means from two independent groups; also called "two sample."

Indirect spirometry calorimetry Measurement of a person's oxygen consumption, used as an alternative to directly measuring the heat produced.

Inferential statistics Statistics that allow us to infer things about a population based on what we learn about a sample. Also refers to using statistical probability tools to help analyze data.

Internal consistency reliability   Reliability that is estimated by measuring the internal agreement between subparts of a measurement instrument.

Interpolation   A process of "reading between the lines" or estimating a value between two known values.

Inter-rater reliability   Objectivity considered as a special case of reliability.

Interval numbers   Numbers that are separated by equal intervals; also called scalar numbers, because they often derive from a scale.

Intraclass correlation   A statistical technique for computing the reliability coefficient to assess the relationship between measures of the same class (i.e., measures of the same thing), as in a test–retest study.

Lack of discrimination   In measurement, the inability to differentiate among people's abilities.

Learning effect   An improvement in scores as test-takers become more familiar with a test. The learning effect can reduce test–retest reliability.

Leptokurtic distribution   A very narrow curve with the data clustered near the mean.

Likert-type scale   A scale that asks the respondent to rate items on a horizontal, usually five-point scale.

Load-cell   An electronic device that measures strength by detecting the force applied to it.

Mathematical range   The result of subtracting the minimum score from the maximum score in a distribution and adding one.

Mean   The average of a set of numbers.

Measurement   The process of assigning a value (a number or quality) to the characteristic being measured.

Measures of central tendency   Statistics that describe the center of a distribution. The mean, median, and mode are referred to as measures of central tendency.

Median   The middle number in a set of numbers.

Mode   The most common number in a set of numbers. Also called the modal score.

Multimodal distribution   A curve with more than one peak.

Multiple correlation   The prediction of some variable of interest from several more readily measured variables.

Muscular endurance   The ability to exert a force repeatedly.

Muscular strength   Maximal force output, usually related to a specified muscle group.

Nominal number   A number that is a substitute for a name.

Norm-referenced measurement   Measurement of an individual's performance in comparison to that of others.

Normal curve   A symmetrical curve with most scores clustered around the curve's midpoint and with all measures of central tendency—the mean, median, and mode—falling in the exact middle of the curve.

Norm table   A table that provides criteria for evaluating a score relative to the scores of others of the same population.

Objective measure   A measure that is wholly independent of who is doing the measuring. This is a different use of the word "objective" which can also mean a goal.

Objectivity   The degree to which a measurement is free from bias. Objectivity can be considered a special case of reliability; it is often called inter-rater reliability.

One-tailed t-test   A test that indicates whether the mean of one data set is higher *or* lower (but not both higher or lower) than the mean of another data set. This increases our ability to find differences between means compared to a two-tailed t-test.

Ordinal numbers Numbers that reflect rankings, giving the place in line but no information about the distance between the performances that have been ranked.

p value The probability that two sample means are different only by chance. Chance is involved because many different samples can be drawn from a population with each sample potentially yielding a slightly different mean.

Paired t-test A t-test comparing two group means collected on a single sample group; also called "single sample."

Pearson Product-Moment Correlation A statistic used to measure the strength and direction of relationship between two variables.

Pedometer A small pendulum, attached to clothing or a belt close to the waist, which registers any up-and-down movement.

Peer review Refers to research investigators' evaluation of others' written research reports.

Percentile A particular score, on an ordered list of scores, at or below which a given percent of the other scores fall.

Percentile rank The percent of scores that are lower than, or equal to, the specified score.

Pilot test The test of a newly developed measure, intended to identify any problems or errors in the measurement procedures.

Platykurtic distribution A curve that is very flat, with the left and right extremes far apart.

Population Any designated group that shares common characteristics of interest to measurers.

Primary trait rubric A set of several rubrics that cover each subpart of the performance or ability being measured.

Qualitative assessments Efforts to understand the processes that underlie various behaviors, through detailed, verbal descriptions of characteristics, cases, and settings, using observations and interviews to collect data.

Qualitative research Research that seeks to understand human behavior and the reasons that motivate this human behavior; typically employs small but intensely studied samples.

Quantitative measurement Gathering numerical data that can be quantified, often so that it can be analyzed statistically to test hypotheses.

Quantitative research Research that uses quantitative measures to test hypotheses, usually with the goal of extrapolating results to a larger population.

r value A statistical expression of the relationship between two variables. Also termed the correlation coefficient.

Range The scores over which data are dispersed. Statistically computed by subtracting the minimum score from the maximum score and adding one.

Range of motion The normal range of movement for a joint, also called flexibility.

Rating of perceived exertion (RPE) scale A scale developed by Gunnar Borg that is used to subjectively monitor exercise intensity by allowing the subject to assign a rating of perceived exertion.

Rating scale A scale used for assessing subjective qualities in the affective domain.

Ratings system A system used to rate employees on various aspects of their performance; similar to a rubric.

Ratio number A number that can be divided into another ratio number to form meaningful ratios.

Regression The process of finding the line of best fit for a set of data with two variables.

Regression to the mean The tendency for extreme scores to move toward the average the second time a test is taken.

Reliability The degree to which a measure can be repeated over and over again with similar results each time; dependability or repeatability.

Reliability coefficient A ratio that shows the relationship between two measurements, indicating the consistency (reliability) between the two measurements.

Rubric A ranked set of descriptors that specifies the components of a skill.

Sensitivity The degree to which a test will give a positive result when the subject does have the condition or disease.

Significant digits The number of digits in a measurement or calculation result that can be accurately estimated.

Skewed curve A curve with a peak that is not exactly in the middle.

Spearman-Brown Prophecy Formula A formula used to estimate the impact on reliability of increasing the test length.

Spearman's rho A special correlation used in cases wherein one of the variables is an ordinal number.

Specificity The degree to which a test will give a negative result when the subject does not have the condition or disease.

Split-half reliability Reliability that is estimated by comparing one half of a test with the other half.

Standard deviation A measure of the variability in a distribution of scores, showing how individual scores vary from the mean.

Standard distribution A common distribution of scores in which the mode lies right in the middle, along with the mean and median. In a z-score distribution, the mean, median, and mode are all zero and the standard deviation is one. Also called a normal distribution and a "bell curve."

Standard error of estimate The estimated standard deviation of the error in a prediction.

Standard error of measurement (SEM) An estimate of the error inherent in any individual's test score.

Standard score A score that has been transformed from a raw score using the standard deviation, or reference to some other number.

Statistical power The ability to find the difference between means, if it exists.

Strength The maximal application of force by a specified muscle group.

Subjective measure A measurement that depends on who is doing the measuring.

Summative evaluation An evaluation that typically marks the end of a process and often sums up previous formative evaluations.

Systematic observation The process of first identifying behaviors of primary interest and then recording the presence or absence or the time engaged in those particular activities.

t-test An inferential test designed to compare two sample means to determine the probability that they are different.

Taxonomy of motor performance An ordered hierarchy of information about human movement ability.

Tensiometer A mechanical device used to measure muscular strength.

Test battery   The combination of multiple subtests into a single measure of a more complex characteristic.

Test–retest   Pertaining to repeated tests administered to determine the reliability of a measurement.

Trendline   The straight line (or curve) of best fit that describes the mathematical relationship between two variables.

Two-tailed t-test   A t-test that indicates whether the mean of one data set is either higher or lower than the mean of another data set.

Type I error   The error of assuming, based on the test of a sample, that a difference exists in a population when none really exists.

Type II error   The failure to find a difference between means that really does exist. This error most often occurs in human research because of very small samples.

Validity   The degree to which a measurement measures what it is supposed to measure with acceptable error; in addition, to be valid, the measured data must be accurately interpreted and applied.

Validity ratio   In evaluating the validity of criterion-referenced measurements, the ratio of the number of scores classified correctly to the total number of scores.

Variability   The difference between the extreme high score and the extreme low score in a sample.

Variance   The standard deviation squared.

z-score   A standard score that allows us to compare any score to the mean score by expressing it as a fraction of the standard deviation.

z-table   A table which shows the percentile ranks or probability for a certain z-score down to a fraction, for normally distributed data.

Index